D1473997

LIVING ABROAD IN
HONG KONG

RORY BOLAND

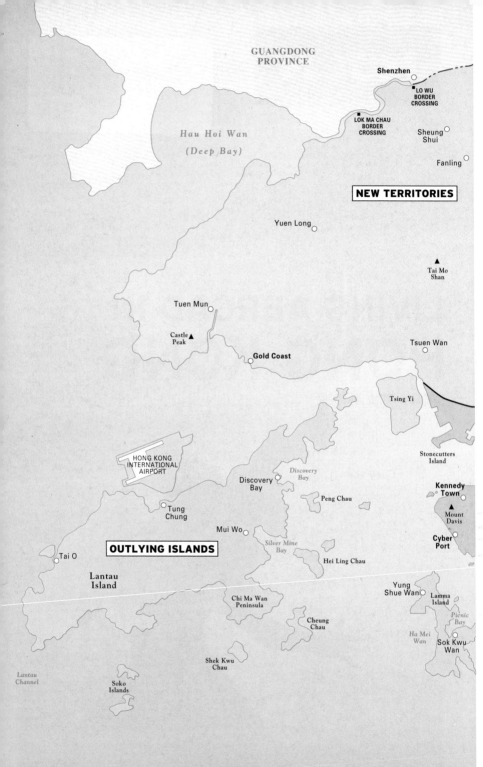

GUANGDONG
PROVINCE

Shenzhen

LO WU
BORDER
CROSSING

LOK MA CHAU
BORDER
CROSSING

Sheung
Shui

Fanling

*Hau Hoi Wan
(Deep Bay)*

NEW TERRITORIES

Yuen Long

▲ Tai Mo
Shan

Tuen Mun

Castle ▲
Peak

Gold Coast

Tsuen Wan

Tsing Yi

HONG KONG
INTERNATIONAL
AIRPORT

Stonecutters
Island

Discovery
Bay

*Discovery
Bay*

Peng Chau

**Kennedy
Town**

Tung
Chung

▲ Mount
Davis

Mui Wo

**Cyber
Port**

Tai O

*Silver Mine
Bay*

OUTLYING ISLANDS

Hei Ling Chau

Yung
Shue Wan

Lamma
Island

Lantau
Island

Chi Ma Wan
Peninsula

*Picnic
Bay*

*Ha Mei
Wan*

Cheung
Chau

Sok Kwu
Wan

*Lantau
Channel*

Shek Kwu
Chau

Soko
Islands

© AVALON TRAVEL

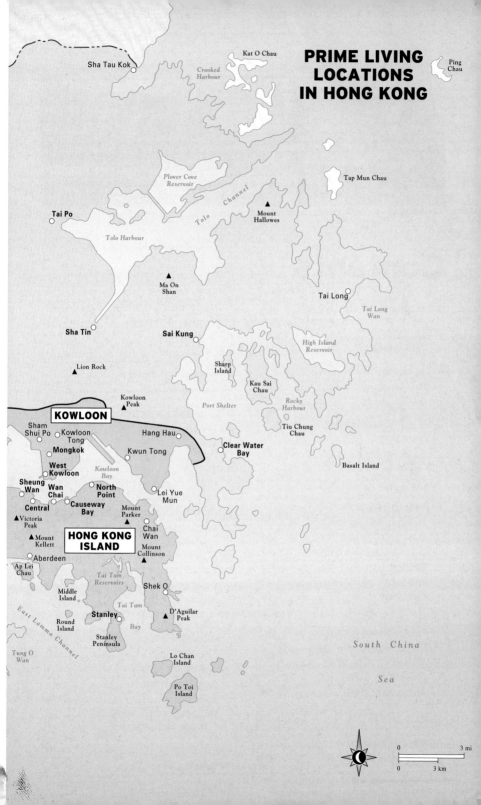

Contents

At Home in Hong Kong

Picture an exotic setting, an international cast, and bags full of money. Few destinations bristle with as much promise and potential as Hong Kong. Synonymous with ambition, success, and adventure, the city has proved irresistible to swashbuckling entrepreneurs and curious globetrotters for generations.

Hong Kong is a city with an incredible fixation on and incredible talent for making money, and at the international firms and multinationals where many expats work, the rewards are handsome. But moving here doesn't need to be about the big bucks. While it was a fantastic bonus, it wasn't money that brought me to Hong Kong. It was opportunity. Moving abroad usually entails compromises on your lifestyle and restrictions on your job options. . .but not in Hong Kong. The city's English-speaking workplace means the job classifieds are plentiful and varied, with opportunities for almost every professional. My partner and I arrived with no jobs and a friend's spare room in which to sling our bags. Within a month we had found work, moved into an apartment, and bought a bag of rice bigger than our bathroom. I can't think of many destinations that can offer a foreigner so much opportunity so quickly.

Hong Kong excited me in a way London, Dublin, and New York did not – or, more likely, could not. It was different and unfamiliar, and it felt like an adventure. No longer a colony but not quite a country, governed by Beijing but not part of China, Hong Kong has dual Chinese and Western identities. For the incoming expat it's hard to know what to expect. No matter what your expectations, though, Hong Kong will almost certainly

confound them. Hong Kong is the contrast of frantic street markets in the shadow of sparkling malls, of sipping on a designer caffé latte frothed by a barista while waiting for your herbal Chinese medicine to be ladled from a steaming cauldron, of the ancestral hall in the afternoon and the cocktail party in the evening. The contradictions are completely maddening and endlessly fascinating. Ultimately, Hong Kong will be as foreign or as familiar as you choose, but the range of experiences on offer is endless. There is no single Hong Kong; it defies simple definition and nobody comes away from the city with the same story.

In many ways Hong Kong is the easy expat choice, requiring the fewest lifestyle sacrifices from those who move here. But it's important that you're motivated by excitement about the differences rather than the similarities, otherwise you're likely to be disappointed. Willingness to adapt is essential. Hong Kong is smelly, noisy, and there is no space; the high-rise apartments are cramped and the streets are uncomfortably crowded.

But if there are reasons to be apprehensive, they are far outweighed by the city's accolades. You'll walk into a well-established international community and its well-oiled social scene. This is a city for living. Endlessly restless, life here moves at an explosive pace that shakes every second from the clock with an energy and enthusiasm that's infectious. Most expats who live here fall head over heels, hopelessly in love.

AT I LOVE ABOUT HONG KONG

- ...shing work in a skyscraper and ...ing on the sand at the seaside in ...ess than 30 minutes

- Life 2.0: Record-breaking internet speeds, cell phones tuned to TV and middle-aged men fiddling with portable game consoles on the MTR.

- Noise, color and community spirit at Chinese festivals.

- *Yum Cha*. Hold on to your belt buckle.

- That you can walk home at three in the morning with your headphones on and never have to look over your shoulder.

- Being able to get your hands on street food anytime, anywhere.

- Junk trips to desert islands.

- Getting out of town: Bargain weekend breaks to Beijing, Bangkok and just about everywhere else in Southeast Asia.

- Being the guest of honor at a feast and trying to work out the rites and rituals and then being forgiven when you break them all.

- Public transportation is nothing short of a miracle.

- Drinking 7-Eleven San Miguel's on the streets of Lan Kwai Fong while listening to Filipino cover bands sing U2 songs better than Bono.

- Simply the best iced tea in the world.

WELCOME TO HONG KONG

INTRODUCTION

Hong Kong is one of the world's most iconic cities, perpetually talked about in superlatives. Famed for its skyscrapers, stock market, and shopping, the city has long been a byword for prosperity where bankers and businesspeople spin their fortunes. Constantly seeking the next big opportunity or the next great bargain, Hong Kong is grasped by an almost breathless pace, driven by a furious desire to succeed.

Yet, there's more to Hong Kong than the size of its bank account. It's a city most strikingly defined by its contrasts and contradictions. The two hundred years as a British colony made a lasting impact on the character of Hong Kong and its citizens, and there is a deep affinity here for many Western values and aspirations. At the same time, it remains the most Chinese of cities and, behind the neon lights, swanky shopping malls, and gadget-obsessed locals, is a city that clings passionately to its traditions. Just dive between the skyscrapers to find wet markets where the fish flop around fresh and the chickens come alive and kicking, or watch the locals queue

© MARTYNA SZMYTKOWSKA

at one of the hundreds of temples to ply their chosen deity with fruit and sweets. Feng shui and fortune telling aren't superstitions here; they're just good business practice.

It's this combination of familiarity and exoticness that seems to snag so many expats. You can live in a neighborhood where everyone speaks English or live in a neighborhood where no one speaks English. You can shop for fresh fruit and meat at the chaotic local market or enjoy the bounties of home from the supermarket. You can try some daybreak tai chi or scrum down for Sunday afternoon rugby. Hong Kong lets you explore a new culture without having to surrender your own. It's a rare opportunity and it seems to keep more lifelong expats here than just about anywhere else in the world.

Of course, most of those first attracted to the city haven't fallen in love with dim sum or enjoy a good dragon dance, they're here to earn money; lots of it. For many expats Hong Kong remains the Holy Grail destination. It has a long, powerful, almost mythical reputation for turning dusty bank accounts into treasure troves and coffee carriers into CEOs. And, while Hong Kong remains an outstanding place to put points on your résumé and dollars in your wallet, it's important to be realistic.

The decadent years of boozy afternoons at the club rather than the desk and postings based on how well you wield a cricket bat are firmly in the past. For those who like the idea of living and working abroad, Hong Kong's English speaking workplace offers an unrivalled opportunity to branch out beyond the staple expat trades of teaching and translation, but competition is fierce. If you aren't sent here by a company, the job search will likely be much tougher than at home as you'll be pitted against highly skilled local employees and hungry mainland immigrants who speak English, Cantonese, and in many cases Mandarin. Full expat packages, padded out with housing, schools, and other benefits, have also become thinner on the ground and many prospective employees will now find they earn local wages, which, while often generous, are substantially less than the parachute contracts of yesteryear. Hong Kong is a hard place to enjoy on a tight budget, and while you may think it'll be fine to live on Hong Kong's dirt cheap and admittedly delicious take-away food and rent a broom closet on the edge of town, if you can't go out and play, it can be very difficult to meet friends here.

But don't let this put you off. For the enterprising and the bold there are boundless opportunities to succeed and the rewards are bountiful. If you have an idea or an ambition, Hong Kong is eager to indulge it. Success rarely comes easy, Hong Kongers work brutally long hours, with evenings often spent wining and dining bosses or networking through the city's bars. For many, this 24/7, breakneck lifestyle is exhilarating, something they thrive on; for others, the pressure and stress can be too much and burnout rates are high.

Ultimately, Hong Kong is not just a city, but a way of life. It's brash, noisy, and non-stop hectic. But it's also invigorating, dynamic, and constantly entertaining: a cosmopolitan, international city where the entire world's experiences are thirty minutes from your doorstep. If it hooks you, don't expect to leave any time soon.

The Lay of the Land

The Special Administrative Region of Hong Kong (HKSAR) encompasses a small peninsula and a scattering of over 235 islands, including Hong Kong Island. Located at the southern end of China's Guangdong region, at the entrance to the Pearl River Estuary, the HKSAR is surrounded by the South China Sea and shares its only land border with China in the north. Across the South China Sea, 60 kilometers to the west, is the Special Administrative Region of Macau. While Hong Kongers share much culturally with their Cantonese-speaking neighbors in Guangdong to the north, they don't share a passport, and the crossing between the HKSAR and China is a full international border.

The total territory of the HKSAR is just 1,104 square kilometers. Broadly speaking, it's best to think of Hong Kong falling into four, distinct geographical areas: the New Territories; Kowloon; Hong Kong Island; and the Outlying Islands. Around 70 percent of the land is occupied by the New Territories in the north of Hong Kong, which abuts the frontier with China proper and the Chinese city of Shenzhen. The New Territories are mostly rural, although in the last few decades a number of planned towns have been constructed to act as cheap bedroom communities and relieve some of the pressure on the chronically overcrowded city. The southern end of the New Territories tapers into the Kowloon Peninsula, which, along with Hong Kong Island, is Hong Kong's prime urban area. The main business district and center for administration and government is Hong Kong Island, which is separated from Kowloon by Victoria Harbour.

Despite its reputation as being the ultimate concrete jungle, around 0.75 of the SAR is classed as countryside, and much of the New Territories is a lush landscape of thick forest greenery, soaring mountains, and stretches of golden beaches. Added to this is Hong Kong's 200 plus islands, which range from rocks jutting out of the ocean, through desert islands, to urban settlements on Lantau and Lamma.

COUNTRY DIVISIONS

Hong Kong is a Special Administrative Region of China, which essentially means that, aside from foreign relations and military defense, Hong Kong retains full governmental, legal, and administrative autonomy. Hong Kong and China maintain separate visa and immigration systems and Hong Kong visas cannot be used in China, nor vice versa. Hong Kong is, however, represented by Chinese embassies abroad.

Hong Kong is divided into 18 districts: 4 on Hong Kong Island, 5 in Kowloon, and the remaining 9 in the New Territories. Each district has an elected district council responsible for public works, improving and maintaining community facilities, and administration in its neighborhood.

WEATHER

Perched just below the Tropic of Cancer, Hong Kong enjoys a sub-tropical climate and four distinct seasons that follow those of the Northern Hemisphere, albeit with some noticeable differences. Winters are short, running from just late December to February, and while the locals have few qualms about dressing up like wooly mammoths, the temperature generally hovers around the mid teens (centigrade). On very rare occasions the mercury will flirt with zero, but snow is unheard of. Spring arrives in March and temperatures quickly warm up, heading into the mid-twenties. The temperatures continue their march on the mercury into summer with numbers in the high twenties by June. Unfortunately, summer also signals the arrival of torrential downpours and Hong Kong's dreaded humidity. The humidity reaches its hair-melting high in July and August, when days are

one of Hong Kong's tropical rainstorms

© BARTOSZ KOSCIELAK

marked by dashes between air-conditioned buildings and regular shirt swapping. Adding to the fun is the threat of a typhoon sweeping into town. Hong Kong's typhoon or tropical cyclone season runs from May until September and the city usually gets tickled by at least a couple of typhoons each year. Typhoons bring strong winds and buckets of rain, sometimes forcing the closure of the airport, public transport, and, if you're lucky, offices and workplaces. Occasionally the city falls in the direct path of a typhoon and although they can be incredibly destructive to property, Hong Kong is well prepared and deaths are thankfully rare. The city's favorite season is probably fall, from late September to late December, when humidity eases and temperatures dip back down to the more manageable mid-twenties.

FLORA AND FAUNA
Flora
While you'll struggle to hunt down a blade of grass in the city itself, the diverse landscapes of the New Territories and the outlying islands, from mountains and wetlands to rock formations and beaches, means there is a surprisingly broad range of flora to be found in the territory. These include over 3,000 varieties of plants, including the city's symbol, the Bauhinia, and 300 native species of trees. Hong Kong's sub-tropical climate allows flora from both the tropical south and the more temperate north to flourish here.

The region's vibrant biodiversity owes much to the 24 generously-sized country parks that cover 40 percent of the SAR and offer protection from Hong Kong's land hungry developers. Most of these are found in the New Territories, stretched over a mountainous terrain that's carpeted with lush vegetation and swathes of forest. During autumn and spring the mountains, the highest of which stretches to 1,000 meters, are a popular retreat for hikers and are well served with picnic stops, visitor centers, and other amenities. Also notable are Hong Kong's collection of exotic rock formations, found both in the mountains and on the shores of outlying islands. Their bizarre contortionist shapes are matched only by their curious nicknames, such as Fat Pig Rock and Dragon Descending into Water.

One of the great attractions of Hong Kong's back yard is that it's right on the city's doorstep, often less than 30 minutes away from Central (Hong Kong's business district). This is lucky because in the downtown areas of Hong Kong Island and Kowloon, glass and concrete has swept away just about any trace of mother nature and even the most passionate urban dwellers may find themselves dreaming of skipping through green fields draped in daisy chains. Respite is provided by a number of parks squeezed

© MARTYNA SZMYTKOWSKA

the green expanses of the wetlands

between the skyscrapers. Actually closer to traditional, well-tended Chinese gardens, these parks feature fish ponds, rock pools, and color-coordinated flower beds; and while they lack true wilderness, they are usually stunningly beautiful.

Fauna

Considering its size and reputation as an urban wasteland, Hong Kong has an exceptionally broad range of wildlife and a particularly boastful collection of birdlife. Nearly 500 species of birds have been recorded in Hong Kong, including black-faced spoonbills, imperial eagles, and the Chinese egret. Most use Hong Kong as a bed-and-breakfast, resting here on their migratory journey between North Asia and Australasia. Their favored watering hole is the Mai Po Marshes in the northern New Territories, whose mangroves and mudflats can welcome around 60,000 birds during winter.

Over 50 species of mammals call Hong Kong home, including the barking deer, leopard cat, and a wide variety of bats. Easier to find are the longtailed and rhesus macaque monkeys that hang around in a number of country parks. In recent years their numbers have swelled so rapidly, topping 2,000, that authorities have been forced to introduce a contraceptive program.

Hong Kong has a couple of nasty reptiles you won't want to find in your sleeping bag. These include 14 venomous snakes, such as the king cobra and mountain pit viper, and the non-venomous Burmese python. While you won't find these strolling around downtown Hong Kong Island or Kowloon, they can occasionally be encountered during hikes in country parks. A reptile you'll

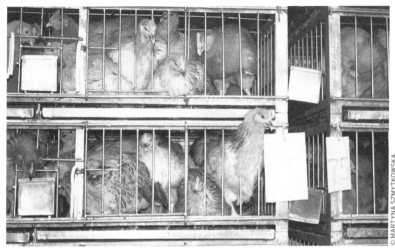

© MARTYNA SZMYTKOWSKA

chickens at a wet market

be happier to see in your home is the Chinese gecko; these small lizards lap up Hong Kong's seemingly ever present mosquitoes and their arrival in a house is said to bring good luck.

Hong Kong's marine wildlife is distinctly less healthy with overfishing and, more recently, rampant pollution causing massive damage to the region's marine ecosystem. Over 1,000 species of marine fish are found in the waters off the Hong Kong coast, but their numbers have suffered a dramatic decline in recent decades. In response, a number of marine reserves have been established, such as Cape D'Aguilar, where 39 varieties of stony coral can be found. Notable marinelife include a variety of rarely seen sharks (the beaches are mostly netted), and green sea turtles, which lay their eggs on Lamma Island's Sham Wan beach. The star of the show, however, is the Chinese white dolphin, better known in the city as the pink dolphin thanks to the pink flush of its skin. The dolphins fool around in the waters off Lantau, although their numbers are also in decline.

Social Climate

Thrown together in a little over 200 years, Hong Kong society reflects the tenacious characteristics of the immigrants who settled the city. Ambition, success, and hard work are the keystones of life here and have helped create a society that very much believes in bettering oneself. If the American dream is based on the pursuit of happiness, the Hong Kong dream is based on the pursuit of success.

Hong Kongers pride themselves on being bolder and brighter than their counterparts and the desire for better exam results and fatter pay checks stretches from kindergarten to the board room. Life is often a constant climb up the career ladder; Hong Kongers endlessly shift jobs on the hunt not only for more money but for a snazzier title, brassier business card, or an office with a view of the harbor. Prestige is as important as pay. It's a relentlessly driven society, sometimes brutally so, but one that encourages its citizens to go from rags to riches in a generation.

This appetite for success is matched by an obsession with consumption. Conspicuous displays of wealth are encouraged in Hong Kong, where owning the newest piece of gadgetry or throwing the most elaborate feast are cutthroat competitions. While Hong Kong's constant desire to parade its wealth may seem crass, in a society that places such importance on success, ownership is proof of one's achievements and is integral to the idea of face (the Chinese concept of social standing and respect). It would also be simplistic to describe this as hollow greed. As immigrants or the children of immigrants, Hong Kongers often have humble histories riddled with uncertainty; wealth offers an insurance against the unknown.

The engine that drives this determination to succeed is faith in the Chinese and Confucian values of paternalism and duty, specifically the desire to earn the respect of one's parents. Hong Kong society remains strongly hierarchical and deference to superiors at work and elders at home is compulsory and universal. And, while older people may grumble that youngsters today

© MARTYNA SZMYTKOWSKA

shining symbols of capitalism in Hong Kong

lack respect, usually citing barbarian manners and an unwillingness to pitch in at the family business, in practice family life is the axis around which the average Hong Konger's daily life rotates. Family life has also kept many traditions and traditional beliefs alive from feng shui to burning paper money for the dead.

The strength of belief in these traditions sometimes shocks visitors who imagine Hong Kong as all skyscrapers and suits. The truth is these beliefs have provided the anchor to which Hong Kongers have clung to through a history of persistent change and doubt. Little in Hong Kong has been constant and the city's identity and very existence has, over the years, been questioned. This has made it tough for Hong Kongers to lay down roots and any sense of belonging is to family, rather than to society. Outside of the family, independence and individualism are prized and there remains a steadfast belief that to achieve something you have to roll up your sleeves and do it yourself. While this spirited self-reliance drove Hong Kong's breakneck transformation, to an extent it's also hampered Hong Kong's sense of community. If you don't know them personally, Hong Kongers can certainly seem a little cool and are rarely expressively happy or helpful to strangers. Don't take it personally. In a city literally bursting at its seams with people, strangers simply don't register on most Hong Kongers' radar; they don't have time both literally and figuratively.

In many ways Hong Kong society is still in its formative years, still defining its identity, and certainly still going through some growing pains. Much of Hong Kong's population has a history here that stretches back only one generation, often less. Hong Kongers come from a wide variety of backgrounds, often raised in other countries. It's this range of experiences and backgrounds that are Hong Kong's great strength. As a city of immigrants, Hong Kong is progressive, tolerant, and, perhaps most importantly, confident in its ability to adapt. The times are also changing; since returning to China, Hong Kong feels more settled and secure, more comfortable in its own skin and confident about the future. Questions of identity are unlikely to evaporate overnight, but in an increasingly globalised world, Hong Kongers have never been more self-assured about their internationalism and multiculturalism.

HONG KONG AND FOREIGNERS

It's fair to say that modern Hong Kong was founded on January 26, 1841, when Captain James Gordon Bremer planted the Union flag at Possession Point on Hong Kong Island and claimed it for Queen Victoria. Thus began

© RORY BOLAND

Hong Kong's multicultural crowds

Hong Kong's intimate, often strained, but ultimately beneficial relationship with the *gweilo* (Cantonese for foreign devil).

Since it was ruled by the British for more than 150 years, Hong Kong's relationship with foreigners has been symbiotic from the very start and it's a city where the dividing line between local and foreigner is significantly blurred. It's freewheeling free-trade status proved a magnet for foreigners over the years, from Baghdad silk merchants to Texan paper-mill magnates and from Dublin doctors to Punjabi police officers. Most of these foreigners would call Hong Kong home for just a few years, until they'd finished their contract, made their fortune or lost it, and then sailed home. But for some, Hong Kong would become home and there are British, Australian, Indian, and other immigrant families who have been here for generations.

This lengthy and continuous exposure to foreigners means Hong Kongers are largely nonplussed when they meet one. Unless you plunge into the very depths of the New Territories, you won't be the first foreign face they've seen and there you can expect little of the superstar treatment given to foreigners north of the border or in some other Asian countries. It would be a stretch to say that the average Hong Konger deals with foreigners on a daily basis, but many do.

Constant interaction with foreigners has made Hong Kong one of Asia's most tolerant societies, although prejudices do remain. The treatment of many Filipino and Indonesian maids has rightly come under heavy criticism and horror stories occasionally hit the headlines. And, while it's important to be aware that Hong Kongers and mainlanders often have very different opinions on world affairs, notably Hong Kongers are far more positive about the United States, there are sporadic outbursts of anti-Japanese rhetoric when Beijing and Tokyo butt heads. One hangover from colonialism is that Caucasians often receive preferential treatment, although outright racism is thankfully rare.

In general, foreigners won't be treated any better or any worse than the locals—at the worst you might be slipped a fork at the local Dai Pai Dong (street food vendor) if the owner thinks you can't drive a pair of chopsticks. One word you are likely to hear thrown around by co-workers and in shops is *gweilo* (Cantonese for foreign devil). Originally used as an insult by the Cantonese Chinese in referring to white residents, these days the word has lost much of its derogatory meaning. Long-term expats still rankle at being called *gweilo,* but for the most part it's simply used to identify a foreigner in a shop or office.

Foreign Population in Hong Kong
Just as Hong Kong's status as a Special Administrative Region is a hybrid of Chinese and British engineering, the question of identity in Hong Kong is a complex one, and defining who is a Hong Konger and who is a foreigner is a potentially tricky task.

In many ways Hong Kong is a tale of two passports. During the uncertain years before the Hong Kong handover, many Chinese Hong Kong citizens obtained British National Overseas passports or took up citizenship in the United States, Canada, Australia, and other Commonwealth nations as an insurance policy, should the communist takeover sink the city. Their fears proved unfounded and many returned, bringing with them their ABC (American Born Chinese), BBC (British Born Chinese), or CBC (Canadian Born Chinese) children. Both children and parents retain strong cultural and familial links with their former home and often consider themselves equally Canadian, American, British, and so on and a Hong Konger. On the opposite side of the equation are the British, Indian, Pakistani, Australian, and various other nationals who were born and bred in Hong Kong, have a right to permanent abode in the city, but retain citizenship of their parents' countries. Both these immigrants and emigrants are Hong Kongers; both are native and foreign. In a city that has traded on and off its twin Chinese and Western identities, dual nationalities are a product of a city that is proud of its multicultural past and puts little stock in crude, gung-ho nationalism.

Aside from Hong Kong's homegrown foreigners, there are also a large number of foreign expat residents in the city. Official figures record around five percent of Hong Kong's seven million citizens as being foreign. The largest minority group is the 115,000 Filipinos and 110,000 Indonesians who mostly work as maids, nannies, or in various other service positions. The number of Western expats has fallen substantially since the 1997 handover, mostly due to tighter work visa restrictions. British nationals, who had free access to the employment market before 1997, were once the largest minority in town but now number just 24,000, followed by 13,000 Americans and 11,000 Canadians. The fact that many Westerners work on short-term contracts means the numbers can be misleading and embassies will tell you the real figures are much, much higher.

The large number of multinationals, international financial firms, and banks based in the city, combined with the fact that English is the primary language of business, makes Hong Kong an attractive proposition for expats. Extensive experience in dealing with foreigners also makes Hong Kong a comparatively easy place to make a new home. Locals are willing to share their culture with you and are also exceptionally patient with the missteps and misunderstandings of foreigners; there is little expectation for you to grasp the intricacies of the Hong Kong workplace (at least not immediately) or start tucking into Bird Nest Soup each lunchtime. There are also fewer of the hassles, frustrations, and government red tape commonly associated with moving and living in another country. Government services, utilities, and service providers are obliged to offer dedicated English-speaking staff and hotlines and are adept at dealing with the special needs of short-term expats.

One grumble is that the city's Western and Chinese citizens continue to nest in fairly separate, independent communities. This is mostly due to language barriers: Few expats, or even long-term transplants, learn Cantonese and most Chinese lack the ability, or more commonly the confidence, to hold a conversation in English. Familiarity with foreigners also means the inquisitiveness that drives locals in other Asian countries to strike up a conversation is absent. In many ways it is refreshing to be treated just like any other resident, but it can be frustrating trying to find non-work opportunities to mix with the local Chinese Hong Kong population. Many Westerners still favor the rugby pitch, English-style pubs of Wan Chai, and the BBQ's at the numerous national clubs. Bridging the gap are the ABCs, BBCs, and CBCs, who have a Hong Kong background but a Western upbringing, can speak both languages fluently, and enjoy a pint as much as they do a dragon dance.

HISTORY, GOVERNMENT, AND ECONOMY

Hong Kong's history is a schoolkid's dream: short. By the time the Opium Wars forced the Chinese into handing over Hong Kong to the British in the 19th century, it contained just a handful of fishing villages, a few thousand inhabitants, and a rampant pirate problem. Hong Kong went from being a far-flung corner of the Chinese Empire to a forgotten corner of the British Commonwealth.

Yet, it was a swap that would secure Hong Kong's success. While China was ravaged by war, revolt, and upheaval, stable Hong Kong attracted the country's brightest and best. These hungry immigrants sowed the seeds of Hong Kong's rise to glory, making their fortune trading first with ships and later on stocks. They would earn the city its unique position as the lynchpin between East and West. It's a position that has often been challenged, not least of all today by a more open China, but Hong Kong is always quick to adapt and be the first to see around the next corner.

Today, returned to the motherland, both country and city are for the first time flourishing together, although, at times it can be an uneasy partnership. Serious

© MARTYNA SZMYTKOWSKA

wrangling over democracy, or the lack of it, remains as residents continue to press their case and Beijing pretends not to hear them. Yet the unease that preceded the 1997 handover to China has been swept away as the world's largest communist country lets the world's most capitalist city do what it does best—make money.

History

EARLY HISTORY

Archaeological digs provide proof of human habitation in Hong Kong stretching back to the Neolithic Period. Setting the scene for much of Hong Kong's history, early settlers relied heavily on the sea, using caves and dunes along the coastline for shelter and fishing for food. Several Bronze Age settlements have also been discovered, most notably on Lantau and Lamma Islands, revealing jewelry, tools, arrowheads, and, most importantly, a number of stone carvings featuring geometric shapes and animals.

© RORY BOLAND

THE CLANS AND CHINA

the sign that once hung over Kowloon Walled City

The first signs of Imperial Chinese presence in the region dates from the Han Dynasty (206 B.C.–A.D. 220) with the discovery of coins and ceremonial artifacts. The most important find to date is the Lei Cheng Uk burial chamber, believed to hold the remains of big shot, Han-era officials and confirming Hong Kong had at least some element of Imperial Chinese administration. Over the following centuries, the power and geographical influence of subsequent Chinese dynasties waxed and waned, as did their control over far-flung Hong Kong, and it wasn't until sometime in the Song Dynasty (A.D. 960–1279) that settlers from the Chinese mainland strapped their suitcases to their donkeys and headed south.

The most important of these new settlers were the Tangs, the first of the Five Great Clan families that settled in the area over the next 400 years. The Tangs

© RORY BOLAND

sturdy entrance to a walled village

were followed by the Hau, Pang, Liu, and Man clans. These Cantonese-speaking clans collectively became known as the Punti (meaning native) and, although there were inhabitants in the region before them, notably the Tanka Boat people, these clans are considered to be the original Hong Kongers. Unfortunately, the clans liked each other as much as they liked the local population of bloodthirsty Blackbeards and they quickly bunkered down behind walled villages—such as that at Kat Hing Wai—for protection. They built schools to teach Imperial education, farmed the land, and supplied subsequent Chinese dynasties with pearls and salt. Their wealth, education, and imperial connections allowed them to dominate the region. At the height of clan power there were a few thousand people living in the region and it was important enough to warrant its own Imperial naval garrison, although it was tasked with protecting the pearls rather than the people.

Village life went on undisturbed until a clash between the waning Ming Dynasty (1368–1644) and rising Qing Dynasty (1644–1911) forced an evacuation of coastal areas, including much of Hong Kong. When the dust settled, destruction in the area deterred many Punti from returning. Instead, the newly-installed Qing Emperor invited the Hakka people, a migratory group of farmers from northern China, to settle in the region. Elements of their distinct culture, cuisine, and language have endured in Hong Kong until this day, most visibly seen in the funeral black, wide-brimmed hats of Hakka women.

TRADE, OPIUM AND WAR

Famously cagey about foreigners bearing gifts, by the 16th century China was coming under increasing pressure from several European nations to swing open the shop door and start trading. The first to wheel in their shopping cart were the Portuguese in 1513, who, along with their persuasive flotilla of ships, quickly persuaded the Ming Dynasty to sign over Macau. By 1714 Britain's East India Company had finally kowtowed (paying homage to the Emperor) their way into

Canton, convincing Chinese authorities to let them build a trading warehouse, known as a factory, along the Canton (Guangzhou) waterfront. Hot on their heels were the Americans, French, and several other European nations, who all established warehouses along what became known as 13 Factories Street.

Eager to limit their influence, the Chinese barred the foreign merchants from the city itself, banned them from learning Chinese, and ensured that contact was exclusively conducted through the Cohong, an elite merchant guide. Despite these limitations, trade flourished, mostly thanks to a keen appetite in Europe for Chinese goods, primarily tea and silk. Unfortunately, the Chinese proved less enthusiastic shoppers and largely shunned the textiles, tea, and spices that foreign merchants offered in return. Instead they demanded silver in payment. As domestic demand for Chinese goods continued to grow at home, governments came to realize that the massive trade imbalance was emptying out their piggy banks.

The solution to the imbalance lay in opium. Unperturbed by a ban on the drug in the Middle Kingdom, the drug barons at the East India Company began shipping crates of the drug in from India. In cohorts with corrupt local officials, who were greedy, addicted, or both, trade in the drug surged, as did those addicted and by the early 1800s several million Chinese were hooked, from peasants and "coolies" to court officials and whole sections of the army. If the Emperor was worried about the debilitating affects of the drug on his subjects, he was equally worried about the dip in his finances. Silver was being used to pay for the drug and the trade imbalance that had once favored the Chinese now flipped in favor of the British.

In 1839 the Emperor dispatched Lin Zexu, a principled and no nonsense Mandarin from Hunan province, to put a stop to the trade. After unsuccessfully petitioning the merchants to stop trading the drug, Lin swiftly began executing Chinese smugglers and setting fire to their boats, before blockading the foreign warehouses in Canton. The British contingent, led by Captain Charles Elliot, held out for six weeks before giving up more than two million pounds' worth of opium, which Lin promptly flushed into the South China Sea. Elliot and the British contingent ceased trade, retreated to Macau, and persuaded London to release the gunboats in the name of free trade. Pitting paddle steamers and rockets against junks and arrows, the British wreaked havoc: destroying forts, occupying strategic ports and cities, and quickly forcing the Chinese to the negotiation table. The first Chinese concession was Hong Kong Island, where a handful of British marines raised the Union Flag on January 26, 1841, on what became known as Possession Point. After Henry Pottinger, Hong Kong's first governor, took a second pillaging-and-plundering joyride up the Chinese coast, the Chinese were forced to sign the Treaty of

Nanking in 1842, which secured British sovereignty over Hong Kong in perpetuity and opened up an additional five treaty ports to foreign trade.

CREATING A COLONY

While Hong Kong might have had a new government and a new governor, there was little to govern. The island itself was a rocky outcrop inhabited by a handful of small villages, home to less than 10,000 inhabitants and an army of malarial mosquitoes. It did offer a deep-water harbor, which, alongside the guarantees of working under British law, persuaded many Hongs (businesses) to set up warehouses along the waterfront. Predictably named Victoria, the new British settlement in Hong Kong erected St. John's Cathedral in 1849 and Government House in 1855 and quickly attracted thousands of enterprising Chinese "coolies" looking to cash in on British trade. Unfortunately, the trade they came for sailed straight past the colony, heading for the five treaty ports and infuriating the influential merchants.

Pressure from the Hongs and an increasingly trigger-happy London meant conflict was inevitable. Both parties found the fight they had been spoiling for in 1856 when China boarded and arrested Chinese crewmembers on charges of piracy aboard what the British claimed was a Hong Kong–registered boat. Joined by the French, the British dispatched the fleet, marched on Peking, and burnt the Summer Palace to the ground.

By the time they hauled the Emperor up to the negotiating table in 1860, the British had dreamt up a lengthy shopping list of demands. Under the Treaty of Tienstin and the Convention of Peking they forced China to open another eleven ports to foreign trade, legalize opium, allow "coolies" to be transported for work overseas, and, most importantly for the future of Hong Kong, cede the Kowloon Peninsula, up to Boundary Street, to Britain.

BECOMING A CITY

Emboldened by its territorial gains and with almost unfettered access to Chinese markets, Hong Kong started to swell. Her Majesty's merry band of soldiers and a handful of civil servants were quickly joined by enterprising merchants, opium addicts, and refugees from the neighboring Guangdong province, and by 1862 the population numbered 120,000. Like all British colonies, Hong Kong was marked by its strict segregation; a handful of British citizens and other white expats wielded a disproportionate amount of influence, and cruelty, over the colony's majority Chinese population. Most Chinese lived on the brink of destitution and, as riots and protests gathered pace, the relationship between Europeans and the Chinese turned poisonous—literally—when the only Chinese baker in the territory to bake Western-style bread tried to slip arsenic into the morning loaves of the whole expat population.

Despite poisonings, strikes, and a dose of the bubonic plague in 1894, Hong Kong continued to grow, both economically and geographically. The British managed to choke more land out of the rapidly expiring Qing Dynasty, who, in 1898, signed over the New Territories (land north of Kowloon up to the Shenzhen River) and 234 islands to London, although crucially it was a 99-year loan this time rather than a "gift." Britain's imperious role in world trade also brought modest wealth to the colony and public services were slowly initiated, such as the Hong Kong Electric Company, switched on in 1890. Colonists erected schools and churches, built their homes around the crown of the Peak, and let their hair down at the exclusive Hong Kong Club or Happy Valley Races.

One prominent Chinese resident of Hong Kong during the period was budding revolutionary Dr. Sun Yat-Sen, today considered the father of modern China. It was in Hong Kong that Sun received his education, was baptized, and first began plotting to overthrow the Qing Emperor. He handed the last Chinese Emperor his pink slip in 1911, but the fatally-divided country immediately descended into a bloody cycle of revolution, revolt, and war that lasted 30 years and brought thousands of refugees to Hong Kong. It reached its bloody nadir in 1937 when the Japanese army raped and pillaged their way through China, forcing a flood of refugees to seek safety in Hong Kong. By 1939, the population had rocketed to 1.6 million, most of whom were sleeping in shanty towns or on the streets, and the Japanese tanks which had reached Canton were swiveling their turrets toward Hong Kong.

JAPANESE OCCUPATION

Despite Winston Churchill's protestations that the colony "resist until the end," it was in effect left lightly defended by an ill-equipped, makeshift collection of Indian, Canadian, and British troops, bolstered by local volunteers. When the Japanese invaded on December 8, just a few hours after their attack on Pearl Harbor, they quickly overran the hastily constructed defenses in Northern Kowloon and in six days captured the whole peninsula. Their final assault on Hong Kong Island was characteristically brutal, including the mass bayoneting of hospital patients. On December 25, Christmas Day, Governor Sir Mark Young was forced to sign the colony's surrender.

British, European, and other "hostile nationals" were interned in camps where imprisonment meant malnutrition, mistreatment, and disease. But what followed was worse. For the next three years the Japanese army terrorized the local population, raping thousands of women, murdering innocent civilians, and razing whole villages in the New Territories. Many Chinese escaped to Macau or to inland China while the occupying Japanese authorities deported thousands more. When the Japanese surrendered Hong Kong on September 16, 1945, Britain's colonial secretary coolly walked out of his prisoner of war camp and reestablished British control, despite U.S. attempts to have the colony reunited with China.

REBUILDING AND THE RISE OF THE SKYSCRAPER

Despite widespread destruction and a population that had dropped as low as 600,000, Hong Kong quickly dusted itself off and rebuilt. North of the border, Mao's communists consolidated their grip on power, spooking the middle classes who bolted to Hong Kong along with their bank accounts and brains. The factories they built and the backbreaking labor of their fellow refugees would make the "Made in Hong Kong" label famous around the world, turn the city into a manufacturing powerhouse, and lay the foundations for its economic miracle.

Yet, while this period is famed for its rags to riches stories, the truth is success was elusive and many lived in shanty towns and worked in conditions that would have embarrassed Dickens. Tensions also bubbled. By 1967, Mao's Cultural Revolution was at its murderous peak and the storm quickly spilt over into the colony. While unions picketed over living and working conditions, communist sympathizers embarked on a campaign of violence that brought the city to a standstill. Lasting just over a year, the British army defused roughly 8,000 bombs, both fake and real, 51 people were killed, and the Hong Kong police returned fire on the People's Liberation Army (PLA) forces across the Chinese border. Hong Kong's economic value to China ultimately forced them to curb the violence. Shook by events, Britain began a series of reforms to improve living and working standards, including the introduction of mandatory high school education and the construction of new towns, such as Sha Tin, to provide public housing.

With the lifting of the international trade embargo on China in 1971 and the liberalization of the country's economy through Deng Xiaoping's Open Door Policy in 1978, Hong Kong's relationship with the communist state blossomed, both on an official and business level. Hong Kong factories shifted across the border to take advantage of an almost endless supply of cheap labor; Hong Kongers supplied the know-how and the capital. And they reaped the profits: Money poured into the city, home ownership rocketed, and locals were introduced to their first supermarket. Encouraged by the city's increasing power in global trade and a string of unprecedented government tax breaks and light regulation, banks and financial institutions shifted their safes to Hong Kong. By the late 1970s skyscrapers had begun to strut along the skyline, the Hang Seng Stock Exchange was on its march to stardom, and Hong Kong had established itself as a financial powerhouse.

COMMUNISM AND COMPROMISE

As the curtains closed on the 1970s, all eyes were fixed on London and the impending expiration of its 99-year lease over the New Territories in 1997. Legally, based on their 19th century treaties, Britain needed only to hand over the New Territories—both Hong Kong Island and Kowloon had been ceded in perpetuity. In reality, half of Hong Kong's population lived in the New Territories and almost all of its natural resources, including water, came either from there or directly from China. Hong Kong simply wasn't viable without the New Territories.

While Margaret Thatcher and Deng Xiaoping eyeballed each other across the negotiating table, Hong Kong wobbled. With a question mark hanging over the city's future, the stock market went into freefall, the Hong Kong dollar fainted, and the city brooded. By 1984, Thatcher, with little other alternative, signed the Sino-British Joint Declaration on the Question of Hong Kong, agreeing to return all of Hong Kong to Chinese rule. The nuts and bolts of the agreement were laid out in the Basic Law of 1988, which stated that the "socialist system and policies shall not be practiced in the Hong Kong Special Administrative Region, and the previous capitalist system and way of life shall remain unchanged for 50 years." It became known as the "one country, two systems" policy and guaranteed Hong Kong's judicial independence, offered extensive self-governance, aside from foreign and military affairs, and even included a few ill-defined notes about democracy.

Despite the declaration, Hong Kongers remained doubtful of China's intentions. Suspicion turned to fear on June 4, 1989, when Chinese troops stomped into Tiananmen Square and massacred thousands of protesting students. While Hong

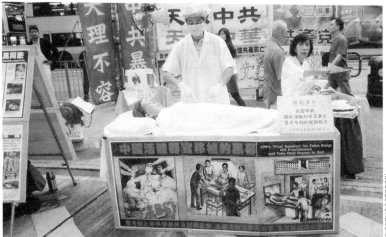

Persecuted in China, Falun Gong protestors are free to protest in Hong Kong – and they regularly do.

© CORY DOCTOROW

Kongers set about smuggling the remaining protestors away from the clutches of China's security services, fear set in. Hong Kongers became convinced that their new masters would burn the Basic Law and strong-arm them into communism with batons and bullets. In response, Hong Kongers reached for their suitcases. Despite bossing them around for more than 100 years, London decided Hong Kongers weren't British after all and only issued a small number of passports. Instead, visa seekers swamped consulates in the city and wealthier Hong Kongers found that a Gold Card could slice through bureaucratic red tape, purchasing passports in a number of small Pacific nations. During the worst of the crisis, hundreds of locals waved goodbye each week, as did some of Hong Kong's top companies.

THE HANDOVER AND A NEW HOME

To try and shore up confidence in Hong Kong's future, Britain introduced a Bill of Rights, which enshrined human rights and placed limitations on the powers of the police and government. They also introduced a limited democracy, allowing 18 of the 60 members of the Legislative Council to be directly elected for the first time. While it helped temper the panic and pulled the economy out of its nose dive, Hong Kongers remained anxious.

It was into this atmosphere of suspicion and doubt that in 1992 Britain dispatched its last governor, Chris Patten, a career politician with the right of center Conservative Party. Eschewing the consensus-building diplomats of the past, the combative Patten did what Britain had failed to do for two centuries and what China feared most—delivered democracy, sort of. In 1995, for the first time in Hong Kong history, the Legislative Council became a fully elected body, although only 20 of the seats were delivered by direct election, another 30 coming from functional constituencies and 10 by an election council.

Britain's sudden and much belated fondness for democracy in Hong Kong enraged the Chinese who called Patten a long list of naughty names before sulking off and setting up their own provisional Legislative Council in Shenzhen, stuffed with Beijing loyalists who'd lost in the recent election. Although Patten and his drumbeat for democracy were popular with ordinary Hong Kongers, he gave the city's powerful business community—who were already flashing their legs and flirting at the future keepers of the city's purse strings in Beijing—the jitters. As the handover loomed, Britain and China agreed to disagree and an uneasy truce descended. The city held its breath.

In comparison to the soap-opera buildup, the official handover was a damp disappointment, not helped by a truly thunderous tropical downpour. Amongst the pomp and circumstance of army bands and yo-yoing flags, Chinese President Jiang Zemin and Prince Charles grimaced at each other while Chris Patten wept

THE HONG KONG HANDOVER

During the sultry summer of 1967, Hong Kong shook to the sounds of bullets and bombs as the worst of the leftist riots gripped the city. Inspired by the Cultural Revolution and its Red Guards across the border, communist sympathizers in Hong Kong organized a constant stream of strikes, protests, and riots against colonial control. As the summer heated up, so did the protestors: occupying and barricading themselves inside the Bank of China building, intimidating and murdering editors and media commentators who publicly disagreed with them, and planting thousands of bombs.

As Hong Kong simmered, what wasn't clear was just how far up the puppet the Chinese had their hand. It was easier to read tea leaves than the official communications from the famously opaque communist government and the British couldn't be sure what the Chinese reaction would be to their arresting of the protestors, many of whom were Chinese citizens by birth. This was made all the more difficult by the fact that several factions inside the Chinese Communist Party were jostling for control of the country and it was hard to know who was really in charge. Initially, the Chinese watched and waited, but as it became clear that the bulk of the Hong Kong population were against the protests, Premier Zhou Enlai withdrew his support and the protests crumbled. But, it was a closer call than many people believed.

High-ranking mainland official Lu Ping, who led the Hong Kong handover negotiations with Governor Chris Patten, revealed that at the height of the riots a fanatical faction of the People's Liberation Army (PLA) were only hours away from invading Hong Kong. It's believed that hardcore Maoists, keen to export Maoism by book or by gun, had been whispering sweet nothings into the ear of the PLA Commander responsible for the neighboring Guangdong Province, who only took the key out of his tank after a last ditch phone call by Zhou Enlai.

And that wasn't the only time the Chinese considered an unannounced jaunt across the border. Lu also revealed that during the negotiations leading up to the Hong Kong handover, Premier Deng Xiaoping was so concerned that announcing a fixed date for the return of the city would spark unrest that he somewhat ludicrously considered the idea that reunification by force would be cleaner and quicker. Deng is said to have told Margaret Thatcher that "I could walk in and take the whole lot this afternoon." To which she replied, "There is nothing I could do to stop you, but the eyes of the world would now know what China is like." Deng apparently agreed because he never gave his men their marching orders and the only explosions on the night of the Hong Kong handover were the celebratory fireworks.

as he was swept off aboard the Royal Yacht Britannia. China, true to its word, dismissed the elected Legislative Council and swore in its own hand-picked provisional council and installed Tung Chee-hwa as Hong Kong's first chief executive, an event which, in a final dramatic flourish, Britain boycotted.

Parachuted in from Shanghai, multi-millionaire shipping mogul Tung was almost immediately sabotaged by the Asian Economic Crisis and as the stock market went south so did his popularity. Rightly or wrongly, Tung was consistently handcuffed to his masters in China and perceived as little more than a mouthpiece for the Chinese Communist Party. His attempt to introduce a public security bill at the behest of Beijing brought half a million out in protest, while further blunders over infrastructure and the SAR's crisis forced him to resign in 2005. Chastened, Beijing this time swallowed its pride and appointed local boy and stalwart of Hong Kong's British-era civil service, Donald Tsang.

HONG KONG TODAY

Known as Bow-Tie Tsang by locals thanks to his fondness for togging out in snazzy bow ties, Tsang has led a Hong Kong that has rarely been as confident or successful. Despite forecasts of doom and destruction on the eve of the handover, Hong Kong has undoubtedly flourished. The economy, aside from some minor swerves, is once again motoring, fuelled by China's miraculous growth. Beijing has, for the most part, resisted sticking its wooden spoon into Hong Kong affairs and ties between the two are as genuinely warm as they have ever been. That's not to say it's been all holding hands and teddy bears, battles still loom, not least of all over Beijing's continued reluctance to grant Hong Kong full direct elections and universal suffrage despite frequent protests and an increasingly impatient electorate.

Government

Cooked up by the odd-couple pairing of Beijing communists and London parliamentarians, Hong Kong's governmental structure is unsurprisingly unique and complex. Independent from China, both judicially and legislatively, Hong Kong is governed by its mini constitution, the Basic Law, and led by a chief executive and a legislature known as the Legislative Council (LegCo). Both the chief executive and legislators are nominally "elected," although Hong Kong's novel brand of limited democracy means Beijing gets to keep both hands firmly on the city's steering wheel. It is the twin and intertwined questions of democracy and control exerted by Beijing that dominates Hong Kong politics. In theory, the city is supposed to be skipping down the path to universal suffrage and full, direct elections; in reality, Beijing keeps tripping it over.

That's not to say that the Chinese Communist Party has been heavy-handed in its treatment of Hong Kong; with just a few notable exceptions, it has let Hong Kong politicians run Hong Kong. However, it continues to stage-manage the election of the chief executive, stuff the legislature with pro-Beijing loyalists, and ensure that most major polices in Hong Kong are introduced with the tacit approval of the big wigs in Beijing. This gives politicians in the city the unenviable task of trying to keep both Beijing and their own citizens happy.

GOVERNMENT STRUCTURE

The executive branch of government is headed by the chief executive, a presidential post that replaced that of governor following the handover, and his 29-member cabinet. The chief executive is "elected" by an 800-member election committee formed from and selected by Hong Kong's 28 functional constituencies, groupings carved from certain industries and business blocks, such as Financial Services and Transport, but also include religious groups and political parties. While the process is called an election, it is in fact deeply undemocratic. Aside from 800 people disenfranchising 7 million, the manipulation of functional constituencies means the committee is stuffed with pro-Beijing loyalists who take their voting orders from Beijing. But China hasn't orchestrated everything. After the first three chief executive elections were held unopposed, in 2007 Alan Leong managed to muster the 132 votes necessary from the Election Committee to stand in Hong Kong's first contested election. The outcome was a foregone conclusion, but Leong's participation on a universal suffrage platform was a substantial step forward in Hong Kong's move toward democracy.

Hong Kong's legislative branch, LegCo, debates and passes laws, approves budgets, and, at least in theory, acts as a check and balance on the power of the chief executive. Of LegCo's 60 members, half are directly elected and the other half are appointed by functional constituencies with terms for all set at four years. In recent years, LegCo has shrugged off its rubber-stamp reputation and become a battleground for its two major political blocs: the pro-Beijing bloc led by the snappily-named Democratic Alliance for the Betterment and Progress of Hong Kong and the pan-democrat camp led by

The contrasting faces of Hong Kong: the colonial LegCo building shadowed by the soaring Bank of China skyscraper.

© MARTYNA SZMYTKOWSKA

the Democratic Party. While the pan-democrat camp has consistently obtained more of the popular vote, the disproportionate distribution of functional constituency seats to the pro-Beijing bloc means they retain a majority of seats.

At the local level, Hong Kong also has 18 district councils, part elected and part appointed, who advise the government on neighborhood issues as well as maintain and improve public works in their area and organize community events. Mostly filled by political appointees, the district councils wield little real power.

A strong rule of law has traditionally been one of Hong Kong's great strengths and its judiciary has an enviable reputation for impartiality and as a champion for human rights and freedom of speech. Based on British common law, it functions in both Chinese and English and is independent of both the legislative and executive branches of the Hong Kong government and wholly separate from the legal system in China.

THE QUESTION OF DEMOCRACY

Disenfranchised for centuries by its British colonial masters, Hong Kongers' first taste of real democracy came in the late 1990s with the first direct elections to LegCo. It didn't last; after the handover in 1997, China swiftly axed the majority of direct elections and instead implemented a semi-appointee system to guarantee their control over the territory. Since then the journey or battle—depending on which side you're on—for democracy in Hong Kong has become the city's defining political question.

Enshrined in Hong Kong's Basic Law is the statement that the "ultimate aim" for the selection of the chief executive and the Legislative Council is "universal suffrage"—in between are a litany of caveats and clauses. Both the Chinese Communist Party and consecutive chief executives claim to be heart and soul fundamentalist democrats, committed to helping Hong Kong achieve democracy; but progress has been painfully slow. It would be unfair to say Beijing is opposed to introducing universal suffrage in Hong Kong, but it has a couple of reasons to be apprehensive. Firstly, it fears that if it delivers universal suffrage to Hong Kong it will inspire democrats in mainland China to press their demands more forcefully. Beijing is also reluctant to surrender its indirect control over the Hong Kong government, fearing universal suffrage will vote in a group of subversive democrats who won't ask "how high?" when Beijing tells them to jump.

That's not to say all Hong Kongers are do or die democrats. They aren't. In fact, opinion polls show support for immediate universal suffrage in Hong Kong to be, at best, luke warm, with the majority of citizens more comfortable with a slower transition. But, as the mountain of missed dates and promises stack up, Hong Kongers have become increasingly impatient and protests, both by ordinary citizens and by the pan-democratic parties in LegCo, have grown. Frustrations usually boil over in the wake of clumsy attempts by Beijing to coerce the Hong Kong government into passing laws against widespread public opposition, such as the failed anti-subversion law of 2003. While Hong Kongers may not yet be pitching their tea into the harbor, the demand for more concrete democratic reforms continues to escalate.

Economy

Comparable in size to Samoa or the Faroe Islands and with virtually no natural resources, Hong Kong, with its rags-to-riches story, is nothing short of astonishing. While it's hard to imagine now, post-war Hong Kong was ravaged by poverty, unemployment, and, in parts, almost medieval squalor, with a GDP that had been flatlining for years. Yet, built on the backs of its Chinese refugees, Hong Kong quickly established itself as one of the world's top manufacturers and through the 1960s and 1970s it posted growth averaging 6.5 percent. And it wasn't done yet. As China emerged from its self-imposed sulk in the late 1970s, Hong Kong repositioned itself as the gatekeeper to the Middle Kingdom and both the goods and the money flowed through Hong Kong hands. Its pivotal role in world trade, rule of law, and swelling piggy bank soon turned it into a desirable destination for banks, financial houses, and other money managers. By the 1980s the Cinderella story and most of the skyscrapers were complete.

Between 1961 and 1997 Hong Kong's GDP swelled 180 times its original size. In 1960 Hong Kong's per capita income was 28 percent that of Great Britain; by 1996 it was 137 percent. According to the International Monetary Fund (IMF), Hong Kong's current GDP per capita of $43,000 ranks it sixth in the world, second only to Singapore in Asia and trailing the United States by just one place. Somewhat incredibly, given it's a city not a country, it is the world's 13th largest trading economy and boasts the world's busiest international cargo airport and its third biggest container port. More famously, the city is home to swashbuckling stockbrokers, has the world's seventh biggest stock market, and is arguably the world's third most important financial center, after New York and London.

After taking a considerable knock to its confidence in the wake of the

© RORY BOLAND

Ever since the British arrived, Hong Kong has been dumping mud into Victoria Harbour to create more prime real estate.

Asian Financial Crisis in 1997, Hong Kong regained much of its mojo, piggybacking on China's outrageous growth, and posting regular growth figures of 4 and 5 percent. The city's more integrated relationship with China has brought undoubted benefits and growth through tourism, trade, and the lowering of tariffs, particularly the Closer Economic Partnership Arrangement; but it's also brought challenges. Hong Kong's privileged role as China's bridge to the world is collapsing thanks to an increasingly open China. It's particularly mindful of losing its status as an international hub for trade and finance and being downgraded to just another Chinese city. The doomsayers point at Shanghai, which by some measures surpassed the Hong Kong economy in 2009, as proof. Yet Hong Kong's familiarity and experience in dealing with international markets, well educated and extensive skills pool, and strict adherence to the rule of law mean Hong Kong remains the region's premium city of finance.

CUTTHROAT CAPITALISM

Rated as the world's freest economy 16 years in a row by the American think tank Heritage Foundation, Hong Kong likes its capitalism bloody and raw. Unlike other tiger economies of the 1970s that developed with central government planning, Hong Kong's Governor John Cowperthwaite promoted a policy of positive non-interventionism. It was a bold step that reduced taxes to a minimum, resisted government borrowing, and cut almost all red tape. Designed to give entrepreneurship a free hand and stimulate competition, this cutthroat capitalism delivered Hong Kong's economic miracle and remains the cornerstone of the city's economic policy.

What does this mean in a practical sense? It takes an average of 6 days to set up a medium-sized business in Hong Kong, filling out two forms and obtaining a company stamp, compared to 38 days in China and 23 in Japan. The city is regularly ranked as one of the easiest places to do business in the world and the government works hard to keep it that way, streamlining everything from employment law to construction permits and keeping regulation to an absolute minimum.

Inequality

It's important to note that not everyone is a cheerleader for Hong Kong's laissez-faire economic policy. All this talk of success paints Hong Kong as a city full of citizens rolling around in safes stuffed with money; that's certainly what the government would like you to believe. But not everyone succeeds. The GDP may be one of the highest in Asia, but the gap between rich and poor is, according to the U.N., the widest in the world, with pots of money concentrated in the hands of tycoons and high-flying professionals. Those at the margins of Hong Kong society are rarely talked about in a city where poverty is a cardinal sin. Despite around 17 percent of the population living below the poverty line and booming government bank accounts, public welfare is downright miserly. The relationship between government, the majority of which are selected from the business community, and business is not so much close as making out in the locker room. Traditionally there has been little popular discontent about the gulf in living standards, with poverty seen as failure of the individual rather than society, but Hong Kong's increasing democratization is sure to bring more vocal demands for a fairer spreading of the wealth.

BANKING AND FINANCIAL CENTER

The backbone and brain of the Hong Kong economy is its service industry, an intricate web of businesses that employ 88 percent of the Hong Kong workforce and account for a staggering 92 percent of the GDP. Alongside the key areas of trade and tourism, the single most important sectors are banks, real estate, and other financial services.

Often mentioned alongside New York and London, Hong Kong is a crucial cog in the wheels that keep the world economy spinning; it is Asia's top exporter of financial services and handles more foreign direct investment than anywhere else in the region. Of the world's 23 largest financial institutions,

DUMPING ON HONG KONG

While Victoria Harbour might have been the waterway that helped float the city's fortunes, this once grand port has been on the receiving end of some equally grand downsizing, reducing it from endless ocean to roaring river and some say a future as a trickling tap. The culprit? Ever since the 1850s the Hong Kong government has been dumping earth into the harbor to create more premium-priced flat land to build on. Incredibly, the harbor is already half the size it once was and it's not only here that the government has been making Hong Kong bigger. Over the years, roughly 70 square kilometers of land throughout the whole territory were reclaimed (just shy of the 76 square kilometers of Hong Kong Island's total size) and they include flagship projects such as Hong Kong Disneyland and Hong Kong Airport, which were both built on land reclaimed from the sea.

The reason for this land fabrication project is lack of space. When the British army first splashed ashore onto Hong Kong Island in the 1840s, they would have found room to plant their flag, park their suitcases, and little else. Victoria Peak sloped into the sand around a kilometer from the shoreline, leaving just a sliver of land for development. At the time, the seafront on Hong Kong Island would have run just in front of Queen's Road Central, where many of the first warehouses and piers were built. The addition of equally inhospitable Kowloon and the New Territories to her Majesty's real-estate portfolio provided little extra flat land and as an increasing number of traders and merchants arrived and the demand for space became more pressing, they decided to start giving the hills a haircut and dumping the earth into the water. It's a program of land reclamation that has continued in fits and starts to this very day.

You'll find indicators to the shifting shoreline throughout the city. Look for Tin Hau temples, such as the one on Queen's Road East in Wan Chai, that pay homage to the goddess of the sea. These once stood within spitting distance of the sea, but some now find themselves marooned behind 10 blocks of city concrete or more. The same has happened to some of the city's most prestigious buildings, such as the Mandarin Oriental, which were once perched on the seafront but now have to peek through blocks of skyscrapers to get a sea view. With land prices responsible for much of the Hong Kong government's pocket money and some of the most densely populated neighborhoods on the planet, it's not surprising that the government continues to reclaim land. While the projects usually throw up little controversy, protestors have become increasingly vocal in their demands for the quickly disappearing Victoria Harbour to be spared any more slimming. Come back in a few years and you might just be able to walk from Central to Tsim Sha Tsui.

19 have their regional headquarters in Hong Kong, while more than 705 international banks have offices in the city. For matadors who like the bullpen, Hong Kong is Asia's ultimate arena.

Hong Kong's magnetism for companies is once again merged with the city's hand-and-glove relationship with China. Determined to tap China's massive market potential, U.S. and European companies, wary of dealing with the big red monster that is China's bureaucracy, set up in Hong

Kong. The city offers a familiar English-speaking business environment, rule of law, and light regulation and taxes, as well as preferential access to the mainland.

To an extent, much of China's rise to a world economic superpower has been stage-managed through Hong Kong and the city has grown rich through hand-holding the country into capitalism. China's limits on foreign investment means many of the country's biggest companies have bypassed the Shanghai Stock Exchange to place their initial public offering on the Hong Kong Stock Exchange, usually bringing in blockbuster profits. Foreign firms are also barred from listing on the Shanghai Exchange, so if they want to reach the mainland's eager and increasingly prosperous investors, they have to head for Hong Kong. Times are changing, as the Chinese government becomes more comfortable with foreign capital, but Hong Kong's experience and pedigree as a center for international finance means it's unlikely to surrender its crown easily.

MANUFACTURING

Hong Kong's days as a manufacturing superpower are long behind it with just two percent of the GDP now derived from manufacturing. The production that remains is still based around Hong Kong's traditional products, primarily textiles, clothes, and plastics. Most of the factories that were once in Hong Kong have now shifted just across the border to the Chinese side of the Pearl River Delta in an area that has become known as the workshop of the world. Many of these factories and warehouses remain Hong Kong–owned and 60–70 percent of the region's yearly Foreign Direct Investment comes from Hong Kong pockets.

EXPORT AND TRADE

While the production may have shifted, Victoria Harbour remains a major departure point for the goods churned out by China's manufacturing machine. As the world's 11th biggest exporter and 10th biggest importer, topping both Canada and Russia, Hong Kong punches well above its weight in international trade. Much of the export total is actually re-exports, goods produced in China, primarily clothing and electronic equipment, and shipped to the world via Hong Kong or raw materials and consumer goods imported into Hong Kong and re-exported to China. As it has done for centuries, the city continues to act as a massive shipping firm for the mainland, although it's facing increasing competition from Shenzhen and Shanghai.

PEOPLE AND CULTURE

There are few places in the world as culturally complex as Hong Kong. Combining a Chinese cultural heritage and a Western lifestyle cultivated under British rule, Hong Kong truly is where East meets West: where businesspeople think nothing of consulting both the *Wall Street Journal* and their family fortuneteller before taking a punt on the stock market; where water cooler conversation over health ailments can seamlessly slip from new treatments at the city's world-class hospitals to new concoctions cooked up at the local Chinese herbalist. The contradictions are constant and startling.

At first glance it's the West not the East that sets the scene. From the suited and booted brokers weaving through jungles of gleaming skyscrapers to the designer-dressed *Tai Tais* (women of leisure) stalking the city's luxury malls and upmarket boutiques, Hong Kongers are unrepentantly materialistic. This is a city that thrives on its ability to make a buck. But stay a little longer and dig a little deeper and you'll find a culture fixated on its traditions.

Hong Kong remains the guardian of China's cultural heritage, where

thousands rise at dawn to stretch out to tai chi in the city parks and the constant click of mahjong tiles fills the side streets and markets. This reverence for tradition is best seen at one of the many festivals, which are celebrated with color, noise, and passion. Confucianism and paternalism remain ingrained in the local character and Hong Kongers are always deferential to their superiors at work and their elders at home. Despite brutal working hours, family life remains pivotal and the eight-seater swivel tables found in thousands of neighborhood restaurants are a testament to the many times a week families meet to eat and connect. It's said that sons and daughters, looking to prove their success to demanding parents, drive the city's seemingly endless ambition.

This cultural stew between East and West can, at first, be confusing and even frustrating to outsiders, as Hong Kongers switch so frequently and freely between their two cultural identities. But as expats become more comfortable in the city, this chameleon character quickly transforms into one of its greatest attractions. Hong Kongers can understand and accept your home culture and they will go out of their way to accommodate you and make you feel at home in their city.

Ethnicity and Nationality

Around 95 percent of the population of Hong Kong is Han Chinese, followed by 1.6 percent Filipino, 1.3 percent Indonesian, 0.5 percent white, and 0.3 percent Indian. On paper this makes Hong Kong remarkably ethnically homogenous. It's only when you arrive that you notice just how much more visible and prominent the international community is, despite the statistics.

Communities of whites (British and Commonwealth), Pakistanis, Indians, and other South Asians trace their beginnings back to the British colony and are very much part of its fabric. These communities enjoyed equal footing during colonialism, at least in the sense that they were all equal under the British, and although the city has become noticeably more Chinese since the handover, they continue to thrive. The notable exception is the white community that suffered an exodus after the handover. Yet, while there has been a steady and noticeable decline in the numbers of white residents, the community remains intact and influential. In recent years, Hong Kong has attracted more traditional economic immigrants, mostly Indonesian and Filipino maids who have had a bumpier landing.

Considering the city's long and storied multicultural history, it can be somewhat surprising just how separate the communities remain. This has little to do with race and everything to do with language. Under the flag of official bilingualism, most of the international community, even long-term residents, stubbornly refuse to learn Chinese. On the other side of the divide, few Chinese feel confident enough to speak English in social situations. As a result both communities gravitate to those who speak their language. The exceptions to the rule are the ABC (Australian/American Born Chinese), BBC (British Born Chinese), CBC (Canadian Born Chinese), and other BC acronym combinations. Born to Hong Kong parents abroad, they are ethnically Chinese but comfortable in both Western and Chinese cultures and fluent in both English and Cantonese. Similar are the large number of Eurasian children, the product of European and Chinese marriages. They have grown up and entered the workforce and are as confident at the bar as they are around the dim sum table.

WHO IS A HONG KONGER?

Thanks to the exceptional and sustained double act of ineptitude from Britain and China, the issue of nationality in Hong Kong is a muddy mess. First a colony, now a Special Administrative Region, Hong Kong has never been an independent country and there is no such thing as a Hong Kong nationality. The closest equivalent is to become a Hong Kong permanent resident, which, as the name suggests, wins you the right to live in the city permanently. Since 1997 and the handover, this status has been definitively slanted towards the city's majority Chinese population who earn permanent resident status by birth in the city or through their parents. For non-Chinese citizens the picture is somewhat less clear and less favorable. They can earn permanent resident status if they have lived in the city for seven years; this also makes their children eligible as long as they take up the status before they hit age 21. Got a headache yet? You aren't the only one.

While the rules brought in 1997 did give most of the population, Chinese or not, a place to reside and work, it didn't give them nationality. Thanks to the ethnic dimensions of China's nationality laws, only Chinese Hong Kongers automatically became Chinese citizens when the bells tolled 12 on the night of the handover. Ethnic minorities in the city were less lucky. While most could claim citizenship in their home countries or through ancestry, thousands had been here for generations or had children who were no longer entitled to an ancestral passport. The BNO British National Overseas passport they carried was about as useful as a bus pass and didn't confer the right to abode in the United Kingdom or Hong Kong. They effectively became stateless. It may sound like splitting hairs when they still had the right to live and work in Hong Kong, but it had practical implications. You can only gain a HKSAR passport if you are also a Chinese citizen, work at certain levels of the civil service, and receive consular protection.

China pointed the finger at Britain, and as Hong Kong was a British colony and its residents British subjects until 1997, many believed London should provide the solution. But, like a cheap nightclub lothario, as the handover approached, Britain tried to sneak out the window before anybody woke up, continually ignoring, dodging, and rebutting requests for full British passports. In a diplomatic game of pass the parcel, Britain and countries such as India and Nepal butted heads over nationality laws. The argument has continued to rumble on until recently with Britain grudgingly giving out passports. This highlights just how complex being a Hong Konger can be.

MAINLANDERS

Considering 95 percent of Hong Kong's population originally arrived from mainland China, the term mainlander can, at first, be confusing, especially when you consult a map and see that Hong Kong remains very much bolted on to mainland China. As both the residents of China and Hong Kong are Chinese, the word is actually used in Hong Kong to differentiate between the Hong Kong Chinese and the Chinese from the People's Republic of China. A mainlander is simply a citizen of China.

Unsurprisingly, given that one group is made up of confirmed capitalists and the other convinced capitalists, there are many things Hong Kong and the mainland don't see eye to eye on, from freedom of the press to spitting on the street. Although the handover to Beijing was back in 1997, there is a sense that these newlyweds are still trying to feel out the rules of the house and find each other's boundaries. And, while there is an undoubted commitment to making it work, there are also misunderstandings and frustrations that occasionally lead to one partner sleeping on the sofa—usually Hong Kong.

There is a concern in Hong Kong that the increasing number of mainland immigrants coming to the city because of loosening work visa restrictions and Hong Kong's growing dependency on ties with China is a combination that's undermining Hong Kong culture and the Cantonese language. Behind this is a gap in backgrounds, values, and culture, not to mention two completely different languages, Mandarin and Cantonese. As a result, mainlanders in Hong Kong are not always made to feel overly welcome; they are stereotypically characterized as rude, uncultured, and loud. Watch a mainland tourist jump a Hong Kong bus queue and the situation will quickly deteriorate into a UFC (United Fighting Championship) throw-down. There can be substantial animosity between the two groups.

EXPAT PROFILE: MIKE ROWSE

Mike Rowse arrived in Hong Kong from Britain in 1972 with little more than his backpack and a passport. After spells as a tutor and tabloid journalist, he ultimately joined the government and became a career civil servant. He was one of just a handful of expatriate officials to continue in his role after the Hong Kong handover. With stints as director of the financial secretary's office and Hong Kong's first commissioner for tourism, in 2001 he made history as the first expatriate civil servant in Hong Kong's history to naturalize as a Chinese citizen. Now retired with a wife and four kids, he is a regular contributor to the *South China Morning Post* and *Hong Kong Economic Journal* and author of *No Minister & No, Minister: The True Story of HarbourFest.*

Since arriving in Hong Kong, you've worked your way up from tutor to serve in some pretty heavyweight positions in the government. Is this proof that Hong Kong lives up to its hype as the land of opportunity?

Every job I have obtained in Hong Kong is because people were prepared to give me a chance. Very often I knew nobody at all on the inside, and even when I did, the appointment was made in open competition with others. This very openness helps a lot. Once inside an organization, merit is nearly always the main criterion for advancement: If you are getting the job done, you will be recognized. For me, Hong Kong has turned out to be the land of opportunity.

You witnessed the handover of Hong Kong from Britain to China firsthand. What are your memories of the months leading up to the handover and the day itself?

I remember the feeling of excitement, and the thrill, like just before the rollercoaster goes in for a big drop: Here we go – no turning back now. On the day itself I remember the Judiciary being sworn in before the (Chinese) President Jiang Zemin, first in Putonghua (I could only hear one judge speak it), then in English, which all the judges spoke, and I thought "Damn it, this could work."

You're one of just a handful of Western expats to have taken up Chinese citizenship. What triggered your decision and how has your new nationality been received?

It was a voluntary decision on my part since Hong Kong had given me everything and I thought I would be a more convincing spokesman and advocate if I carried a Hong Kong passport. (You need to be a Chinese citizen to be eligible for a Hong Kong passport.) A lot of people were surprised because they thought you had to be ethnic Chinese to qualify for Chinese nationality which I had known for a long time was not correct. I never felt ethnicity was a factor at work, but language ability or lack thereof did affect potential postings.

Do you consider yourself British, Chinese, a Hong Konger, or a mix of all three?

I am a mix of all three. I have British heritage and some British traits. I have come to respect and stand in awe of China. I love Hong Kong, simple as that.

Who is a Hong Konger?

A Hong Konger is someone, anyone, who has made Hong Kong his home.

Hong Kong is often said to have a dual identity, both Western and Chinese. What's your opinion?

Hong Kong does have dual identity and it is always catching you off guard. When you think it is modern and Western, it will suddenly be Chinese and vice versa. As an example, I was stunned by the demonstrations in 1989. One minute we thought we lived in an apolitical city, the next there were one million marching to show support for the students in Tiananmen Square. They were marshalled by 900 policemen who made a point of leaving their weapons in the police armories for the day. Not a single arrest, not a single act of violence, no windows broken – I cannot think of any other city in the world where this could have happened. Again in 2003 when a demonstration was being organized on civil rights, when the police said they would only count marchers who left Victoria Park through a particular gate, ordinary men and women queued for hours to enter the park via other gates so that they could leave through the designated gate and the police would be obliged to count them. Chinese determination combined with a British sense of justice.

What is it you love about the city and what would you say to expats considering moving to Hong Kong?

I love the sense of vibrancy, the feeling – backed up by experience – that there is always something happening. I love the impatience of the place: When people want something, they want it right now. A friend who went back to the U.K. told me two business meetings per day were considered flat out in his company there, whereas in Hong Kong he would expect to conduct eight or nine. Partly of course this is because of Hong Kong's compactness and the incredible public transport network. If you're thinking about a move here, come and look, then jump right in.

For non-Chinese living and working in the city, the differences and friction between Hong Kongers and mainlanders can be somewhat baffling. The most important thing to remember is that while Hong Kongers and mainlanders can rant, scream, and pitch pots and pans at each other, foreigners who get in the middle will soon find the kitchenware flying in their direction. This is essentially a family argument.

Class and Communism

All of Hong Kong's bragging and blustering about capitalism and being the freest economy in the world paints the city as full of citizens rolling around in safes stuffed with money; that's certainly what the government would like you to believe. But not everyone succeeds. The GDP may be one of the highest in Asia, but the gap between rich and poor is, according to the U.N., the widest in the world, with pots of money concentrated in the hands of tycoons and high-flying professionals. Those at the margins of Hong Kong society are rarely talked about in a city where poverty is a cardinal sin. There is little in the way of a social security net and housing programs are woefully

underfunded. Yet, despite around 17 percent of the population living below the poverty line, there is comparatively little popular discontent about the gulf in living standards. Both the government and society at large tend to believe poverty to be a personal failure rather than an issue for the state.

In fact, most Hong Kongers remain wary of state control and there is an aversion to government intervention. This is a legacy left over from the immigrants who fled Communist China. Many older Hong Kongers who had firsthand experience living under the mad and bad years of communism, including Mao's ill fated Great Leap Forward, remain particularly wary

© MARTYNA SZMYTKOWSKA

Everyone in Hong Kong works hard to make a living – but not everyone has the perks of big business.

of China's role in Hong Kong. Attempts by the big bosses in Beijing to impose stricter press controls or security measures are usually met with a sea of protests. Rule of law, freedom of press, and other Western principles gained under British rule have had a profound and lasting influence on Hong Kong and they are principles locals are unwilling to compromise on. While undoubtedly proud to be reunited with China, Hong Kongers exhibit less enthusiasm for the boys in the big red club and the strings they grip in the Hong Kong government.

Social Values and Etiquette

As with many things in Hong Kong, the city's social values and customs are like an orange: Peel away the Westernized skin and you'll find a traditional Chinese center. At the core of many local beliefs and values is the influence of Confucianism, which promotes social order and peace and the primacy of the community over the individual. It is also rigidly hierarchical and age, position, and relationship tend to rule interpersonal interactions. These relationships are dictated by the murky waters of face and *guanxi*, best explained as the status of a person and the respect he or she is due, and their

a small Tin Hau temple squeezed in amongst Hong Kong skyscrapers

© MARTYNA SZMYTKOWSKA

related spinoffs which dictate how you should act. For Westerners, trying to understand these concepts can be like twisting a rubik's cube: When you finally get one side to click into place, you've mangled everything else into a mess.

One potential source of confusion is that many of the Hong Kongers you meet are confident enough to code-switch between Western and Chinese culture. It's also worth noting that like anywhere, Hong Kong is always modernizing and beliefs and values once prevalent are becoming increasingly relaxed.

ETIQUETTE

Nuclear meltdown arguments about the perceived rudeness of Hong Kongers are regular fixtures on the letters to the editor pages of the English-language press. And, while Hong Kongers certainly don't walk out the door each day plotting to step on your toes, there is certainly an indifference to strangers on the street. While face demands an almost embarrassing amount of politeness to people you know, strangers aren't due any and can be ignored—and they are. Rudeness trench warfare is out on the street, where you'll likely be knocked around like a pinball by ignorant pedestrians and have to dodge dagger blows from reckless umbrella-wielding folks. Down on the MTR you'll find the frontline, where boarding and disembarking commuters are regularly caught in a Mexican standoff at the doors. Queue-jumping, seat-stealing, and lack of courtesy towards those with young children are all fodder for the letters pages. Are they worse than other big cities? Probably not. Will they annoy you? Absolutely.

Another change that can take some getting used to is Hong Kong's better-out-than-in philosophy when it comes to bodily functions. While Hong Kongers don't spit on the street, a good hock into a handkerchief is not uncommon and you'll occasionally see locals go deep-sea diving into their ears and noses to retrieve lost treasure. To experience culture shock at Defcon 5, the full blast of a belch delivered inches from your face will stretch your intercultural understanding to the limit. In fairness, most locals also consider much of this behavior rude.

In private, with people you know, the playing field is drastically different and there are a few rules of etiquette that are worth following. First of all, don't do a Broadway bow when you meet your hosts. You're not a samurai and this isn't Japan. If you have to drop something, a small head nod and lowering the eyes will be appreciated when you first meet someone. Otherwise, Hong Kongers have mastered the handshake, although it will usually be a little weaker than the arm pumping you're accustomed to. Deference to elders and superiors is important and if you are meeting anyone older or more senior than you, they should set the tone for how formal or informal the meeting should be. Failing to show the proper respect will be construed as a slight. You should allow them to walk through doors first, sit first, and eat or drink first. They will be aware that you aren't accustomed to Chinese etiquette so these small efforts can go a long way.

When you first meet someone, you may well receive a grilling on how old you are, what's your position at work, how much you earn, and whether you're married. Usually delivered at rapid-fire questionnaire speed, these questions can seem a little intimate for a first meeting, but are used to discover your standing, your *guanxi,* and how much face you're due. Without this information, Hong Kongers will find it difficult to know how to act around you.

DINING ETIQUETTE

Much of Hong Kong life seems to revolve around the dining table and communal eating is essential to everything from family life to concluding business deals. Evening meals and business lunches are often done in groups and food is shared, as evidenced by the spinning tables used in restaurants to deliver grand feasts to up to eight people. Communal dining is a highly ritualized experience; there are a few rules and customs worth following to make sure you end up with food—and not your foot—in your mouth.

Whoever is oldest, or at business meetings the most senior, acts as the host. You should wait for the host to sit at the head of the table and invite

a classic Hong Kong meal: Blue Girl beer and noodles

© AGNIESZKA SZMYTKOWSKA

you to sit, before taking your seat. It's normal for the host to order for everyone and although they will usually ask for suggestions, it's best to keep your arm down. It's considered good form and food face to let them do the ordering. In general, a good host will not order anything normally seen between the pages of *National Geographic,* but there are occasions when an honor meal will be served, usually involving something rare, pricy, and potentially displeasing to a Westerner's palate. Shark Fin soup is the most popular and fairly inoffensive, at least to the taste buds. Unfortunately, there is little room here to escape eating without causing offence. Health reasons or allergies are the best excuse, although both can be a tough sell for the snake course special. Tea and water are usually provided as communal drinks and, at business dinners, wine or a spirit, though rarely beer.

Once the food arrives, resist the temptation to spear the nearest piece of meat with your chopsticks. instead, wait for the host to dig in. Food generally comes in small bowls, along with side dishes of vegetables, various sauces, and rice. Health scares mean communal chopsticks are now used to serve food. It's best not to treat the table as a roulette wheel and instead wait for the host to spin the table and deliver a different set of food within striking distance of your chopsticks. Don't be afraid to get your hands dirty when dining. Slurping, chomping, and lip-smacking are considered celebrations of the quality of food and you can feel free to lift soup bowls to your lips to lap up the leftovers or suck any bones dry—everybody else will. Next to your bowl you'll be provided with a small plate to deposit any bones, gristle, or other leftovers. Avoid sticking chopsticks upright into rice, which signifies death, or laying them across the top of your bowl. Instead, set them to the side on your plate.

The bill is the responsibility of the host and splitting the bill is very rare. Instead, you can reciprocate the offer of a meal sometime in the future, if amongst friends.

FACE

The key in the clock that winds Chinese society, the importance of *face* in Hong Kong is hard to overstate. It subtly but strongly governs the interaction and relationships between individuals, from your friends and co-workers to your doorman or driver. It decides who pays for dinner, what sort of gift you should give, and how to accept compliments and deliver criticism, as well as infinite other social interactions.

What is it? It's a good question and one that has kept Western philosophers locked in debate for centuries. The barstool definition is the status of someone within society or a particular community and the respect that they are due. For a foreigner it can initially be impossible to tell just how much face someone has. Hong Kongers on the other hand are always assessing, always measuring. Basic indicators are wealth, family history, profession, and position, the big four that Hong Kongers will ask you about to get an idea of your social standing. But it's far more than a class distinction. At its nuts-and-bolts level, when you really get to know people, it's about your achievements, relationships, and behavior. It's a top-to-toe personality assessment and the more face you have, the more respect and honor you are due from those around you.

Unfortunately you can't buy face at your local 7-Eleven. It has to be earned. Aside from gift-giving, promotions, and widening your circle of influential friends, the most common way to gain face is to be given it by someone else when they show respect to you. For example, say your mother-in-law visits: In this particular relationship, as the elder, she holds the power and the face. When she says she enjoyed the meal you cooked she is giving you face, but you can't simply say, "Yes, it was bloody good." Face relationships are based on reciprocity and you must first claim modesty and then return the compliment, saying you only wish you could cook dumplings as well as her. And *boom,* everybody has bagged some face. Not showing the proper respect or breaking this reciprocity causes people to lose face, which is where all your troubles will begin.

So far everything is probably sounding pretty familiar; show respect to people and compliment your mother-in-law—easy. The difference is that Chinese society has a much more fixed code that must be followed when being respectful. People are more sensitive to perceived slights and the consequences can be much more drastic. Not dumping your colleague's, friend's, or mother-in-law's face down the drain is a constant pitfall that stalks all expats and it's here that Western values and Chinese values often clash. While Western culture stresses the right of the individual and encourages him or her to express their opinion, Chinese culture places more value on the community and maintaining peace. Confrontation and disagreement are to be avoided at all costs. This can prove a difficult trick to learn for Westerners who are used to addressing problems head on, but bulldozer showdowns are considered rude by Hong Kongers. Upsetting group harmony will result in a loss of face for both parties involved. Instead, issues are approached gently and dealt with by suggesting improvements, rather than by reprimands and accusations.

Fear of upsetting group harmony or causing a loss of face by disappointing someone also mean Hong Kongers are very reluctant to use the word *no*. Instead, they will use *if, but,* and *maybe,* ignore the issue, and occasionally tell the odd white lie. This can lead to major misunderstandings, where an expat thinks they got the thumbs up and the Hong Konger thinks he said *no*. Ultimately, unless you specifically hear the word *yes,* everything else should be considered a delicately delivered *no*.

GENDER EQUALITY

Traditionally Hong Kong has, like Chinese society as a whole, been a masculine society with sons prized over daughters and men expected to head into the workplace and women into the kitchen. Things have changed drastically over the decades and Hong Kong now comes near the top of gender-equality rankings in Asia. While ordinances and laws that prohibit discrimination based on gender have helped, the real change has come from Hong Kong's success-hungry employers who are more interested in who can do the job best, not which bathroom they use. Women make up nearly half the workforce and although men still dominate the top positions and politics, many glass ceilings have been shattered. Careers are considered as important to women as they are to men and families will usually pass the baby on to grandparents or employ a domestic helper.

Conversely, the expat world is mostly, although not exclusively, male. While expat women will encounter few problems in the workplace, much of the expat social scene revolves around drinking, sports, and "picking up" women (or at least trying to), and it can be harder for women to find friends. Female expats also decry the Hong Kong dating scene with expat men often preoccupied with local women and interested local men hard to find.

Religion

Hong Kongers take a pragmatic and intelligent approach to religion, combining the beliefs, values, and practices of Buddhism and Taoism with the superstitions of ancestor worship. For Westerners used to religions having very clear and often bloody lines drawn between them, this elasticity towards worship can seem strange but also attractive. Taoism, and to a lesser extent Buddhism, is far less doctrinal than its Western counterparts; adherents in Hong Kong don't attend temple at a set time as a group, but as individuals. Taoism and Buddhism stress values and principles that should be followed, many of which dovetail with Confucian teachings.

With few ritual practices, rights of passage, or even the weekly milestone of Mass, it can be easy to think Hong Kongers are Mickey Mouse worshippers. This is a mistake. Despite Hong Kong's external modernity, religion and superstitions that have accumulated over the centuries are taken very seriously. The number of followers of each religion is hard to estimate because everyone has their own cocktail of beliefs, but there are over 600 temples and smaller shrines in the city and they are rarely quiet. Festivals to the various legendary gods, from the Tin Hau Festival to the Mid Autumn Festival, are celebrated energetically and often bring the whole city to a standstill.

Hong Kong's dual personality also extends to religion. Thanks to colonialism, you'll also find a thriving Christian community and substantial congregations of Muslims, Sikhs, and Jews.

TAOISM AND BUDDHISM

While there are strict Taoists and strict Buddhists in Hong Kong, Taoism and Buddhism tend to be treated as a package deal and many temples contain deities and statues from both religions and locals frequently intermix the two faiths.

Meaning the way or the path, Taoism was originally a collection of beliefs and values, a philosophy intended to guide individuals on the right path. Helpfully, Taoism is often described as indescribable, as simply the beginning and end of everything. Broadly speaking, it is non-interventionist, nonconfrontational, and

© MARTYNA SZMYTKOWSKA

The Po Lin Monastery on Lantau is one of Hong Kong's largest Buddhist complexes.

advises allowing life to take its natural course and acting in accordance with nature. It promotes balance through yin and yang, and feng shui and tai chi are two common ways of restoring harmony. Taoism lacked a divine and revelatory figure like Jesus Christ or Muhammad and instead developed over time through the teachings and thinking of many leaders. Although, Lao-tzu is still considered by many to be the father of the movement and his writings *Tao Te Ching* the seminal text. It was only later that Taoism incorporated temples and legendary gods and most of the temples in Hong Kong are Taoist, each home to a number of deities. The most popular are Tin Hau (Goddess of the Sea), in a nod to Hong Kong's seafaring past, and Kwan Tai (God of War).

To bring luck and good fortune, Hong Kongers pray to certain gods or, more commonly, slip them some goodies. Say Mr. Tang has an examination coming up to become a police detective, he'll go down to a Taoist temple and offer up a few oranges to the God of Education. I've even seen a Big Mac served up to the hungry God of War, who must be appeased. Temples are open throughout the day and you're always free to visit, just keep in mind people are worshipping.

Brought to China from India sometime in the fifth century, Buddhism commands a considerable following in Hong Kong and the Lord Buddha's birthday is a public holiday, when statues of the fat fellow are taken out for their annual bath. Hong Kong Buddhists follow the Mahayana branch of Buddhism that preaches that enlightenment (true peace from the suffering in the world) can be achieved through compassion, wisdom, and meditation. Many of its teachings interlock with those of Taosim and Confucianism. Buddhism does tend to be more organized and there are several Buddhist monasteries and nunneries in Hong Kong, where they run courses and meetings. Buddhists are also involved in schools, charities, and, to a limited extent, politics. Most Buddhist temples are found in secluded areas, to promote peace and tranquility, and are usually less ostentatious and much quieter than their Taoist counterparts.

ANCESTOR WORSHIP

The oldest of Chinese beliefs, ancestor worship requires that you pay respect and reverence to the dead, even long-gone ancestors. Showing family ties go beyond the grave in Hong Kong, ancestor worship is also motivated by the fear that spirits can come back to haunt you (not in the *Beetlejuice* sense): that a restless spirit can bring bad luck and make a business lose money or a marriage fail. In bad news to altruists, philanthropists, and those who were honest on their tax returns, the belief is that the spirit world is very similar to this one and spirits need to be made comfortable. During the Hungry Ghost Festival, spirits are supposed to be able to cross between the worlds and Hong Kongers burn fake money, known as Hell Bank notes, as well as miniature paper cars, houses, and even smart phones to appease them.

CHRISTIANITY

Protestants and Catholics both rowed into Hong Kong with the British Army and the religions have a history in Hong Kong dating back to 1841. Today there are around 600,000 Christians in the city, close to 10 percent of the population, evenly split between the Catholic and Protestant faiths; most are practicing Christians. The Catholic Church has 41 churches, as well as smaller chapels and halls, and the Protestants have at least twice that number split between Baptists, Lutherans, and Anglicans, as well as other branches. Most services are in Cantonese, although many, if not most, churches also provide English-language services and there are numerous foreign priests and pastors. Both the Catholic and Protestant churches are heavily involved in the community, running a number of schools, hospitals, and various social welfare programs. In a testament to the city's healthy attitude to freedom of religion, Hong Kong Chief Executive Donald Tsang is a practicing Catholic.

OTHER RELIGIONS

Christianity wasn't the only religion to arrive in Hong Kong courtesy of the British Army, Pakistani recruits brought Islam and Indian recruits Hinduism and Sikhism, and all three have continued to thrive in Hong Kong thanks to subsequent immigrations.

While official government statistics record 90,000 Muslims in Hong Kong, it's believed the true figure could be as high as 200,000, swelled by a large Indonesian community, many of whom are undocumented. The vast majority of Muslims are non-Chinese, mostly migrants from Pakistan and the Middle East, although there are an estimated 30,000 Chinese adherents. There are five functioning Mosques, the most important of which is the Kowloon Mosque and Islamic Centre that acts as a de facto community center. The Hindu community of Hong Kong numbers some 40,000, mostly Nepalese and Indian followers centered on the Hindu Temple in Happy Valley. Smaller still are the city's 10,000 Sikhs, who are almost all Indian and worship at the Sikh Temple in Wan Chai. Jews also arrived in Hong Kong a short time after the British colony was set up, but as traders rather than soldiers. Today there are around 3,000 Jews, mostly temporary expats who worship at the Ohel Leah Synagogue.

The Arts

Despite accusations that it has all the cultural capacity of a whoopee cushion, Hong Kong is not the artistic wilderness critics would make it out to be. This is after all the city that gave the world John Woo, the kung-fu flick, and Cantopop (Cantonese popular music). While Hollywood and hip hop are certainly popular, movie screens are dominated by high-flying martial arts and the airwaves by the fresh-faced crooners of Cantopop, and Canto-culture is able to brag regional influence.

FILM

The undoubted king of culture in Hong Kong, the city's prolific film industry produced a string of global blockbusters and made household names of stars such as Jet Li and Bruce Lee and directors John Woo and Wong Kar-wai. Much of this success is due to the kung-fu film and their jaw-dropping fight

Bruce Lee, Hong Kong's most famous son (sculpture by Cao Chongen)

© MARTYNA SZMYTKOWSKA

sequences; Hong Kong directors have proved masters of this genre. *The Way of the Dragon,* with Bruce Lee and Chuck Norris squaring off, is still considered by many to be the seminal martial-arts film. But it's not all about beating people up. Sometimes it's about shooting them. Few directors since Shakespeare have managed to rack up a higher body count than John Woo, whose smart action films have made him one of Hollywood's most sought after directors. Other major names to watch are the critically acclaimed Wong Kar-wai and comedy king Stephen Chow.

Unfortunately, cinema schedules that were once stacked with locally produced films in Cantonese have been looking somewhat lean lately and the industry has been in crisis. Thanks to the relaxation of censorship laws, the Chinese mainland film industry boomed and attracted Hong Kong's brightest and best up north, tempted by bigger budget films, fatter pay checks, and

THE QUICK AND EASY GUIDE TO HONG KONG FESTIVALS

Hong Kong's straight-laced, buttoned-down business reputation suggests a city that's idea of a party is champagne, cheeseboards, and a soothing Chris de Burgh cover band. Don't be fooled. Beneath their suits, Hong Kongers have a party animal ready to escape – and it frequently does. This is, after all, the city that perfected the dragon dance, sends people clambering up 60-feet towers to pluck off buns, and has never seen a firework it didn't like – or light. Hong Kong has long been a stronghold of Chinese culture and its traditional festivals are celebrated with energy, color, and lots of noise.

Because most Chinese festivals are linked to the phases of the moon, dates vary from year to year. For the following festivals, months are listed.

• **Chinese New Year** (Jan./Feb.): The year's biggest celebration can be somewhat of a disappointment from a party point of view.

The city shuts down for three days and most people either jet off to somewhere warmer or stay at home with families; much of the life is sucked out of the city. That said, both the annual parade and fireworks display are spectacular.

• **Spring Lantern Festival** (Jan./Feb.): Also known as Chinese Valentine's Day and marking the end of Chinese New Year, the Spring Lantern Festival sees colorful lanterns fill parks, streets, and villages.

• **Ching Ming** (Mar./Apr.): An important day for families who trek to graveyards to clean their ancestors' tombs and burn paper offerings, frequently setting half the hillside alight in the process.

• **Birthday of Tin Hau** (Apr./May): The Goddess of the Sea – Tin Hau – is much revered in Hong Kong and her birthday is a day of widespread celebration, especially in fishing the chance to play for a much bigger audience. This is much to the chagrin of Hong Kong audiences who largely don't speak Mandarin. Local films appear in Cantonese only; so if you want to see them, you'll have to wait for the DVD release, which usually comes with English subtitles.

Admiration for Hong Kong's film industry is usually a great icebreaker at parties. That is, of course, as long as you don't mention Jackie Chan. Ever since the star expressed his doubts in democracy—"I'm gradually beginning to feel that we Chinese need to be controlled. If we're not being controlled, we'll just do what we want"—he's been public enemy number one.

MUSIC

The soundtrack to your Hong Kong adventure: You can't escape Cantopop, no matter how hard you might try. Found blasting from shops, taxis, and, if

communities. It's like looking at the Love Parade on boats: Hundreds of vessels are decked out in colorful ribbons and bright banners and loaded with offerings for Tin Hau. At Tin Hau temples expect elaborate and noisy ceremonies and dragon dances.

- **Cheung Chau Bun Festival** (Apr./May): Hong Kong's oddest festival and one of its best, the Cheung Chau Bun Festival is celebrated on its namesake island with a carnival parade that includes children dressed up as ghosts "floating" on stilts and the famous bun climb, where participants pitch themselves up a 60-foot bun tower and battle for the buns.

- **Dragon Boat Festival** (May/June): Centered around the International Dragon Boat Races, this festival is the culmination of some serious gym time and weeks of training as competitors go paddle to paddle in these breakneck boat races. For spectators, it's about hitting the beach, the beer

tent, and, for some, the floor, with revelers spending as much time admiring each other as the intricately carved wooden boats.

- **Hungry Ghost Festival** (Aug./Sept.): Hong Kong's very own Halloween – it's believed that mischievous and malevolent spirits try to return from the spirit world during the Hungry Ghost Festival. To appease them Hong Kongers burn paper offerings of essential items needed in the afterlife, including money, cars, and of course iPods.

- **Mid-Autumn Festival** (Sept./Oct.): Second only to Chinese New Year in importance, the Mid-Autumn Festival is famous for its spectacular lantern displays, winding dragon dances, and, most importantly, diet-ruining mooncakes.

- **Chung Yeung** (Sept./Oct.): Similar to Ching Ming, Chung Yeung is another day for dusting down ancestors' graves, and also for hiking and picnicking on hilltops.

you're very unlucky, radios at your workplace. Cantopop is a hybrid of Western pop and Chinese influences, as well as hip hop, rock-and-roll, and possibly vuvuzelas. Crooning in both Cantonese and English, Cantopop's carefully packaged stars dominate both the charts and the tabloids, not only in Hong Kong but across many Asian countries.

TRADITIONAL CHINESE CULTURE

Hong Kong has been a guardian for Chinese culture ever since Chairman Mao and his fanatical red book–flaunting henchmen took a hatchet to Chinese traditions and art during the dark days of the Cultural Revolution on the mainland. You'll see tai chi, feng shui, and other time-honored rituals, such as the noisy dragon dances made famous by Chinatowns around the world, continuing to flourish. Cantonese Opera also has a home in Hong Kong. The art form had all but flatlined in the past decade, but Hong Kong is attempting to breathe new life into it with subsidies, school projects, and more performances. Its staid plots of damsels in distress and dastardly villains told through martial arts, acrobatics, and singing have changed little over the years, and the sleep-inducing four-hour shows may be too much for the BlackBerry generation.

WESTERN CULTURE

Many Western art forms enjoy a strong presence in Hong Kong, from a professional comedy club to the full-blown Hong Kong Philharmonic. Theater has become particularly popular in recent years; alongside performances of classic and contemporary-classic plays, a number of more cutting-edge and innovative groups have received plaudits. Productions may be in Cantonese or English or alternate on different nights and English subtitles are widely available. You'll also find regular music festivals dedicated to jazz, classical music, and just about everything in between. World famous names in theater, opera, and music regularly visit the city; there is no shortage of events to keep your calendar ringed red.

SPORTS AND RECREATION

Hong Kong is fanatical about sports. Well, it's fanatical about one sport: horse racing. Following it with an unrivalled passion, thousands of punters pack out the weekly races at Happy Valley and Sha Tin. While the sport might have noble overtones, much of this enthusiasm is driven not by the thrill of the race but the thrill of betting your house on the outcome. Gambling on horse racing is rampant in Hong Kong and the Hong Kong Jockey Club is by far the city's largest single tax payer, filling the tax collector's pockets with more than HK$10 billion annually.

PULL ON YOUR PARTY PANTS FOR THE HONG KONG SEVENS

Officially a rugby tournament, unofficially an annual effort to drain Hong Kong's beer reserves dry, the Hong Kong Sevens is not only a magnet for fans around the world, beamed out to over 200 million homes, and Hong Kong's biggest sporting event, but more importantly it's the city's biggest party and one that's hugely popular with expats. While the rugby may be the reason to gather, for many the sport is simply a sideshow; the Mardi Gras atmosphere, pitchers of beer, and the chance to pull on a cowboy outfit are the real attraction.

If you're not familiar with the game, Rugby Sevens is basically a trimmed down, souped-up version of full rugby union. Played over 14 minutes on full rugby pitch with 7 players instead of 15, it's faster, sharper, and more exciting. The Hong Kong Sevens tournament is the flagship event in the International Rugby Board's Sevens Series and attracts teams like England, Australia, and the United States.

If you'd rather wash your eyes out with bleach than watch sports — let alone rugby — don't fear; you shouldn't let a little thing like the game get in the way of a great day out. The Sevens is revered for its legendary Carnival atmosphere with the fans in the infamous South Stand dressing up as cartoon characters, superheroes, and naughtier R-rated costumes to cheer on their favorite team. Completing the experience are pitchers, parties, and pictures that shouldn't find their way onto Facebook in the bars and pubs of Wan Chai over the Sevens weekend in March.

Despite Hong Kong stadium holding 40,000 people, tickets are harder to get hold of than unicorn horns and most are smuggled out under the table to corporate sponsors. If your company doesn't have tickets, you can cross your fingers and toes and try the limited release public sale. Otherwise, ask friends and colleagues in the run-up to the tournament; someone always knows someone with an extra ticket.

Beyond that, Hong Kongers generally feel they have better things to do with their time than to spend it glued to ESPN. The Hong Kong team does participate as an individual nation in most sports and competitions but, not surprising given both its size and the city's indifference, it has struggled to make a mark, with table tennis being a notable exception in both popularity and success. British sports continue to hold a lot of sway in Hong Kong and English Premiership soccer, or football as it's known here, is arguably the most popular spectator sport, judging by the hundreds of TVs dedicated to screening games at dozens of bars across Wan Chai and Lan Kwai Fong. A number of cricket and rugby clubs have also survived since colonial days and, while the majority of players and spectators remain expats, the city's blockbuster sports event is the sold-out Hong Kong Rugby Sevens in March, which draws a crowd from all over the globe.

Sport for the sake of keeping fit and staying healthy rather than competition is more common and Hong Kongers are fairly active. While gyms have become increasingly popular, traditional sports are still widely practiced. Hong Kong's reputation as a center for martial arts is undimmed and many different disciplines retain widespread appeal. The most prominent is tai chi, which is practiced by thousands of people in parks around the city and valued for its health benefits to the body and mind, particularly amongst seniors. Those looking for more competition and to squeeze a little more horsepower from their muscles are increasingly turning to dragon boating, one of the world's fastest growing sports and one reborn in the modern era in Hong Kong. Particularly popular with young professionals, it sees teams of up to 20 paddlers, pitched against each other in 40-foot-long dragon boats in a frantic, mad splash and dash to the finish line. Colorful banner flags, deafening drummers, and the intricately carved boats, crowned by a dragon's head, all add to the drama and the annual International Dragon Boat Races draws massive crowds.

Community

Undoubtedly one of the most challenging aspects of moving to a new country is waving goodbye to your family and friends at the airport. Once you've arrived in Hong Kong, getting out and meeting people should be a priority; being able to relax with new friends, ask questions, and share common frustrations and experiences about your new home helps ease culture shock considerably. Making new friends is one of the most important, yet overlooked, aspects of moving abroad. People dedicate time and energy to setting up a new house and settling into their new jobs, yet they don't make a priority of making friends. Trying to meet new people can be equally difficult and frustrating and often requires the same proactive spirit.

Luckily, there is perhaps no city in the world better to get expats clinking drinks than Hong Kong. The number of clubs, organizations, and circles in the city is endless, many of which are directly aimed at the expat community. Perhaps the most popular way to meet new people is through the city's vibrant sports clubs, where life is as much based around the bar as it is around the ball. If your appearance on the football pitch is likely to signal broken windows and several months off work, there are alternatives. Private members clubs continue to dominate many people's social circles, while mixers organized by consulates, chambers of commerce, and various cultural organizations are a good place to meet like-minded people (and climb the career ladder at the same time). If you've got a passion, a move to Hong Kong does not mean you need to surrender it at customs. Expat and English-speaking groups exist for everything from amateur dramatics to gluten-free dining. When all else fails, fall back on your passport. Almost every nationality has its own clubs and neighborhood meet-ups.

Old clubs close, new organizations open, and it's impossible to list them all. A couple of good resources when you arrive are *Hong Kong Magazine* and *Time Out,* which both have classified listings. Over on geoexpat.com, you'll find expats of every hue willing to point you in the direction of the group you want and, if not, probably three or four who'll help you set one up.

MEETING THE LOCALS

Hong Kong is a fantastic place to meet people from all over the globe, from countries you've never heard of and, in at least one example I've experienced, countries that don't exist anymore. Your Facebook friend list will read like the opening ceremony of the Olympics. Perhaps surprisingly, given its geographic positioning, it's not a great place to meet Cantonese people—or locals as they're better known. The reason is language. While many Hong Kongers can speak decent, even fluent, English, speaking a second language is always a challenge and they are understandably more comfortable having friends with whom they can speak Cantonese. Very, very few expats speak Cantonese, which means English-speaking expats and Cantonese-speaking locals tend to run in different groups and the two communities live fairly separate lives outside of work. This is a real shame because to really get to know a place you need to know the locals. All of the groups and events that follow offer the chance to meet locals, to one extent or another—although, mom and toddler groups tend to be specifically aimed at English-speaking expats and, to a lesser extent, so do some of the cultural and art organizations. Sports teams are a better bet, while volunteer organizations will usually be made up mostly of local Hong Kongers.

WHERE TO MEET PEOPLE
Sports Clubs

Sports clubs have provided a place for expats to meet up and get muddy since the city's colonial days and are still very much an integral part of expat life in the city. Their solid attendance figures are as much due to a commitment to partying as they are to practicing and they are a great place to make new friends. Few sports don't have at least one team in Hong Kong, although soccer, rugby, and hockey are some of the most popular and can boast dozens of clubs and competitive local leagues. The dedication required in joining varies from a lazy kick about on Sunday to well-established clubs with coaches and

EXPAT PROFILE: ANGIE WONG

As the first food editor for *Time Out Hong Kong* and editor of the city's first Zagat Guide, Angie Wong is one of Hong Kong's best known and best loved food writers. Born and raised in New York City to a Hong Kong Chinese family, she is currently working on her first book about being "Almost Chinese." Passionate about Cantonese food and Hong Kong, you can find some of her finest work and insights into Hong Kong's most exclusive kitchens over at www.angiewong.com.

What made you decide to leave the United States and move to Hong Kong?

I had just graduated from journalism school and started working at an international magazine in New York. I had to get in a very long line if I wanted to write for this publication. My then-boss told me if I ever wanted to get published, it would be an advantage to leave the United States and get my start in a the market that wasn't so saturated with reporters. So I bought a ticket.

What were your first impressions of living in Hong Kong? How have your impressions changed over time?

There was so much energy running through Hong Kong when I first landed. You can literally feel it pushing you. I knew I wasn't going to get much sleep while I was here. Between work and going out, I was clocking around four hours a night for my first year. There is a lot of drinking and lots of meeting new people. At one point I felt like if I didn't go out for one night, I might miss something. It's New York times 60.

At first you do the city life, but then if you are like me, you need an escape. And when that happens, there is no better place: Just jump in a taxi in Central and within 20 minutes, you are at a beach or on a mountain top somewhere.

managers who will expect you on time—every time—for training and not to light up at half time. The more serious teams, such as Kowloon Cricket Club and Valley Rugby Football Club run teams in several sports and often several teams in the same sport at different levels. Their membership fee wins you access to the training ground, leisure facilities, and clubhouse bars and restaurants. They have a strong sense of tradition and belonging and organize regular social nights, member events, and their much-celebrated end-of-season galas and balls. It's not unfair to say that most social events are fueled by alcohol, and nights often have all the hallmarks of spring break in Cancún.

Joining a club is fairly straightforward, especially with a range of teams at every ability level. Almost all teams and sports also run women's teams, which are no less intense on the pitch or on the bar stool. Before you pick a club, ask around at work; many larger companies enter teams in various leagues. Most clubs run recruitment drives in September, just before the season kicks off, but

Why is food such an important part of Hong Kong culture?

Food in Hong Kong is more than just eating. Food is entertainment here. Food is political. Food gives identity to a society searching for one just a decade after the handover. It is the means for having a social life. Along every step of getting food, from chatting it up with the vegetable lady at the wet market to sharing a table at a cha chan teng, you must engage with others.

Also, in Hong Kong, people pretty much eat out all the time. Kitchens are generally tiny and food costs are high. It would cost less for most people to eat out than to cook. Cooking at home here is a luxury. There are over 14,000 restaurants on the concentrated island of Hong Kong. And at least seven new restaurants open every day. This gives you a clue into the importance of food to people here.

What are three or four dishes that you would recommend beginners to Cantonese cuisine try?

Go to a chop shop and get a plate of roast pork, roast goose, and steamed chicken over rice. Yup, the ones hanging in the windows. One of the best meals you'll ever have. Then look for a beef brisket noodle shop, one with a long line, and go to town.

Can you see yourself moving back to the States and leaving Hong Kong any time soon?

Someday I will go back to the States. That's still home. But living there will never be the same, not after all that I've experienced, and not with my new set of references. I believe every American should leave the comforts of their home for a few years to live abroad. I will return to the States with a deeper appreciation and a better understanding of nearly everything.

you'll be able to try out at any time. As a starting point, try the local clubs in your area; Happy Valley and Kowloon are two of the most notable.

Alternatively, if the only thing you want to be lifting are pints, you can sign up for a club's social membership, which will see you included on all their beer-fueled adventures. Those who are training-shy and want something on a more casual basis should check out expat forums, such as geoexpat.com, or ask around at British pubs.

Private Members Club

For many foreigners, particularly Americans, private member clubs have associations with cloak and dagger rituals, secret handshakes, and the kind of initiations that could land you in prison, hospital, or at the psychiatrist. Yet, behind the covert operations that an increasing number of clubs are now eschewing, Hong Kong's private member clubs still play a pivotal role in the

HOW DO YOU DIM SUM?

Less of a culinary experience, more of a dining adventure, Hong Kong's celebrated dim sum culture is as renowned for its atmosphere, rituals, and traditions as it is for its spring rolls and pork buns. But for first-time visitors faced with a raucous dining room, stony-faced staff, and no idea about the rules, it can be a daunting prospect. Here's what you need to know.

Dim sum is a social experience, an excuse for family and friends to catch up over food; dishes are served in small bite-sized portions that are designed to be shared and tables are often eight-seater affairs with table tops that can spin to deliver dishes to everyone in the group. While you can dim sum solo, and restaurants are increasingly adding tables to accommodate couples, you'll be able to try far fewer dishes and will have to share your space with fellow strangers going stag. You should also be prepared for noise. The first time I entered a dim sum restaurant I thought there was a fight going on. Cantonese is not a lullaby language and when 50 plus families are all screaming to be heard above the clatter of cutlery and the thunder of trolleys, it can feel more like dining on the deck of an aircraft carrier.

You'll get little help from the staff, who generally consider customers an annoyance to be actively avoided. Top dim sum restaurants in Hong Kong live and die on the quality of their food, but even here you shouldn't expect bow-tied waiters swooning

city's business and social life. For wealthy professionals, expats and locals alike, membership is essential as both a sign of status and as an opportunity to wine and dine with all the right people. Long known as bastions of fine dining and lounge room drinking, modern Hong Kong clubs now offer first-rate leisure facilities, such as state-of-the-art gyms, swimming pools, and spa facilities, as well as an exhaustive activity program.

Which club you want to join will very much depend on what sort of rewards you are hoping to reap—is membership an investment in your career or your family? Some of the longer-standing clubs, such as the Hong Kong Club or Foreign Correspondents Club are still very much rooted in the clubby atmosphere of men propping up the bar, armed only with a newspaper and a pint. They have a regular schedule of business lunches and dinners and often invite heavyweight names from the world of politics and economics to give speeches. They remain an unrivalled place to meet the city's most influential and powerful people. Of course, even if the head of the IMF gives a real crowd pleaser of a speech, your three-year-old child is likely to be unimpressed. Your other option is family-orientated clubs where the focus is on events and facilities, such as yoga studios, tennis courts, ice skating rinks, and bowling alleys. Many clubs now offer a balance of business and pleasure, and all will have extensive and usually first-rate over you. You'll need to be demanding and leave most of your manners at the door if you want to get a seat, eat, and even pay. The maître d's who guard the door at the most popular dim sum places are notoriously hardnosed, ushering regulars past long lines of malnourished customers who've been reduced to chewing their own finger nails. Be patient, the busier the place, the better the food. If there is no maître d', you're on your own. Hover like a hawk around diners ready to leave and expect to fight with someone who arrived after you but spins tales about being first, their reservations, and their terminal disease, depending on how naive they think you are. Just sit down.

Unfortunately, the traditional dim sum cart that was once wheeled around table to table has been retired in all but a handful of places. Instead, you order by ticking what you want on a small menu card, which is then handed to the waiter. Whether an English menu is on offer very much depends on where you're dining, although, assuming you can convince the waiter to put in the leg work, even the smallest of places should be able to rustle one up. Once you're ready to pay, the waiter will tally up the ticks on your menu card and hand you the bill. The service charge may or may not be added. If it's a place you think you'll return to, consider dropping a few notes so you can at least get the maître d' to acknowledge your existence the next time you visit.

dining options. There are also clubs geared towards certain hobbies and sports, such as golf clubs and yacht clubs, which will usually offer exactly the same sort of extensive facilities mentioned and a dedicated golf course or marina.

Unfortunately, like at high school, just because you've found a club you want to hold hands with, it doesn't mean they'll want to hold hands back. The fearsome selection policies of yesteryear, when quality was measured through the amount of blue blood in your veins and the size of your moustache, may have waned, but potential members still have to endure a selection process similar to a poodle at a dog show. Different clubs enforce different rules, but some of the hoops you'll be expected to hop through include a formal nomination by members, an introductory cocktail party, and a thorough interview. Clubs try to maintain a steady number of members and the waitlist can be biblical, sometimes years long, sometimes closed. This is despite membership fees that often run upwards of HK$1 million. Some clubs offer debentures that give red-carpet access to their waiting list and these can swap hands on the black market for millions.

Of course a club is never really closed, but they will only admit the right caliber of member. Perhaps the simplest way to gain membership in a club is through your company. Corporate memberships are frequent and many of Hong Kong's most influential companies maintain debentures with a club or several clubs that

INSIDE HONG KONG'S CLUBS

First set up by the city's colonial elite around the turn of the century, Hong Kong's clubs were inspired by and modeled on the gentlemen's clubs that flourished in London. Intended to be fine dining and drinking societies – a home away from home for gentlemen – they provided a place for men of blue blood who had nothing to do all day to meet other fellas with too much time on their hands to do nothing together while drinking whiskey. The London clubs were highly discerning in their selection of potential members, frowning on membership by the aspiring middle class and men who actually earned their money rather than pocketed it from daddy. From their very start, Hong Kong's clubs were more practical.

Opened in 1846, the Hong Kong Club was Hong Kong's first gentleman's club, and while it attracted the city's titled civil servants, the fledgling colony was decidedly short on barons and dukes, and membership was instead dominated by prominent merchants and traders.

Thanks to its influential members, it was often said – only half jokingly – that it was the real seat of power in the colony and it was from here over lunches and sundowners that a handful of people plotted the success of empire, the colony, and, perhaps most importantly, how to line their own pockets. Like those opened across the British Empire, the clubs were bastions of Britishness and a badge of authority. Membership was racist, sexist, and thoroughly Victorian. Women were barred, although they at least had their own clubs, unlike the city's Chinese population who couldn't get a membership card no matter the size of their bank balance. Even British men who married Asian women were often handed their box of belongings and shown to the door while their Eurasian offspring were a constant source of scandal and usually given the cold shoulder.

This may all sound like tales from the far, forgotten past, but while private member clubs around the world folded along with the Union

guarantee entrance. Even if they don't have reservations, they might still be able to secure you a seat at the table through some subtle influence. It's also worth keeping club membership in mind when choosing your apartment complex; many maintain slimmed-down clubhouses that offer many of the benefits of club membership as part of your rent. Information about clubs is far easier to come by than it once was, although a handful still wrap themselves in James Bond secrecy. M for Membership (www.mformembership.com) has a list of around half of Hong Kong's clubs along with their membership types and fees.

Volunteering

Not only is volunteering a great way to give something back to your community, for expats it's an unrivalled way to get under the skin of the city and meet the people who live here. Don't be discouraged by not speaking Cantonese, while this is a prerequisite for positions in some organizations, there are many

Jack as the Empire retreated, Hong Kong's clubs managed to not only survive but thrive. Untouched by the collapse of the British Empire and seemingly unmoved by the modern world's changing attitude to race, at Hong Kong's clubs it was very much business as usual. The clubs continued to revel in their separation: coats of arms remained stapled to the wall, cricket was on the TV, and men of substance could sink into the same worn armchairs they'd inhabited for the last dozen years. Some had become more egalitarian in their membership, but they remained predominately white. The flagship Hong Kong Club actually had nothing in its rule book stating that they didn't admit Chinese members; they simply weren't nominated.

By the 1980s the change that the clubs had resisted was already turning Hong Kong on its head. Many of the colonial-era Hongs (major business houses) had been taken over by local Chinese businessmen and as the Hong Kong handover approached, the British establishment who frequented the clubs was set to sail off into the sunset. This forced the clubs into a fundamental change and, while a sprinkling of Chinese members had already taken up membership, by the mid-1980s clubs had thrown open the doors and started actively recruiting. Today the majority membership at most clubs is Chinese, although white members are still proportionally over represented. Some bemoan the loss of the clubby atmosphere and the camaraderie, claiming that club members no longer know one another and that clubs have become extravagant leisure centers. One constant is that membership is still exclusive and that clubs remain a haven for the wealthy and the privileged. Entry to certain club social events are still the hottest ticket on the calendar and their hallowed halls and hushed dining rooms are still where many of Hong Kong's biggest deals are brokered by its most influential movers and shakers.

opportunities where the position doesn't require the language or even where speaking English is an advantage. Friends I've known have been involved in everything from serving food at shelters to serving champagne at art fundraising events, from leading a sewing class to leading a guitar class. In some circumstances speaking English is a unique advantage, such as visiting elderly people at an English-language care home or helping disadvantaged primary school children learn the language. Almost all charities and projects are looking for help with English-language copywriting and editing. How much of a commitment you make to an organization is really up to you and volunteering can range from a long-term undertaking to a one off event.

The easiest way to start volunteering is to register at one of the organizations in Hong Kong that help match volunteers and charities. Their online websites offer listings from hundreds of charities and nonprofit organizations and they have a searchable database which lets you narrow down positions based on specific skills and availability. While it might sound obvious, most volunteers usually get the greatest rewards through volunteering for causes and issues that affect them and there is nothing wrong with picking and choosing where you want to volunteer. Some organizations that have online project databases are Hands On HongKong (www.handsonhongkong.org), Ho Sum (www.ho-sum.org), meaning Good Heart, and the more Chinese-language-orientated, government-run Volunteer Movement (www.volunteering-hk.org). Other groups and clubs, such as the American Women's Association of Hong Kong, have ongoing charity commitments and are always looking for more volunteers, as are churches and more established, international organizations such as Oxfam and the WWF.

Professional Mixers

If you're working in Hong Kong as a professional, you'll likely end up at these things whether you want to or not. As a city that thrives on business and the importance of *guanxi,* the greasy wheels of the city's PR machines never stop turning and it will likely be an integral part of your job that you climb on board and go for a spin. In recent years, networking events have become increasingly clever at masquerading themselves as social events and Hong Kong's PR firms are masters at the art. Eschewing PowerPoint presentations and formal speeches in favor of laidback lunches and dress-down drinks all washed down with fountains of champagne, professional mixers are ultimately a chance to shake the right hands and complete your business card collection. The fancy food and fine wine is certainly a draw, but try not to get drawn into making tours of the PR parties every night, unless you want a heavily skewed vision of the city. If you are overexposed, and most professionals are, you'll probably find you're often plotting an excuse not to attend, lusting after a night on the sofa, with a pizza and television.

Culture, Education, and Hobbies

Whether you've always dreamed of pulling on an apron and learning how to bake or pulling on a costume and playing Cinderella, most hobbies and interests are catered for in Hong Kong by English-speaking expat groups. For arts and culture, the Hong Kong Fringe Club (www.hkfringe.com.hk) does a very good job of supporting local bands, artists, and drama groups, and is a useful point of first contact. One of the city's most high-profile and talented groups are the Hong Kong Players, who put on a number of plays each year and an annual pantomime. Other popular groups include photography, book, and film clubs, although you'll also find groups dedicated to less-celebrated activities, such as role-playing and kite-flying. Many are organized on an ad-hoc basis and if you can't find your particular passion, post on www.geoexpat. com—even the oddest hobby will have a few keen expat fans. More actively, there are several long-standing groups devoted to getting grass-shy city slickers beyond the city limits. Try Hong Kong Outdoors (www.hkoutdoors.com) to find groups of various abilities dedicated to hiking, biking, and diving.

The classroom is always a good place to meet new people and you can check out the education chapter for a blow-by-blow account of what the city has on offer to help swell you head. For casual courses on everything from making pottery to valuing it, the YMCA (www.ymcahk.org.hk) should be your first point of contact.

Baby and Toddler Groups

Negotiating a new city and culture can be tough enough, but when you've got a pair of rug rats trying to perforate your eardrums—screaming about the strange smells, loud noise, and everything else they don't like—it can be downright daunting. Expat parents can often feel a little adrift when they first arrive in Hong Kong with a spouse who is working long hours and little to fill the days except cleaning up paint spills and humming along to Sesame Street. Mom and toddler/baby groups or playgroups are plentiful (although less geared towards fathers), and can be a great place to meet fellow expat parents and share experiences. These groups are also goldmines of insider information and advice on everything from finding a good babysitter to negotiating the city's combative education system.

The range of groups is extensive and are as casual or involved as your time allows, with most offering weekly or bi-weekly get togethers. Mothers with membership at private members clubs may find a mom-and-tots group on offer there, as well as daycare facilities and play areas. With its location in Mid Levels, the Ladies Recreational Club (www.lrc.com.hk) is a convenient option, while the Aberdeen Marina Club (www.aberdeenmarinaclub.com) has a particularly wide selection of programs for moms and kids. If you aren't a private club member, there is no need to plunder the family fortune just to gain access to their mom-and-tots group. There are dozens of independent, English-speaking groups throughout the city and if you're in an expat area such as Happy Valley or Stanley, you'll find several in your neighborhood. Long-standing groups that regularly enjoy high praise are those run by the American Women's Association (www.awa.org.hk), which has several groups open to all nationalities, and the YMCA (www.ymcahk.org.hk) and YWCA (www.esmdywca.org.hk), which offer a series of mother and toddler programs, from straight out playgroups to organized gymnastics and football. All of these require a small membership fee and you should register early as they are oversubscribed. For listings and more suggestions ask the helpful parents over at www.geobaby.com.

PLANNING YOUR FACT-FINDING TRIP

It's impossible to truly get a feel for Hong Kong until you get your boots on the ground. If you're planning to make the city your home, it's essential to visit at least once before you sign up for a move. The noise, pace, and crowds of Hong Kong can't be captured in books, photos, or even on the silver screen. It won't be until you've tried to buy a durian—and smelled one—at a local market, elbowed your way around a few corners, and been hustled onto a commuter-stuffed train that you'll have a firm idea about whether you want to live here.

Hong Kong's long opening hours, excellent public transport system, and compact size mean you can pack a lot into a short visit. But alongside snapping photos of the city's tourist sights, be sure to explore areas where you're considering living and where you're likely to work. Try the food and transportation, and walk the streets. Hong Kong's tourist areas are a stark contrast to its grittier neighborhoods; after all, there's no point in only visiting Manhattan if you're going to live in Brooklyn.

© MARTYNA SZMYTKOWSKA

Preparing to Leave

WHAT TO BRING
Documents
Citizens of the United States, Canada, Australia, New Zealand, and the European Union can stay up to 90 days in Hong Kong visa free, while British passport holders win 180 days. All visitors require a passport, ideally with six months validity remaining. Some airlines may request proof of return or onward travel when travelling to Hong Kong, although this is rare. It's usually sufficient to tell them you plan to purchase travel tickets in Hong Kong, travel onwards to Macau, or at worst sign an airline waiver form. If you do plan to travel north to the Chinese mainland, you will need a visa. Single-visit Chinese visas can be obtained easily in Hong Kong, although generally not on the same day and if you have time to get one from your nearest Chinese Embassy before departure, it may save on stress and hassle. Although you're unlikely to be stopped by police, you are required to carry your passport at all times as proof of ID.

Clothing
Hong Kong's seasonal weather means you'll need to powwow with the weather forecaster before stuffing your suitcase. That said, you're unlikely to be breaking out the fur-lined fleeces. With much of the year marked by hot weather

HOW BAD IS THE HUMIDITY?

Neatly described by the brains at Merriam-Webster's Dictionary as a "moderate degree of wetness, especially in the atmosphere," humidity in Hong Kong can be characterized as the experience of walking into a steamy bathroom where the hot water has been left running. Once outside, the humidity will start you sweating as if you were smothered in deep heat and swaddled in cling wrap, and by the time you arrive at work you'll look like you fell down a well. It's not like this all the time: The humidity arrives in late April/early May, peaks through the summer months of June, July, and August, and falls away again in October.

Just how unpleasant is the humidity? It depends on the individual. If you're already sporting wet patches in Chicago in April, Hong Kong's steamy summer is likely to see your eyebrows slide off. Of course the heat can be avoided with the Artic air-conditioning fitted in all buildings and public transport, but, at some point, you'll need to go outside. For some expats, humidity ranks as the worst aspect of living in Hong Kong; for others, well, they're happy they never have to trudge around in the sludge and the snow.

and humidity that could melt the wax off crayons, you'll want to bring light, breathable clothing and plenty of T-shirts and shorts. Despite this, it's also worth packing a couple of sweaters, even in the height of summer, to withstand the Artic air-conditioning in shopping malls, offices, and on public transport. The dress code in Hong Kong is pretty much the same as in Houston or Helsinki, although Hong Kongers do tend to dress a little more conservatively. So, leave your favorite Hawaiian shirt at home. If you plan to attend interviews or business meetings, a suit is an absolute must and can be picked up for a bargain at one at the city's famous tailors.

Miscellaneous

No business meeting is complete in Hong Kong without the swapping of business cards and it's hard to overstate their importance. If need be, you can have them printed up in 24 hours. Job hunters may also want to pack their laptop, as email correspondence is likely to be your primary form of contact with prospective employers and realtors.

MONEY

If you believe the headlines, Hong Kong will swallow your money like a slot machine. It's certainly an expensive city, but just how much you spend here is very much within your control. Flex your Gold Card and you'll find Hong Kong's high-end hotels, restaurants, and bars have the prices to give it a ruthless workout. More realistically, staying at a midrange hotel, eating and drinking at more moderately-priced restaurants, and enjoying the odd beer should keep your daily outlay to somewhere around HK$1,000.

Accommodation is usually the real budget buster, but if you're willing to sacrifice a little comfort and occasionally air-conditioning, it can be surprisingly cheap. Eat only at local rice and noodle joints and prices can tumble down even further.

Currency, Exchanges, and ATMs

If you have an ATM card with access to the Cirrus or Plus networks, the easiest, safest, and usually cheapest way to access your money is to simply use your card. ATMs are ubiquitous. Aside from smaller shops and restaurants, credit cards are almost universally accepted and also offer favorable exchange rates. Cash can come in handy for bargaining at markets and shops, and is essential on some of the far-flung islands. Dollars, euros, pounds, and most Asian currencies are easy to exchange, with individual money changers boasting better rates than banks. If you're changing U.S. dollars, the greenback is pegged to the Hong Kong Dollar at HK$7.8.

WHEN TO GO

If you've ever wondered what it would be like to be steam-cooked, come to Hong Kong in summer (June–mid-Sept.). The soaring humidity levels turn the city into a sticky, sweaty sauna and even a short walk down the street can leave you and your clothes looking like you've taken a tumble in a washing machine. As if the thermonuclear temperatures weren't enough to contend with, you can also look forward to frequent monsoon downpours and the occasional typhoon (typhoon season runs May–Oct.). That said, if you plan to live here, some would argue it's best to tangle with the city's weather at its most dastardly.

The best of the weather comes in fall (late Sept.–early Dec.), when the humidity has subsided, the rain has cleared, and it remains T-shirt weather until the end of the season. Spring (early Mar.–May) also offers more manageable humidity, especially early spring, and less rain, as well as a host of traditional festivals and events. Winter (mid-Dec.–late Feb.) is little more than a word in Hong Kong and temperatures usually bob around the mid-teens. The crisp, clear days make it a perfectly feasible time to visit.

Many tourists are tempted to visit Hong Kong for the massive Chinese New Year celebrations. While the dragon dances and fireworks are impressive, most shops, business, and services are closed down from three days to a week, and dodging illegal firecrackers is only fun for so long.

Arriving in Hong Kong

ARRIVAL AND IMMIGRATION

Unless you've spent the last few days on a train, you're likely to land in Hong Kong at its award-winning airport. Immigration services are professional, efficient, and in English, and entry stamps are usually issued with no questions asked. You will fill out an entry card on arrival and you should keep the carbon copy until you exit the city, although if lost, you simply fill out a new one on departure.

Many people who come to Hong Kong do so in some form of official capacity for their company and are often unsure about whether they require a business visa. Hong Kong immigration specifically allows for those here as visa-free visitors to conduct a certain amount of "business related activities," such as contract negotiations, trade fair attendance, and product orientation. You're not, however, allowed to take up employment or involve yourself in direct selling to the public. For those who are coming to talk to possible employers or simply see the city with a view to moving here, you are perfectly entitled to do so. However, you don't need to give the immigration officer your life story and it will save hassle for all involved if you just say that you're a tourist.

TRANSPORTATION

Hong Kong Airport has a fireplace stacked with awards and trophies for its first-class service, not least of all commended is an enviable public transportation system. If you're staying in Kowloon or on Hong Kong Island, your best bet is to hop onto the futuristic Airport Express, which runs every 12 minutes and will whisk you from the airport to Kowloon Station or Hong Kong Station in 24 minutes or less. From those two stations a fleet of free shuttle buses ferries passengers onwards to almost 100 hotels in the city. Tickets for the Airport Express can be bought from the machines on the station concourse. Although, a better plan is to pick up a stored value Octopus Card, from the customer service desk, that can be used on all forms of transport and recharged when needed.

Alternatively, while it can't match the ruthless efficiency of the Airport Express, the A11 bus is the way I like to take first-time visitors to Hong Kong. Taking a more leisurely 40 minutes to an hour, the A11 bus boasts panoramas over the South China Sea, bird's-eye views of the streets of Central and Wan Chai, and is a much better introduction to the city. For those who can't resist the exclusive appeal of a taxi, Hong Kong cabs are cheap, well regulated, and, unlike other cities, you won't find any cowboys at the airport. However, the location out on Lantau means your trip will be lengthier than on the Airport Express and substantially more expensive.

Those plotting a quick escape to China will find coaches and ferries at the airport ready to shepherd them onto the mainland, as well as bonded ferries that travel directly to Shenzhen, Guangzhou, and Macau without the need to pass through Hong Kong Immigration.

Sample Itineraries

How long you spend on any research trip to Hong Kong is a personal decision and very much depends on your individual circumstances. Those who find themselves flown out for an interview usually only have 72-hour stop in the city. If you can, try to schedule more time in the city; people spend longer than that deciding what to buy a friend for his or her birthday, so picking up and moving halfway across the world is not a decision that should be rushed. Realistically, the least amount of time you should consider is a week. Hong Kong's 24-hour lifestyle means you can fit a lot into one day; seven days would give you the opportunity to taste some Hong Kong food, get shoved around on the subway, and sweat your way around some of the city's backstreets (just don't expect to see much of your pillow). A more relaxed time frame of two weeks will give you a far better picture of the city. You'll have time to adjust to the pace of the city, explore areas where you're likely to be based, both for home and work, and slip in some sightseeing as well.

the IFC2 tower in Central

© BARTOSZ KOŚCIELAK

For those that are job-hunting in Hong Kong, you won't find work in a week or two. Ultimately, like with most cities, to get a job you'd be well advised to move here for a month or two and be available for interviews and make contacts face to face.

ONE WEEK
Day 1

Ideally you'll arrive into Hong Kong just as the sun is making an appearance, giving you a full day—jet lag allowing—to explore the city. After 15 hours strapped into a jumbo jet, the only place you'll want to be is in a shower. So, clear immigration, jump on the Airport Express, and hit your hotel, where you can also dump your bags. Try and ignore the siren calls of the pillow menu and dive into the guts of the city. For breakfast, ask your concierge to point you in the direction of his favorite *cha chaan teng* (tea café). These bare-bones diners are where the Hong Kong workforce enjoys a breathless breakfast, filling up on Hong Kong–style French toast (a stack of bread slices deep fried in egg, layered with peanut butter, and swimming in butter), washed down with Hong Kong milky tea.

After you've rebuttoned your trousers, take the MTR over to Central, Hong Kong's gleaming business district, and find Exit B to emerge in its beating heart: Des Voeux Road Central. Home to banks and multinationals, the streets here are flanked by a sheer wall of skyscapers, more than anywhere else in the world. It's impossible not to be impressed, and there is an undoubted appeal to punching into work amongst some of the world's most glamorous buildings. Jostling through the swarms of sleep-deprived office rats clinging to their BlackBerries on Des Voeux Road will also give you a fleeting feel for the furious pace of a city that only has one speed: sprint. Continuing west along Des Voeux Road Central you'll reach Statue Square, the crux of the city, where the colonial-era Legislative Council (LegCo) building rubs shoulders with the exceptional Norman Foster–designed and feng shui–arranged HSBC headquarters. Spend your day exploring the district. This is the Hong Kong from the brochures, the Hong Kong that attracts brokers, bankers, and everyone in between. If you don't get a buzz from the energy and power of Central, Hong Kong might not be the place for you.

As night falls, take a short walk up to Lan Kwai Fong, a den of over 100 bars and restaurants, and perhaps the only place in the city where expats outnumber locals.

Day 2

Hong Kong's much maligned other half, the Kowloon Peninsula, has long played the stepsister to Hong Kong's Cinderella. While you're unlikely to end up living here—although that's a situation that's changing—its built-up districts and frantic street-life capture the spirit of Hong Kong, and its overflowing markets remain an attraction for tourists and shoppers alike.

Spend the morning taking in a couple of the area's more maverick markets. Start at the covered Jade Market, where sellers haggle over 19th-century necklaces and try and hock 21st-century junk to unsuspecting tourists, before moving on to the more interesting Bird Garden and Market on and around Yuen Po Street. From mahjong to dai pai dongs, much of Hong Kong's socializing is done outdoors; at the Bird Garden and Market owners arrive to chat, smoke, and pitch their birds into impromptu American Idol–style singoffs.

Your options on where to eat in the area are limited but excellent. Hundreds of noodle shops and chop shops serve up no-nonsense Cantonese dishes, arguably the city's best, but you'll need to be big enough and brave enough to point and pick inside because English menus are rare. If you need a break from the sweaty streets and want something more formal, Ming Court, inside the pristine Langham Place Hotel in Mongkok, offers award winning dim sum.

After seeing the cramped streets and creaking buildings that were traditionally the signature of Kowloon, step out of the past and into the future with a trip to West Kowloon. Underwater 20 years ago, this reclaimed land is now home to designer-built office blocks and swanky residential buildings and is fast emerging as a genuine rival to Central across the water—it's already stolen the city's tallest building. Don't miss a chance to explore some of the apartments

© BARTOSZ KOŚCIELAK

Lan Kwai Fong is Hong Kong's busiest bar and club district and a major draw for local expats.

that are on offer; their generous sizes have made them popular with expats. You can also take a trip up to the top of the ICC for a 100th-floor view over the city and, on a clear day, all the way up to China.

As evening falls, stroll back up to the Yau Ma Tei district to take in the street party that is the Temple Street Night Market. At Hong Kong's biggest and brashest market, aside from the blocks and blocks of stalls selling everything from power drills to powdered rhino's horn, you'll find Hong Kong's celebrity fortune tellers and outdoor Cantonese Opera karaoke. Do some bargain shopping and tuck into the alfresco dai pai dongs for freshly hooked seafood and a cold Tsingtao.

Day 3

Hong Kong is keen to present itself as a sophisticated, cosmopolitan, and international outpost in the chaos of Asia, yet this is only part of the picture. Beneath the business suits and beyond the cocktail parties, Hong Kong has a deep traditional streak and there is no better place to explore it than Sheung Wan. Hunched beneath the skyscrapers of Central, this is Hong Kong's oldest neighborhood and its knot of streets are stuffed with dried seafood sellers, scruffy dim sum joints, and low-rise—by Hong Kong standards—residential buildings, all humming to the strains of aging air-conditioners.

Start off at the Sheung Wan MTR Station and strong-arm your way along Hillier Street, before swinging west onto Bonham Strand and into the heart of the dried seafood district. If you want a bite to eat, try Sheung Wan Cooked Food Market—the Hong Kong answer to a food court. The communal tables are usually packed at lunchtime with Hong Kong office workers shoveling down cheap noodle and rice dishes. From here, head south to Hollywood Road, a street renowned for its antique dealers, to find the beautifully ornate Man Mo Temple, one of Hong Kong's oldest. Temples continue to play an active role in many Hong Kongers' lives, particularly on holidays; past the haze of smoke swung out by the beehive-sized incense rolls are police officers, triads, and coy librarians plying the gods of literature and war with flowers and fast food to bring them good fortune.

There is no better way to contrast a visit to Sheung Wan than with a trip up to Mid-Levels, Hong Kong's expat heartland. Camped out half way up Victoria Peak, this forest of high rises is almost exclusively residential and the easy access to Central has long been a pull for international residents. There is relatively little in the neighborhood aside from residential buildings, but as Hong Kong's prime expat neighborhood it's worth exploring and, if possible, seeing a few apartments. Complete the expat community tour with a slide down the Mid-Levels Escalator, a near-kilometer system of outdoor escalators that sweeps Mid-Levels office rats to their offices in the morning and back to their bedrooms in the evening. Stop off in SoHo, beneath the escalator around Staunton Street, for dinner; you'll find a broad selection of moderately-priced Western restaurants.

Day 4

There is no better place for a crash course in Hong Kong street life than from the top deck of the city's double-decker trams, or the ding ding as it's known locally. Tracing the island's north coastline at a slothful pace, it's an artery running through the heart of the city's key neighborhoods and a great place to catch an eyeful of the bustling streets.

Pick up the tram in Sheung Wan and watch old become new as you creep into Central. Jump off in Wan Chai, opposite the Wan Chai MTR station, to explore one of Hong Kong's most engaging districts. Famed as the stomping ground of Suzie Wong and for its boozy nightlife, Wan Chai actually trails only Central for skyscrapers, which rub shoulders with a ramshackle mix of mom-and-pop stores, markets, and older residential buildings. Head up through the fruit and vegetable market on Gresson Street and see if you can pick up something tasty, before turning east onto Queen's Road East to find the Hopewell Centre, once the tallest building in the city. Tie down your stomach and take a trip up Hopewell Centre's glass elevator for Godzilla views of Hong Kong Island and beyond. Ignore the tourist-trap restaurant at the summit and instead head for Fat Angelo's at the base of the skyscraper and across Spring Garden Lane. This chain of Italian American restaurants will never win a Michelin, but they offer some of the most reliable Western food at fair prices in the territory.

Once you've waddled out of Fat Angelo's, make your way back to Wan Chai Station and catch the tram for your next stop in Causeway Bay, Hong Kong's shopping headquarters. Anchored by the SOGO department store, the district hasn't been lost to exclusivity and its independent retailers are still able to trade punches and prices with the big brand chain stories. Catch your breath and plunge into the crowds of shoppers for a full-blooded shopping experience. If you've got real estate on your mind rather than Levis, head back to the tram and follow it along to Quarry Bay—a mid-priced middle class district which gains a lot of praise for its honest prices.

Whatever you've spent the afternoon doing, don't miss a chance to see Causeway Bay by night, when it descends beneath a glow of neon and groans amidst the swelling crowds. Hidden halfway up the skyscrapers are numerous bars and restaurants that cater to a local Chinese crowd and charge sensible prices. For a true Hong Kong–style night you shouldn't leave before you've embarrassed yourself in a karaoke bar. Wildly popular, Hong Kong karaoke bars tend to favor separate rooms for groups of friends to punish each other, but some also have open mic lounges. Butchering an Elvis number can be a great way to meet new friends.

Day 5

If the noise, grime, and crowds of the sweaty city already have you plotting a move to Maine instead, it's time to see Hong Kong's backyard. Even for confirmed urban jungle gorillas, like most people who move here are, Hong Kong's real jungle is an essential part of life in the city, with many Hong Kongers taking to the hills, beaches, and waters of the New Territories and Outlying Islands each weekend to clear their heads and clean out their lungs. One of the most popular retreats is Lamma Island, which has long lured Bohemians, beatniks, and hippies who like to swap their suits for sandals and enjoy the mellower lifestyle and strong sense of community. The sleepy one-street capital, Yung Shue Wan, is the kind of town that makes you want to slip into a hammock and slip on some Bob Marley. Instead, settle for a drink with a fancy umbrella along the seafront before slapping your legs awake for the 90-minute hike over to Lo So Shing Beach. Stretches of golden-sand beaches are one of Hong Kong's most underestimated qualities and this is one of the best. After you're fully cooked, continue your march another 30 minutes to the village of Sok Kwu Wan, celebrated for its humble yet excellent seafood restaurants. From here, take the ferry back to civilization.

Day 6

If Day 6 is a Saturday, there is no better place to put some food in your belly than one of Hong Kong's five-star brunches. These gluttonous feasts are a rite of passage in the city and we know several expats who list buffets under hobbies. They are served every day of the week, but the best crowds really come to swing from the chandeliers on Saturdays. Most of the best buffets are inside five-star hotels, including the truly breathtaking banquet at the Intercontinental Hotel, where you can crack lobsters and swill champagne while enjoying postcard views over the skyline.

Once you've had your fill or the chair has collapsed, whichever comes first, dip into the MTR, head for Central, and then make your way to The Peak Tram. Climbing the side of Victoria Peak at a steep angle, the tram will deliver you to Hong Kong's biggest tourist attraction and its most exclusive living location, The Peak. The properties here are dollar for dollar the priciest in the world and if you're interested in nosing around the sprawling mansions you'll need to contact a real estate agent in advance. Otherwise, take a stroll around and enjoy the views or, as is more common these days, play Where's Waldo with the skyscrapers hung forlornly in the gathering clouds of pollution.

Back down the mountain, head for Central and the Star Ferry Pier. Hong Kong's answer to New York's yellow cab or the London double-decker, only with a dash of Victorian style, the Star Ferry has been plying Victoria Harbour for more than 100 years and, aside from being one of the city's top tourist attractions, remains an integral part of many commuters' blitzkrieg battle to work. From the top deck you can watch the Hong Kong skyline being unwrapped behind you and if you've timed it right, you'll pull into Tsim Sha Tsui just before 8 P.M. to watch the Symphony of Lights from the Avenue of Stars. This laser and lights spectacular is a fitting goodbye to the city.

© RORY BOLAND

a golden stretch of beach on Lamma Island

Day 7

Depending on your destination and

the time of your flight, you may have anything from a few hours to a full day left in the city. Those that do have some of the day to enjoy before jetting off should start by using in-town airport check-in. This simple but sublime system lets you dump your bags and get your boarding card at Hong Kong Station up to 24 hours in advance with most airlines—leaving you baggage-free for your final day. If you're likely to be lynched back home unless you cough up a few presents, it might be worth heading to Cat Street in Sheung Wan to pick up chopsticks, Mao statues, and Buddha heads.

TWO WEEKS
Day 1
For anyone fresh off the plane in Hong Kong it's practically impossible to ignore the irresistible draw of the skyscrapers, so don't. Spend your first day soaking up the atmosphere and sucking up the fumes in Central, Hong Kong's premium business district and home of the skyscraper. Arrive in style aboard the iconic Star Ferry, which sets sail from Tsim Sha Tsui and lets you watch the world's most incredible skyline unfurl before you as you pull into Central. The key that winds Hong Kong, Central put the city on the map, keeps it in the headlines, and lets it play on the world stage. In Central, home not only to skyscrapers but the swankiest shopping malls and most exclusive restaurants, you can easily lose a day just marveling at its opulence. If you fancy knocking chairs with some of Central's mandarins and moguls, you'll find them lunching inside the exclusive Cuisine Cuisine inside the IFC Mall or picnicking on its 4th-floor roof garden.

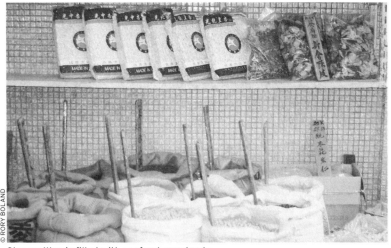

© RORY BOLAND

Sheung Wan is filled with seafood merchants.

Set amidst the soaring skyscrapers and hair-trigger hurrying, the stately LegCo building in Statue Square, seat of Hong Kong's legislative branch of government, and St. John's Cathedral, perched on the hill above, are reminders of the city's British influences. Nearby, the powwowing journalists and diplomats inside the Foreign Correspondents Club continue to capture the clubby atmosphere of colonial times gone by. If you don't have a friend or a story that can get you past the cloakroom, head next door to the Fringe Club, a bastion of the city's much maligned cultural scene and a good spot to enjoy some live music, exhibitions, or theater. Pick up a *Hong Kong Magazine,* which has event listings and expat-orientated job postings, before retiring to the rooftop terrace where you'll be able to hear the cat calls of the nearby Lan Kwai Fong district, the city's prime watering hole.

Day 2

Assuming you didn't spend your first night frozen inside Lan Kwai Fong's ice vodka bar like so many illustrious expats before you, Day 2 should be all about business. Ideally, before you arrive, you will have read our prime living locations chapters, picked a few neighborhoods you might be interested in, and contacted some real estate agents in advance. If not, consider heading to Caine Road at the Mid-Levels Escalator intersection with Shelly Street, where you'll find a cluster of real estate agents who deal with the nearby Mid-Levels property market, a bedroom community for many of the city's expats. Flash them a smile and they'll be only too happy to usher

Hong Kong Star Wars–style Symphony of Lights Show

© BARTOSZ KOŚCIELAK

you around a few properties either on the spot or the following day. But don't stop there.

Apart from the high-end market of royal residences and Hollywood homes, most agents specialize in the neighborhood where they are based. They'll likely spin you a fable about knowing the entire city's property market better than their own mother, but in truth most Hong Kong Island–based agents think Kowloon is a restaurant. With each neighborhood you're interested in you'll need to wash and repeat the process. Always see at least two agents in each area so you can compare and contrast contracts, prices, and service—it reduces the chances of you ending up with a cowboy who'll sell you Alice in Wonderland prices.

Days 3-4

Spend the next couple of days visiting neighborhoods you're interested in and try and see at least half a dozen flats. Even if you haven't reached a stage where you're committed to a move here, it's a good opportunity to nose around a few apartments and get an idea of what cramped quarters Hong Kong living looks like. It'll give you a handle on what you'll be paying and what you'll get in return.

Do take the time to see a couple of different neighborhoods. Even if you fall head over heels for your first neighborhood, you should always see more so that you have a more rounded view of what's on offer. If you're stuck for choices, consider investigating Mid-Levels and Kowloon Tong, two fairly different areas popular with expats. Alongside the actual apartment viewings, be sure to play PI around the neighborhood; see what amenities are available and at what distance, check out the local shops, and investigate local schools, setting up a visit, if appropriate. For those who already have a work address, try out the commute from possible neighborhoods, ideally during rush hour.

Spend at least one of your evenings enjoying some BBQ meat at one of Wan Chai's top notch, low-maintenance chop shops (you'll find recommendations in the restaurant listings) and then researching the sociable, expat-filled bars around Lockhart Road.

Day 5

With Day 1 spent amongst the skyscrapers of Central and Days 2, 3 and 4 likely dining on steak in one of the city's residential expat enclaves, it's easy to get a picture of the city as a slice of the West. Yet, once you live here, you will quickly discover just how staunchly traditional Hong Kongers can be and the importance of tradition in local life. For a firsthand example, roll out of bed early and head to Victoria Park to watch the groups of graceful tai chi practitioners in action at sunrise. Popular with older Hong Kongers

© MARTYNA SZMYTKOWSKA

view over North Hong Kong Island from the Peak

for its association with longevity, this mellowed martial art is good exercise for both body and brain and if you know what you're doing, some groups won't mind if you jump in. Reward yourself afterwards at the frills-free neighborhood canteens, on Tung Lo Road just behind the park, who serve up steaming pots of congee and other local breakfast favorites. The food inside the ramshackle Hong Kee congee shop on King Road has been impressing breakfast fans for ages.

Even for those who consider shopping the ninth circle of hell, there is an urbane appeal to the crowds, noise, and after-dark neon glow of a shopping trip in Hong Kong. The selection and prices make shopping a national sport and nowhere is it more fanatical than Causeway Bay. Here you'll find the city's flagship department stores, several shopping malls, and an endless selection of independent shops. At the very least, you can look around and get a handle on prices.

From Causeway Bay, head north to the Happy Valley neighborhood, an upmarket, residential area popular for its leafy streets, space—at least by Hong Kong standards—and village-like appeal. If you're interested in nosing around a few apartments, you'll find several real estate agents along the main street, Sing Woo Road. Otherwise, the best way to get to know the place is by quizzing the regulars sipping Guinness and talking sport at The Chapel Bar or The Jockey, the neighborhood's British-style pubs. Happy Valley's centerpiece is the Happy Valley Racecourse, which gets busy each Wednesday night with tens of thousands of screaming punters who come to drink cheap beer, bet on a few horses, and enjoy the big screens and big game atmosphere. If it's on, don't miss it.

Day 6

Playing Brooklyn to Hong Kong Island's Manhattan, Kowloon is often overshadowed by glitzy Hong Kong Island, but the clutch of working-class neighborhoods at its core, sprawling satellite suburbs, almost endless streets of family-run shops, bare-bones restaurants, and rambling markets tell a far more typical story of the average Hong Konger's life.

The artery that runs through the heart of Kowloon and the Tsim Sha Tsui tourist district is sparkling Nathan Road, known as the Golden Mile. A tribute to Hong Kong's shop-till-you-drop spirit, it's jammed with jewelers, tailors, and electronics stores. The clutter of neon advertising signs that hum above the shabby buildings are a classic Hong Kong scene captured in a thousand centerfolds. Possibly the shabbiest and certainly the most famous is Chungking Mansions, a dingy and somewhat intimidating maze of a building, stuffed with strip-lit corridors, dripping air-conditioning units, and sardine-sized elevators. Brave the scrum of hawkers outside the building to find multicultural Hong Kong at its most vibrant. With an estimated 120 nationalities bartering over currency exchanges, trying to fire up cell phones, and cooking up the best subcontinent cuisine in the city, many people consider this the true spirit of Hong Kong's success. Grab something to eat at the snack bars or head upstairs for an authentic Indian meal.

If you're going to live in Hong Kong, noise and crowds are sure to be a constant source of annoyance and there is no better place to get a taste for them than in Mongkok. Officially the planet's most densely populated piece of real estate, the streets are teeming with people, hawkers, and food stalls. Deploy your elbows and explore the area's markets, including the Ladies Market (clothing), Goldfish Market, and Mongkok Computer Market. After a few hours you'll probably feel like you've swallowed a car engine, so head back into Tsim Sha Tsui and Aqua in the stylish One Peking Road building for some rest and relaxation. Set on the crown of the building, this swanky bar/restaurant offers floor-to-ceiling panoramas of the skyscraper skyline across the water. While the cocktail prices reflect the setting, it's worth splashing out to enjoy the view.

Day 7

Clear the cobwebs from the night before with a trip to the top of the Peak on the Peak Tram. Once reserved for Europeans only, the Peak remains an exclusive residential enclave accessible only to those with bullet-proof bank accounts. Real estate here is often the priciest per square meter in the world, with similarly astronomical rents, and if you want to see inside any of these luxury pads, you'll need to contact realtors in advance. On the increasingly-rare smog-free days, the Peak also boasts an unrivalled view over the heads of the skyscrapers below towards Kowloon and occasionally as far as the border with China.

After lunch, drop down to the other side of the Peak to see how the other half lives in Aberdeen, a former fishing village. Reached by number 7 bus from the Central bus terminus, Aberdeen is a working-class, although not poor, district nestled on the south side of Victoria Peak that's detached enough and substantial enough to feel like its own town. Hong Kong's fishing industry is in decline, some say terminally, but the docks here still splash to the sound of fishing trawlers and play host to Hong Kong's dwindling number of boat people, who live and work on their cramped junks. Here you can hire a sampan for a heart-stopping swerve around the swell of cruise ships and breathtaking darts in front of oncoming oil tankers to a destination of your choice. Popular spots include desert islands, where you can enjoy the golden sands and clear waters alone, or the excellent seafood restaurants on nearby Lamma.

Day 8

With 14 days in Hong Kong, you shouldn't ignore Hong Kong's sister SAR, the older but far more beautiful Macau. Just an hour away by ferry, the city in recent years has become known as the Las Vegas of the East, with branches of The Sands and The Venetian, as well as local casinos, such as Casino Lisboa, attracting an increasing number of tourists. Even if you plan to keep your dollars in your wallet and shirt on your back, step inside to soak up the big-show atmosphere, free drinks, and live shows. Just as big and brash as their Vegas cousins, the casinos are liveliest by night when the cover bands pull out their guitars and the cancan dancers pull up their skirts.

By day, don't miss exploring Macau's Portuguese past. The city has done an impeccable job of maintaining its colonial buildings; the cobblestone squares, wooden shuttered verandas, and pastel-splashed churches combine for a lazy, laid-back atmosphere you simply can't recreate in Hong Kong. Those that are truly bowled over by the architecture or committed to losing their house could stretch a stay overnight, but accommodation options aren't fantastic and there are all-night ferries returning shipwrecked and shirtless gamblers back to Hong Kong.

Day 9

Start your day over in north Kowloon at the Wong Tai Sin Temple, a strutting, grandstanding showboat of a building that has come to be the focus for many of Hong Kong's festivals. A visit here reveals just how broad an influence tradition and superstition have in Hong Kong society and the role they continue to play on everyday life. During the day a steady stream of fisherfolk, factory workers, stockbrokers, and lawyers arrive to pray for good fortune or find out what their future holds by having their chim sticks read. Like everything in Hong Kong, visits are lightening quick, squeezed in between lunch or picking the kids up from school, but remain part of a daily or weekly ritual. Assuming you aren't handed tonight's winning lottery numbers by a talented but selfless fortune-teller, try lunch in nearby Kowloon City. The no-nonsense restaurants here are run by refugees and immigrants from Thailand and Vietnam and their authentic dishes are as good as you'll find in Ho Chi Minh or Bangkok.

Leave the city behind in the afternoon by taking the number 92 bus from the Diamond Hill MTR station to see the seaside town of Sai Kung, set amongst the lush greenery of Hong Kong's great green lung, the New Territories. Not unknown but not yet overrun, Sai Kung has reinvented itself in recent years as a day-tripping destination, combining the laidback atmosphere of Hong Kong's traditional fishing villages with a dash more sophistication—although don't expect Malibu. Its affordable houses have also become popular with rat-race refugees. If you're not interested in the real estate, soak up the atmosphere with a stroll along the waterfront and enjoy the fresh seafood served up at the alfresco joints on the promenade.

Day 10

If you've read the book, you'll have understood that Hong Kong is keen to distinguish itself as Hong Kong, different and separate to China. Hong Kong is Hong Kong. Find out why with a trip across the border to Shenzhen. The cradle of China's capitalist jackpot, Shenzhen is a town that feels like it's set on the edge of the future. You've heard the hype and read the newspapers about China's economic miracle; a visit to Shenzhen is a ringside seat. In recent years, as the city turns increasingly respectable, some of the hard edges have been hammered out of this frontier town's "anything goes" attitude and amongst the rising sky-scrapers and smell of freshly-laid tarmac there remains an unshakable confidence in tomorrow and belief in success. Nowhere is China's ambition more brazen than in Shenzhen. Over the years, the two cities have grown increasingly close, not only economically but culturally. Yet the differences remain stark. Even superficially there are different haircuts, different clothes, and different cultural norms—say goodbye to queuing and hello to spitting.

Incredibly easy to reach, Shenzhen is connected to Hong Kong via the MTR at Hung Hom to the Lo Wu border crossing. The journey only takes about an hour, but remember a full international border straddles the two cities and you'll need a visa to enter China. Citizens of most countries, but not Americans, can opt for an on-the-spot SEZ visa from the China Travel Service office at the border crossing, good for access to Shenzhen and the surrounding area but no further. Once in Shenzhen, do what Hong Kongers do and fill your boots and your suitcases with cheap goods. For the lazy, Commercial City—a five-story behemoth of a building stuffed with hundreds of independent retailers—is set next to Lo Wu Station and draws bargain hunters for everything from suits to massages. More interesting and less stressful is the SEG computer market in the city center. This is believed to be the largest collection of independent computer and electronics retailers in the world and if you're a geek, bring a brown paper bag in case of hyperventilation. There is little to catch your eye in the city center, but it's worth parking yourself at a roadside café just to people watch.

Finish your day with dinner and a drink over in the Western district of Shekou. Not necessarily a sign of progress, but a mighty declaration of the city's ambitious intentions, Shekou is home to dozens of Western restaurants and bars that initially catered to Shenzhen's sizable expat population but have swelled their ranks in recent years, thanks to a booming class of Chinese professionals who've developed a taste for both their disposable income and for champagne. From Shekou you can grab the ferry back to Hong Kong; just be sure to check the time as they don't run especially late.

Day 11

Home to the airport and Hong Kong Disneyland, Lantau Island has started to shed its backwater beginnings and taken on a more prominent profile in the development of the city. With a bridge and MTR connection to Kowloon and Central respectively, its real estate market is also attracting a broader audience.

First stop on Lantau should be Hong Kong's very own slice of American Pie suburbia, Discovery Bay. For those that have been following the itinerary, you'll have been in Hong Kong for a quite few days and stepping into the weird world of Discovery Bay will make you feel like Neil Armstrong on the moon. Forget what you've seen so far, Discovery Bay might be in China but it thinks it's in Cleveland. The synchronized sprinklers, polished street lights, and nuclear families speeding around on golf carts can be a little, well, sinister, but keep an open mind. DB, as it's better known, garners a lot of criticism, but you'll find very few residents, past or present, who don't sing its praises. The main plaza is the hub of the community and you'll no doubt find some lunch regulars only too willing to walk you through the plus points.

Spend the rest of the afternoon exploring Lantau's great outdoors. Reached by shuttle bus from DB, the island's main town, Tung Chung, is largely forgettable, but from here you can pick up the Ngong Ping 360 cable car which will elevate you high above Lantau for stunning vistas of the mountainous interior, framed by the South China Sea. Once you've reached the summit, skip the cynical tack that's marketed as a "cultural village," and head straight for the Big Buddha, a 34-meters-tall, 250-ton gleaming statue of Buddha, part of the Po Lin Monastery. Visit the monastery proper for some excellent vegetarian dishes.

Day 12

Hong Kong's answer to Malibu only with less bikinis, the southern belly of Hong Kong Island is where you'll find the city's most exclusive communities, attracted by a sun-drenched coastline that's been left relatively unmolested by developers. Despite being within spitting distance to Central, it's an attractive area and a welcome break from the city. Spend Day 12 exploring potential nesting grounds and enjoying the unhurried pace of the seaside villages.

One of the reasons the south side hasn't ended up inside a bulldozer's bucket is because it lacks an MTR connection—something which is set to change. Your best bet is to catch the number 6 buses that depart from in front of Admiralty MTR station. Most are double-deckers, so secure the binocular seats on top to enjoy superb vistas over the lush countryside and sparkling South China Sea as the bus snakes its way through Repulse Bay and Deepwater Bay to the seaside town of Stanley. Both Deepwater Bay and Repulse Bay have first-rate beaches to flop down on and their 15-minute commute from the city makes them popular with work rats; but unless you have an interest in them for their real estate, stay in your seat until you pull into Stanley, the only major town in the area. As the hub of south side life, Stanley is an enjoyable muddle of low-rise side streets with a bustling market and attractive seafront promenade lined with tourist-orientated restaurants and bars. If you're considering the south side as a place to live, take a peek around Stanely's small mall for an idea of what amenities are available.

Those solely seeking the sun and sandcastles would be better off travelling a little farther to the southeast of the island to find lesser-explored Shek O. It's far from a travel trade secret—it gets rammed with locals on weekends—but its distance from town and low-key appeal does mean it's largely overlooked by tourists. Almost completely undeveloped, it feels more local and more authentic and is home to what is arguably Hong Kong Island's best beach. With neither the pretention nor prices of the communities near Stanley, Shek O's houses are much sought after and demand far outstrips supply. Very few properties actually make it onto the open market; so, if you're interested in renting, you'll need to ask around in the local shops, as most rentals are by word of mouth.

Day 13

On your last full day in Hong Kong, tie up any loose ends. You'll have seen a couple of neighborhoods, so today is a good day to revisit those that really appealed to you. Be sure to follow up with any real estate agents you've made contact with and, if appropriate, ask them to continue sending you listings in areas in which you have shown a firm interest. If you have a job offer or are expecting one, now is the time to visit a few serviced apartment complexes and choose where you want to park your suitcase in the first few weeks after you arrive, while you continue the apartment search. Those planning on an everything-and-the-kitchen-sink move may want to talk to a removal company or relocation firm about their services and prices. This can obviously be done on the phone, but a face-to-face meeting saves on confusion and soothes nerves.

Day 14

Many people will have a full day in Hong Kong before they meet their jumbo jet, so the first thing you should do is dump your bags and check in (up to 24 hours in advance with some airlines) at the in-town check-in at the Airport Express at Hong Kong Station.

Hopefully you'll have had all your questions answered by this stage and know whether Hong Kong is somewhere you could call home. If not, consider a day taking in some of the things Hong Kong is most celebrated for. Revisit Central and slide into the fast lane as the suits steam their way to work. Have a class A, blowout meal in one of the district's superb restaurants, or go for a cheap meal. Hong Kong is one of the few major cities in the world where truly good and memorable food doesn't need to cost the world. Just hit a chop shop or noodle shop in Wan Chai or grab some dim sum. Take a trip across Victoria Harbour on the timeless Star Ferry and watch the flawless skyline unfold behind you. But don't sugar coat it. Go get pushed around in the crowds in Mongkok or try asking for directions or anything in Sheung Wan.

Before you head for the plane be sure to pick up a copy of *Time Out Hong Kong,* which, alongside feature articles on the city, contains expat contacts. It's something to read on the plane journey home.

Practicalities

Accommodation prices in Hong Kong can aim a tank turret at your budget and blow a hole clean through. If you want to stay in the city's rightly-lauded five-star hotels, expect to be treated like escaped royalty, but also expect to pay for the privilege. Thankfully, there is often little to separate the five-stars and Hong Kong's better mid-range hotels, bar pillows stuffed with fancy feathers, a pair of bananas in your fruit bowl, and a few hundred dollars. If you avoid high occupancy periods, such as major exhibitions and conventions, Chinese holidays, and the Hong Kong Sevens, you might be able to haggle up to 30 percent off the standard rack rate. Before you buy, it's also worth doing some shopping around online; Zuji.com, an online travel agent, offers far better prices on Hong Kong hotels than its U.S. and European competitors and its deals can sometimes take a huge chunk off of rack rates.

If you're counting pennies, Hong Kong's much maligned selection of budget accommodations is as broad as it's ever been and surprisingly affordable. The city's guesthouses, once only fit for and only visited by the rodent population, have cleaned up considerably and many offer decent, if low frills, stays. Unfortunately, the gap—or gulf—in guesthouse quality remains frightening, from the bottom of the market where you'll have no air-conditioning, no windows, and a receptionist who doubles as your prison warden, letting you in and out at certain times, to Rolls Royce experiences with en suite showers and free Wi-Fi. Be sure to do your research. Those planning to stay in the city for a couple of weeks should almost certainly consider the extra facilities, such as a kitchen, that a serviced apartment offers.

ACCOMMODATIONS

Big spenders determined to put Hong Kong's lauded five-star properties to the test won't have to search long; most are set on prime real estate surrounding the Central and Tsim Sha Tsui waterfronts. On Hong Kong Island the **Four Seasons** (8 Finance St., Central, tel. 852/3196-8888, www.fourseasons.com, from HK$4,500 d) regularly muscles its way on to lists of the world's top hotels, partly thanks to its unbeatable harbor views. For something a little more charismatic, ignore the chain brands and instead book a room at the **Mira** (118 Nathan Rd., Tsim Sha Tsui, tel. 852/2368-1111, www.themirahotel.com, from HK$1,700 d) in Tsim Sha Tsui. Straight off the catwalk, this stylishly different hotel has an intimate, boutique atmosphere with amenities to embarrass its bigger competitors, including sophisticated rooms that feature PCs, a Sony entertainment system, and Blue Ray DVD player. More modest rates can be found at the **Novotel Century Hong Kong** (238 Jaffe Rd., Wan Chai, tel. 852/2598-8888, www.novotel.com, from HK$1,200 d) in the heart of Wan Chai, which offers well-appointed rooms and enviable amenities, such as a rooftop swimming pool. While the name may suggest dusty dorms and scouts planting tepees, the **YMCA Salisbury** (41 Salisbury Rd., Tsim Sha Tsui, tel. 852/2268-7888, www. ymcahk.org.hk, from HK$800 d) in Kowloon is one of Hong Kong's great secrets, boasting harbor views to rival its neighbor the Peninsula, a whirlpool tub,

Wi-Fi, and straightforward rooms at straightforward prices. Those planning to brave Chungking and Mirador Mansions could do no worse than the **Cosmic Guest House** (12F, Block F1, Mirador Mansions, 54-64 Nathan Rd., Tsim Sha Tsui, tel. 852/2369-6669, www.cosmicguesthouse.com, from HK$200 s), which offers secure surroundings and clean rooms. If, however, you took one look at Chungking Mansions and decided you'd rather sleep inside a trash can at the railway station, the **Alisan Guesthouse** (Flat A, 5F Hoito Ct., 275 Gloucester Rd., Causeway Bay, tel. 852/2838-0762, http://home.hkstar.com/~alisangh, entrance on Cannon St., from HK$300 s) in Causeway Bay is one of the few guesthouses on Hong Kong Island and substantially better than the bulk of its competitors, with well-kept rooms and friendly service.

FOOD

Much of Hong Kong revolves around the dining table, from business deals to family meals, and it's hard to stress the importance of food to the Cantonese. With kitchens in many of Hong Kong's suitcase-sized apartments consisting of a rice cooker, microwave, and a can opener, it's little surprise that locals eat most of their daily meals in restaurants; the popularity of eating out is also reflected by the sheer number of eateries found on every corner.

As the cradle of Cantonese cuisine, the fresh seafood, BBQ meats, and bite-size dim sum should be the first things between your chopsticks. When you're noodled out, the city also has Asia's best selection of Western restaurants. Dining out can be as expensive or as cheap as your wallet allows, with some of the tastiest Cantonese dishes costing little more than pocket change. More than just a meal, dim sum—better known as *yum cha* (drink tea)—gives Hong Kongers the chance to meet up, share food, and make a mess. Popular for lunch times or lazy Sunday afternoons, the concept revolves around the social aspect of sharing several small snack-sized portions of food. That said, there is nothing, but the number of notches in your belt, stopping you from tackling some dim sum alone.

Tim Ho Wan (G/F, Tsui Yuen Mansion, 2-20 Kwong Wa St., Mongkok) recently made the headlines as the world's cheapest Michelin-starred restaurant and despite the now hour-long waits to get a table, the dim sum pork buns and beef balls in this threadbare canteen are a just reward. If you want to try a no-nonsense Cantonese restaurant, it's hard to go wrong; the eateries stationed at every street corner in every neighborhood are usually more than decent. If in doubt, follow the crowds. One worth going out of your way to find, although it's handily located in Central, is **Mak's Noodles** (77 Wellington St., Central, tel. 852/2854-3810). This family-owned business has been toiling away in the

DON'T EAT JAWS

Unfortunately, much of Hong Kong's wonderful fauna has a habit of turning up on your dinner plate. There is a Cantonese saying "any animal whose back faces the sun can be eaten," and while Hong Kong's palate is no longer quite so broad, the threat of biting into the rump steak of an endangered species remains. Great strides have been made in recent years by the WWF Hong Kong and other pressure groups to stop the consumption of threatened animals and marinelife, especially sharks used for shark fin soup. Yet the city remains a place to truly watch what you eat. Pick up a copy of the *WWF Hong Kong's Seafood Guide* for an eco-sensitive chaperone through the city's seafood selection.

kitchen for the best part of five decades and is famed for its wonton noodles, a Hong Kong specialty. Be warned: Mak's is little more than a pocket-sized hole in the wall and while prices are small, so are the portions.

For foreigners worried about the mysterious debris floating in their soups or the enigmatic translations of body parts on their menu, the standby option and perpetual favorite is *char siu* (BBQ) pork with rice. Found on most menus and best in the restaurants where you see the cooked animals strung up and chopped up in the window, you'll rarely have a bad *char siu;* but there are some standout options. **Joy Hing** (Block C, 265-267 Hennessy Rd., Wan Chai, tel. 852/2519-6639) is another pit of a place decorated with paper posters advertising daily specials, strip lighting, and grease. The draw is the outstanding *char siu,* which, in a crowded field, is often cited as the best in the city and draws long lines through much of the day. If you want something on more than plastic plates, **Fu Sing Shark Fin Seafood Restaurant** (1/F Sunshine Plaza, 353 Lockhart Rd., Causeway Bay, tel. 852/2893-0881) is a more comfortable sit-down restaurant. Ignore the naughty dish in the restaurant's name, Fu Sing offers a full Cantonese menu and regularly makes it in to top ten lists for both its *char siu* and dim sum, which are all reasonably priced. While much of the best traditional Cantonese food in the city is served amongst shabby surroundings, the city's five-star hotels offer a swankier setting and more innovative cooking. One of the best is **Ming Court** (555 Shanghai St., Mongkok, tel. 852/3552-3300, www.hongkong.langhamplacehotels.com), which is lauded for its delicate, contemporary interpretations of classic Cantonese cuisine served amid hushed tones, starched tablecloths, and a restrained, imperiously turned-out banquet hall.

Breakfast should be done at one of Hong Kong's warp-speed *cha chaan teng's* and you could do no better than wedging yourself into **Australia Dairy Company** (47-49 Parkes St., Jordan, tel. 852/2730-1356). Ignore the misleading name, this place has nothing to do with the land down under and everything to with Hong Kong's traditional morning breakfast—a fusion of Chinese and Western influences. Food is served up at a thunderous pace amid a clatter of customers. The chef here has turned the humble scrambled-egg sandwich into an art form and the restaurant is a Hong Kong institution with a fanatical fan base.

Fresh seafood is perhaps the pivotal feature of Cantonese cuisine and being able to enjoy cheap, high quality fish, shellfish, and other creatures plucked from the deep blue sea is an undoubted advantage of living here. This insistence on freshness means many of the best seafood restaurants can be found in fishing villages along the coast, such as those at Sok Kwu Wan on Lamma Island. These unpretentious plastic-chair restaurants are usually stacked shoulder to shoulder along the seafront and in all honesty there is little to choose between them. **Rainbow Seafood** (Sok Kwu Wan, Lamma Island, ferry available from Central ferry piers, tel. 852/2982-8100) in Sok Kwu Wan is perhaps the most celebrated, although the restaurants nearby are equally as good.

At some point, when either your stomach or pride raise the white flag, you'll tire of dropping your chopsticks. Try and resist the pull of the admittedly excellent but overpriced Western restaurants in the city's hotels and head for the more affordable price tags of Wan Chai, Lan Kwai Fong, and SoHo. For unfussy comfort food, **Jaspas** (28 Staunton St., Central, tel. 852/2869-0733) in SoHo has long been an expat favorite, notorious for its boozy lunches, while **Dan Ryan's** (114 Pacific Pl., 88 Queensway, Admiralty, tel. 852/2845-4600, www.danryans. com) in Admiralty is a convincing recreation of your local neighborhood bar and grill—only with better food. One of the city's truly not-to-be-missed dining experiences is British High Tea amongst the marble floors, gilded columns, and Victorian grandeur of the **Peninsula Hotel** (Salisbury Rd., Tsim Sha Tsui, tel. 852/2920-2888, www.peninsula.com), where you'll enjoy cucumber sandwiches and jam-covered scones, be waited on by straight-backed, bow-tied staff, listen to a live string quartet, and dream of Mr. Darcy.

Colonial cakes aren't the end of the story when it comes to Hong Kong's ethnic options. The city's multicultural population means there is an A-to-Z of cuisines on offer. If you've got the backbone to brave the hawkers and dingy stairwells of Chungking Mansions, you'll find a slew of barebones diners here serving Indian and Pakistani cuisine. Don't expect restaurant service, don't even expect windows, but do expect authentic curries and budget prices. One of the more upmarket places—at least by Chungking standards—is **The Delhi Club** (Chungking Mansions, Block C, 3/F, C3, 40 Nathan Rd., Tsim Sha Tsui).

DAILY LIFE

MAKING THE MOVE

Relocating to another country, whether for a year or forever, necessarily involves a large amount of work, money, and upheaval. Not only are you swapping houses, cities, and jobs, but you're locking horns with a new culture and language at the same time. While stress is part and parcel of the experience, there is no need to feel overwhelmed. Hong Kong has a lengthy and successful history of dealing with expat workers and you'll find a wealth of services on offer to help you with moving kids, cats, and the kitchen sink. Paperwork can often be the source of pre-arrival jitters, but the city's immigration system is quick, helpful, and largely painless. For the majority of new arrivals, much of the visa workload will be handled by their company, although it's perfectly possible to navigate the system individually.

The most important thing to remember is that whatever problem you encounter, someone else who has moved to the city has almost certainly faced the same situation and there is always a solution. When the cogs click into place,

© MARTYNA SZMYTKOWSKA

and they always do, you'll find the stress giving way to excitement as you explore your surroundings and get to know your *yum cha* from your *char siu*.

Immigration and Visas

Streamlined and straightforward, the Hong Kong immigration system generally makes the process of applying for an employment visa as painless as possible. That doesn't mean they'll give you one. The days of dropping the right name and shaking the right hands are long gone and unless you're posted here by your company, preferably a multinational with its hands on all the right strings, shaking an employment visa out of immigration can be tough. While being a native speaker of English will still win you a visa for certain jobs, such as copywriter or teacher, it is no longer a golden ticket to the chocolate factory.

EMPLOYMENT VISA

Put simply, to get an employment visa you need a job. Aside from a handful of freelancer visas, you can't apply for an employment visa as an individual. You will need an employer to act as your sponsor. In fact, most of the paperwork is submitted by your employer. In a perfect world the company will apply for the visa before you leave your home country and you'll have it in hand when you arrive in Hong Kong. All you'll need to do is supply photocopies of your birth certificate, passport, degree, and any other relevant training certificates, and you need a clean criminal record. Applications for the visa are processed through the Hong Kong Immigration Service and tend to take 6–8 weeks to be issued. The visa is tied to your employer, so if you get your marching orders from work, you'll have to march right out of Hong Kong. If you want to swap firms, you'll need to reapply.

Job Seekers and Employment Visas

While the preceding information is valid for all applicants, if you've come to seek employment in Hong Kong by yourself, your situation is somewhat different and more difficult. The immigration office measures everybody applying for an employment visa with the same stick; if you're looking for work, it helps to know what they're measuring. The Immigration Service states that applicants should "possess special skills, knowledge or experience of value to and not readily available in the HKSAR." For those of us who don't understand bureaucratic double-speak, that means bums need not apply. The visa is called Employment for Professionals for a reason and this typically means a degree or MBA, depending on the position, although an impressive CV filled with relevant experiences can suffice.

Immigration will also inspect the job offer to ensure that pay and benefits are comparable to local market standards. If it's too low, they will assume that an expat is not really needed. The pay required varies from job to job but the expat grapevine claims that offers with wages less than HK$15,000 are usually rejected. Your employer will also have to prove that the job can't be filled locally. For bigger companies used to dealing with immigration, this can be a formality; but smaller companies who don't frequently employ expats will have a hard time justifying your employment to immigration and rejections are not uncommon. If you and your company are having trouble, there are a number of firms in Hong Kong who specialize in obtaining employment visas, but their services aren't cheap.

One contradiction you'll come up against is that Hong Kong immigration states that those seeking employment should apply for an employment visa *before* they come to Hong Kong; however, all the books, including this one, will tell you that you need to come to the city if you want to find a job. So who should you listen to?

While I can't advise you to break Hong Kong Immigration Law, I can tell you that many, many expats come to Hong Kong to seek work while here as visitors. The generous stays and visa free access allowed by Hong Kong will give you plenty of time to rummage about in the employment pool. If the work search takes more than the three months you're allocated on your tourist visa, you can do a "renewal run." You exit into Macau or China for the day, re-enter Hong Kong and get a fresh stamp. It's a practice largely ignored by Hong Kong Immigration but don't push your luck. Those returning for a third or fourth consecutive visit will likely find themselves in trouble.

OTHER VISAS
Investment Visa

Visas for investment are aimed at those who want to set up business in Hong Kong. The criteria used to evaluate applicants is broadly similar to that used for the general employment visa. However, the "assessment of your contribution to the Hong Kong economy" will focus on the viability of your business plan, your finances, and how many Hong Kongers you are likely to employ.

Working Holiday Visa

Hong Kong has reciprocal agreements with a number of countries that allows for young people (ages 18–30) to take up one-year working holiday visas. Citizens of Australia, Canada, Ireland, New Zealand, and Japan are currently eligible for the one-year visa that allows for part-time employment.

Capital Investment Entrant Scheme

Proving money can buy you love, the Capital Investment Entrant Scheme is the only visa that doesn't require applicants to have a clean criminal record. In fact, it doesn't really require anything except that you have HK$10 million sitting in your bank account.

Quality Migrant Scheme

An alternative to an employment visa, the Quality Migrant Admission Scheme allows immigrants who pass a points-based test to move to Hong Kong, seek work, and take up employment. Aside from being able to seek work while in Hong Kong legally, the main advantage is that you can also jump employers without losing your visa. Scores are based on age, education, experience, and language skills and applications are processed quarterly. Unfortunately, few people are admitted under the scheme and the process and decision process have been criticized as being opaque.

Study Visa

With a number of excellent universities, Hong Kong attracts annual influxes of international students and study visas are relatively easy to obtain. It is the educational institution that acts as the sponsor for the visa and who submits the required paperwork to immigration, so you will need to be accepted into a program before applying for a visa. As a reward for lavishing your college fund on a Hong Kong institution, those that have graduated from a degree course or higher qualification are eligible to work in Hong Kong with very few restrictions.

Dependents

The spouse and children (under 18) of those admitted to Hong Kong with an employment visa, as well as under certain other visa types, are entitled to an automatic residency visa. The spouse is also permitted to take up employment in Hong Kong, but must first notify the Immigration Service. The rules and regulations of this visa, particularly regarding employment, seem to change with the wind, so do be sure to check the current rules.

NET Scheme

This is not a visa, but a program that will get you one. The Native-speaking English Teacher (NET) recruitment scheme is a program aimed at placing native English-speaking teachers in Hong Kong public schools, both primary and secondary. While this isn't the only or necessarily the best way for teachers to find employment in Hong Kong, it does, if you're successful with your application, pretty much deliver a guaranteed employment visa. Applicants need to possess at least a Bachelor's Degree, preferably in English Language, Literature, or Linguistics, a post-graduate teaching degree, and teaching experience, although on occasion some of these requirements are waived. Contracts and, thus, visas are for a period of two years.

CHANGING VISA TYPES

Most visas are highly restrictive and it is not possible to change your visa type without going through the whole application process again. Employment visas

CHINESE VISAS

To the surprise of some travelers and the immigration agents at the border who have to deliver the bad news, entry into Hong Kong and even a visa to live and work here does not win you entry into China. Hong Kong and China have completely separate immigration departments and a full-blown international border between them. So if you want to visit China, as many people do, you'll need to apply for a China visa. Thankfully, Hong Kong has long been a first stop for visitors who need a few days of chopstick-training before plucking up the courage to explore the Middle Kingdom, and Chinese visas are easy to get and cheap.

Your main point of contact will be the **Chinese Ministry of Foreign Affairs** (7/F, Lower Block, China Resources Building, 26 Harbour Rd., Wan Chai, tel. 852/3413-2424, www.fmcoprc.gov.hk), a sort of mini Chinese embassy, where visa prices

are lowest. Visas here take four days with their regular service. For something a little snappier or more complex and longer visas, you can use an agency, many of which can knock out a visa in just a few hours. The ubiquitous **China Travel Service (CTS)** (G/F China Travel Building 77 Queen's Rd., Central, tel. 852/2998-7888, www.ctshk.com), a quasi-government-run organization, is the best known, although not necessarily the best. Many expats swear by **Forever Bright Trading** (Room 916-917 New Mandarin Plaza Tower B, 14 Science Museum Rd., TST East, Kowloon, tel. 852/2369-3188, www.fbt-chinavisa.com.hk), who have managed to sweet-talk visas out of the authorities for even the most unusual cases. Visa prices at both the ministry and the agencies will vary on the visa and your nationality.

It's worth mentioning that the Chinese government officially adare tied to your employer as a sponsor and if you attempt to change companies, you will need to reapply.

VISA FOR CHINA

For the purposes of visas and immigration, Hong Kong and China are wholly separate entities with a full international border between the two. If you plan to go to China during your trip to Hong Kong, you'll need to apply for the requisite Chinese visa. This can be done either at the Chinese Foreign Ministry Office in Hong Kong or at travel agents such as CTS. China currently advises tourists visiting Hong Kong and wanting to visit China to apply for a Chinese visa at the Chinese embassy in their home country. In reality, travelers have reported no problems or issues in acquiring a Chinese visa in the city.

A number of nationalities, although not currently U.S. citizens, are also eligible for the five-day Shenzhen visa, which can be obtained at the Lo Wu

DAILY LIFE

vises people to obtain Chinese visas in their home country and very occasionally, especially during major events, officials will pull the rulebook out, blow the dust off, and point sternly at it. Practically, Hong Kong is rarely affected, especially the agencies, and Hong Kong residents with a HKID always have the right to apply here. Do, however, be warned that Chinese visa rules can be volatile; officials will often tinker with the regulations and, more commonly, the prices and you should always check ahead for up-to-date information.

Most visitors will be looking for the tourist L visa, which can be single or double entry, and allows you to stay for up to 30 days at a time. Multiple entry L visas over 6-months-1-year periods are also available, although they are hard to get in Hong Kong without the help of an agent. If you're heading up to China for business, as many people in Hong Kong do, you'll need an F visa. These again come in single, double, and multiple entry, the latter valid for up to two years, and are usually good for 30 days or more. Again, if you want a multiple-entry visa, your best bet is an agency. Beyond all of these is the resident Z visa, which you will have to apply for at the Chinese embassy in your home country

Usually, if you just want to get your passport stamped and say that you've been to China, most nationalities, although not currently U.S. citizens, can get a five-day Shenzhen visa valid for the Shenzhen Special Economic Zone on the spot at the Lo Wu border crossing. Eager to wine and dine tourists at their glittering new casinos, Macau offers visa-free access on arrival for citizens of the United States, Canada, Australia, New Zealand, and most European countries, for periods of 30-90 days.

Border crossing and is valid for the Shenzhen Special Economic Zone. Other visas can also be applied for in Hong Kong, but in case of delays or problems, it is usually advisable to apply for more complex Chinese visas through the Chinese embassy in your home country.

Moving with Children

Even uprooting kids from their friends, family, and familiarity for a two-week vacation can end up in tear-filled tantrums, so the idea of flying them half way across the world for a year or three can seem daunting. But while you will undoubtedly have to tackle homesickness and culture shock, the benefits far outweigh the disadvantages. Exposure to such an international community is a unique and incredible experience and studies have proven that expat children usually develop into more confident and more successful adults. In all likelihood your move will bring out the best in your kids. Hong Kong also offers fewer of the disadvantages associated with moving to other destinations since it offers an English-language environment, first-rate schooling, and some of the world's safest streets. Few of these reasons are likely to excite your kids, so if all else fails, pull out the pictures of Ocean Park and Disneyland.

kids playing in a fountain

PREPARING KIDS FOR THE MOVE

Some kids will be delighted about moving to Hong Kong, others will swear eternal revenge, and any preparation you undertake should be tailored to your child's reaction and emotions.

One of the most important steps in preparing kids for the move will be familiarizing them with Hong Kong. Give them access to books, DVDs, and

Internet resources which accentuate the positive about the city. Take them to a local Cantonese restaurant at least a few times before you leave; if they have already tasted and started to like the food, it will be one less challenge for them to conquer when they arrive. At the same time, don't gloss over the negatives. It's better to be honest about the changes and compromises they will have to make now, rather than after the move. While children may have had little input into the decision to move to Hong Kong, you can compensate by letting them have their say on schools and accommodation. Make them feel involved. Go online and look up teams and groups that will let them play the same sports or take up the same hobbies they already enjoy at home. It may also be worth organizing a goodbye party or family get-together before leaving; this will give your child a sense of closure and help them prepare mentally for the next stage in their life.

MOVING WITH BABIES AND PRESCHOOLERS

You're unlikely to encounter any major problems in moving babies or pre-schoolers to Hong Kong; their favorite brand of food will be available and restaurants and public transportation are set up to accommodate small ones and the strollers that come with them. Do keep in mind, however, the lack of space and the terrain. Trying to push a stroller down the packed streets of Hong Kong can require the maneuvering skills of a racecar driver, while the steep inclines on Hong Kong Island mean you'll need extra horsepower. These are all factors worth bearing in mind when you are choosing where to live. Public baby-changing facilities can also be few and far between. Many expats and locals alike employ maids, or *amahs* as they are known, to help with childcare. They usually live with you and do the cleaning, washing, and cooking. As most *amahs* come from the Philippines, they will speak English, the downside of which is their Cantonese may be no better than yours.

MOVING WITH ELEMENTARY SCHOOL-AGE KIDS

This is commonly believed to be the best time to move kids to a new country; younger children tend to be incredibly adaptive and will be more open to changes and strike up new friendships easily. School is the likely source for new friend-ships, but also consider enrolling them in sports teams and hobby groups that interest them, especially as there is little room or opportunity to play outdoors freely. The sooner they find new friends the sooner they will feel at home.

MOVING WITH TEENS

Teenagers find moving from the sofa difficult, so it's no surprise that it's this age group that often finds shifting countries the most challenging. They will already have strong attachments to your home country, including best friends, sports teams, and probably the love of their lives, making leaving all the more difficult. Theirs is likely to be a rollercoaster ride of highs and lows. You can ease the transition by picking an appropriate time to move, preferably the end of an academic year, allowing them to say goodbye to their friends and start school in Hong Kong the same time as other kids. Make sure that they have a range of ways to continue communication with friends back home; Hong Kong is well connected and Facebook and Skype have made long-distance communication easier than ever.

School is likely to be a somewhat different experience in Hong Kong, probably involving a uniform and certainly a heavier workload. Be aware of the change and be available to help out if they're struggling. Ultimately, they are also the best placed of all age groups to get the most out of the experience. Once they start making friends at school—and they will—they will be exposed to many, many different cultures and ideas, something that will make a lasting impression. Depending on where you're coming from, teenagers in Hong Kong tend to be given an awful lot of independence, something which will undoubtedly influence your own child and you may well have to loosen the reins a little. Thankfully, the city is very safe and there is less chance for mischief in Hong Kong than in most other countries.

Moving with Pets

It's relatively simple to move pets to Hong Kong with minimal fees, minimal fuss, and generally no quarantine. However, before you stuff Tinkerbell and Macavity into your suitcase it's worth considering the quality of life they'll enjoy in Hong Kong. Almost all aspects of cat and dog ownership are regulated in Hong Kong, ensuring cats and dogs are treated well, but small apartments and lack of access to green spaces are just a couple of the problems you'll need to contend with.

BRINGING A PET TO HONG KONG

Residents of the United Kingdom, Ireland, Australia, New Zealand, Japan, and Hawaii can avoid quarantine for their pets by providing an animal health certificate. This requires you to have your dog microchipped and to get a residence certificate valid for the last six months and a vaccination certificate certifying that all the animal's shots are up-to-date signed by a registered vet.

Check your white pages for vets that specifically deal with the import and export of animals and they should provide you with a one-stop certificate shop. You will also need to notify the Hong Kong Import and Export Duty Officer of your animal's arrival at least two days in advance and present a certificate from your carrier certifying that the plane was a direct flight between your home country and Hong Kong and that you didn't stop off somewhere to pick up a bag of rabies.

Residents of the Continental United States, Canada, and most other European countries will need to collect all of the above plus an anti-rabies certificate from their vet. Somewhat trickier, depending on where you live, is getting a residence certificate that certifies that no domestic animals have had rabies in your state or province in the last 30 days. Any animals that arrive without this pocketful of documentation are subject to being placed behind bars and a lengthy quarantine.

All owners, whether using quarantine or not, need to apply for a permit from the Agriculture, Fisheries, and Conservation Department, which costs HK$432 and takes around five days to process. All dogs in Hong Kong are licensed and mircochipped and dogs must be relicensed every three years at a cost of HK$80. This also involves a health check-up and revaccination for rabies. Thanks to the microchip, lost dogs are usually returned to the owner, but you must notify the authorities promptly if Fido makes a break for freedom or face a fine when he's caught sizing up lampposts downtown. You can find out more about pet import requirements and the microchip procedure from the Agriculture, Fisheries and Conservation Department.

LIFESTYLE FOR PETS IN HONG KONG

While the rules and regulations might make it relatively easy for dogs and cats to relocate, they may not appreciate their new home. Unless you're earning big bucks or willing to live out in the New Territories, the chance of having a garden is almost zero. Combine this with pocket-sized apartments and it means you'll need to take your dog out to exercise and use the toilet at least a couple of times day. There are practically no open spaces in the city and unleashing your dog in public is illegal, so there will be little chance for pooches to stretch their legs, except during weekend trips. With long working hours many locals use dog walkers, but you'll need to assess if this fits into your budget. Dogs with heavy coats can also find the Hong Kong humidity sweaty work and you'll need to keep the air-conditioning on all day. Cats are, as usual, less problematic; although, one issue to keep in mind is that they won't be able to go outside. You'll also need to bar or keep closed any windows and access to balconies, lest Fluffy go skydiving without her parachute. If you're determined to relocate together, be sure that your apartment complex allows animals; many don't.

Vets in Hong Kong are well trained, an education reflected in their charges. If your animal has a condition that requires ongoing treatment you should budget for some highway robbery. Pets with a fussy diet shouldn't have any difficulty with a move as your favorite brands from home are likely to be available. All vets and pet stores are monitored and licensed by the Agriculture, Fisheries, and Conservation Department.

BUYING PETS IN HONG KONG

Birds and fish, particularly goldfish, are popular pets in Hong Kong, as they are thought to bring good luck. You'll find both at the dedicated bird market and goldfish market in Mongkok, while individual pet stores also have a wide selection. If you're considering buying a cat or dog in Hong Kong, make abandoned animal shelters your first call. All animals available for re-housing are screened and should be suitable. You can contact the SPCA, Hong Kong Dog Rescue, and Hong Kong Alley Cat Watch for more details on procedures and shelters.

What to Take

Thankfully, a move to Hong Kong doesn't mean sacrificing the comforts of home. Most of your favorite foods and products can be found in Hong Kong at your local Wellcome or Park N Shop supermarkets. Cheddar cheese, Mexican and Indian sauces, sliced bread, and fresh pasteurized milk are just some of the goods expats lust for when abroad, but all are fairly mundane finds available in most supermarkets. Many expats can replicate their food shop from home with only a few changes and little extra expenditure. For more niche items and a better brand selection, Oliver's and 360 have a selection and prices aimed specifically for expats. As most brands tend to be British or Australian, U.S. expats also rotate the Gateway store in Sheung Wan into their shopping schedule; a sort of imitation Sam's Club that can satisfy your insatiable yearning for Kraft Macaroni and Cheese, Tide detergent, and other familiar U.S. brands.

CLOTHES

The size difference between Europeans/North Americans and Asians is less of an issue in Hong Kong than in other countries in Asia thanks to the wide range of Western brands and shops, but the larger your size, the less choice you're likely to have. Women have the greatest difficulty finding suitable sizes, particularly in trousers and dresses above U.S. size 14/16. European brands such as Marks and Spencer, Zara, and H&M often stock a small selection of larger sizes. Men and women who are plus sizes will find few items that won't look like cling wrap when pulled on and should consider bringing a suitcase stuffed with clothes.

SHOES

Similarly, larger shoe sizes can be difficult to find in Hong Kong and men over a U.S. size 11 and women over size 8 will only have a handful of Western stores to choose from.

ELECTRONICS

Unless you like fireworks, you'd be well advised to leave electronic equipment at home. The voltage in Hong Kong is 220v and 50hz, as opposed to 120v and 60Hz in the United States, and while transformers are readily available they are cumbersome and notoriously unreliable. Everybody in Hong Kong has heard horror stories of the wrong plug going into the wrong hole or the transformer malfunctioning to explosive and expensive effects. For smaller electronics, such as an iron or hairdryer, it's best to pick up a cheap replacement item locally. Larger goods, such as fridges and washing machines, are also best picked up locally. The cost of shipping is prohibitive and repeated use with a transformer is generally ill-advised. If cost is an issue, you can try picking one up from geoexpat.com, where expats who are leaving offload products cheaply.

Tech and computer items are increasingly more flexible on voltage and an increasing number of flatscreen TVs, DVD players, and various other products accept a range of voltage; laptops, for example, are usually compatible with both 220v and 120v. If you do bring multi-voltage items, remember that Hong Kong has British, three-pronged plugs. Both adaptors and transformers can be bought on Apliu Street in Sham Shui Po, as well as in major electronic outlets, such as Fortress.

Buying Electronics in Hong Kong

Sadly, the days of picking up a shopping cart full of computers for the change in your back pocket are long gone. The aggressive pricing of online companies in the United States and Europe means electronics in Hong Kong are no longer as jaw-droppingly cheap as they once were. Still, if you're willing to cut a few corners and know a microchip from a mouse, bargain prices are available.

In general, it is computer equipment and audio/visual equipment, as well as associated gadgets, that boast the best price tags. Second-hand laptops and phones that are less than a year old can be an absolute steal and you can deck yourself out like James Bond for not much money. To find them you'll need to brave one of Hong Kong's cable and computer emporiums, such as the Golden Computer Arcade in Sham Shui Po or Mongkok Computer Centre. Inside these multi-story mazes are shelves creaking with cables, cutting edge microchips, and gadgets even Steve Jobs

© MARTYNA SZMYTKOWSKA

stacks of cheap computer equipment for sale at a Hong Kong computer center

hasn't thought up yet. While products on sale are generally genuine, the grey market in parallel imports also does a booming trade. Computer centers are not places where the customer comes first. You're unlikely to get an international warranty and the returns policy can be as short as seven days to seven steps away from the counter. Be sure you know what you want and how much you're willing to pay. Stories of tourists being ripped off are wildly overblown, but negotiating is the key here. If you don't know the market price for a given item, expect to overpay.

FURNITURE AND HOUSEHOLD ITEMS

For those worried about the cost of refurnishing a home and restocking a kitchen, you won't necessarily need to bend your credit card. Ikea is a good start for furnishings, while Pricerite is cheaper and can help you stock up on kitchen utensils and bed clothes. You'll also find expats regularly offloading their earthly possessions when they leave Hong Kong at buy-in-bulk, secondhand prices. Geoexpat. com and *HK Magazine* are good places to find these fire sale giveaways.

SHIPPING OPTIONS

With a smaller apartment and the low cost of many products in Hong Kong, it will often save you money and a few headaches to just buy what you need in the city. If you do want to ship a few prized possessions or even tip everything in your house into boxes, there are a number of companies who can ship for you.

Unless you really can't live without your Mickey Mouse Alarm Clock and automated toe clipper for a few weeks, give air freight a miss. The price per kilo is prohibitively high for anything other than a few essential items. Shipping by sea is around half the price or less, reasonably straightforward, and takes roughly 8–10 weeks, depending on your location. If you have just a few boxes, consider a company such as Seven Seas World Wide; they will ship a 30kg crate door to door from the United States to Hong Kong for around HK$2,500. If your move is more involved and requires uprooting a whole house, you might consider taking up the services of a dedicated relocation firm. These companies offer storage, packing and unpacking services, as well as advice at both ends of the move. There is no shortage of such firms in Hong Kong and they range from respected international names such as Crown Relocation and Allied Pickfords to local companies like FTC Relocations. Prices depend on whether you're in midtown New York or rural Kansas and it's important to shop around for the most competitive quote for your specific move.

CUSTOMS

Hong Kong is a duty-free port, so nothing you ship here, apart from liquor, tobacco, and cars, requires duty to be paid. Even better news is that Hong Kong's paperwork-shy attitude also applies to customs, and you'll only need to fill out a couple of pieces of paper to get your belongings into the city. Shipping stuff out of the city is also duty free. Although before you start plotting to load up shipping containers with discount clothing and Hello Kitty T-shirts and sail for Seattle, remember you will have to pay import duty back home on anything that you can't prove is your own household goods.

HOUSING CONSIDERATIONS

Hong Kong manages to combine both the world's most densely-populated neighborhood and the world's priciest pieces of real estate. It's far from a winning combo. Space is at an absolute premium in the city, even by Asian standards, and expats, particularly from the United States, can find it quite a shock to downsize half their square feet without getting to downsize their rent. Luckily, there are no truly bad neighborhoods; Hong Kong is an incredibly safe place to live. You'll also find the whole city is pretty much at your doorstep.

Unless you're on a premium contract that will give you access to the handful of houses in seaside communities, most Hong Kong housing consists of bedroom communities stuffed to bursting with high-rise apartment blocks. The upside is many of the higher-end complexes and communities offer an endless list of amenities, from rooftop BBQs and swimming pools to shuttle buses and in-house laundry services. A handful of expats, looking to either

© MAGDA HUECKEL & TOMASZ ŚLIWIŃSKI (MUZUNGU-ART)

escape the suffocating streets of the city or explore a more traditional Hong Kong, head for the New Territories or the Outlying Islands, where they find a more relaxed lifestyle and lower rents, but longer commutes.

The Hong Kong rental market is extremely volatile and prices can fluctuate wildly over just a few months, which, combined with notoriously temperamental landlords, can make finding the right location for new arrivals a difficult task. With that in mind, it's usually best to arrive first and stay in serviced apartments until you've had a chance to look around and get a feel for the housing market.

Housing Options

To borrow a phrase, you can have any sort of apartment you want, as long as it's small. While there are other options available, as listed in this chapter, the vast, vast majority of Hong Kong housing is high rise and close quarters. The price of real estate is one of the greatest hardships of living in Hong Kong and unless your company has opened their checkbook—wide—you should be prepared to downgrade your real estate and escalate what you pay in rent.

APARTMENTS

The age, size, and quality of apartments in Hong Kong span a gulf. At the bottom end of the market you'll find claustrophobic cupboards with no kitchen, no air-conditioning, and enough exposed electrical wiring to jump start Frankenstein. No expats end up at this end of the market simply because getting a job and visa in Hong Kong entails earning enough money to live somewhere better. At the top end are luxury penthouses, popular with expats, that feature sea views, whirlpool tubs, and enough rooms to house the Waltons. Those who end up in one of these Hollywood-style pads

© MARTYNA SZMYTKOWSKA

The apartments in Mid-Levels are some of the tallest in the city.

usually have the astronomical rents covered by the deep-pocketed company director.

In between these two are the more realistic properties. The average Hong Kong apartment will feature one bedroom; a small living room, which doubles as a dining room and corridor; a kitchen, which may only contain a countertop and a microwave; and a bathroom with shower. Almost all apartments will have air-conditioning and those that don't can be struck off your list immediately unless you want to be deep-fried like a dough-nut. Decoration-wise, don't expect the owner to have read Martha Stew-art's guide to interior decorating or to have even flicked through the Ikea catalog; white walls and office blinds are the norm, while humidity makes carpets and wallpaper a very rare and foolish investment. Few apartments have central heating systems as Hong Kong doesn't really get cold enough to justify them. Instead, many people use a small fan heater or oil heater to keep Jack Frost at bay on colder days. Apart from a handful of walk-ups, all apartments will have an elevator.

The mid-range to top range of the apartment market is where most ex-pats land. Within this range there is still a great deal of choice, depending on how much money you want to throw down for rent. While apartments are rarely spacious, you'll obviously find more space for more money, with two or three bedrooms the norm, and sometimes a smaller maid's room. Kitchens will usually be more substantial, set in a separate room and fully fitted, while bathrooms will have a larger shower and occasionally a bath. The living room and dining room are still usually combined, although there should be enough floor space to include a full dining table and chairs without sitting in front of the TV. Because space is still tight, expect stor-age space to be tucked under beds, around the ceiling, and anywhere else that doesn't take up the precious floor space. Many of the apartments in this price range will be furnished, although quite what this means varies from apartment to apartment. For the most part, you won't find apartment parking until you hit the upper end of the market and even then it can have limitations, such as no guest parking.

All apartment buildings will have a management or maintenance fee attached. The cost depends on the size of the apartment and exactly what the building owners provide, but basic cleaning, upkeep of the elevator and common areas, and roach patrol are standard, as is a doorperson on duty around the clock. If you have an inclusive rental agreement, the manage-ment fee and government rates are included in your rent. If it's exclusive, they're not.

LUXURY APARTMENT COMPLEXES

Half home, half hotel, Hong Kong's luxurious apartment complexes not only offer the most square feet but also a long list of extras to justify the expensive rents. Almost all are new and stylishly designed—to one degree or another—with air-conditioned lobbies, security staff, and reception desks. Most also have communal recreational areas, which include gyms, squash courts, and even swimming pools. These facilities are often known as clubhouse facilities, although the clubhouses themselves will often offer a bar, reading room with Wi-Fi, and kids areas. At the very top end of the market, the buildings are like self-contained communities with tai chi classes, toddler groups, and supermarkets on site.

The complexes are popular with expats because these extras can take a lot of the hassle out of renting. Most are owned by a single developer and saddled with evocative names such as Caribbean Coast and Bel-Air or the slightly too evocative The Belchers. Fully furnished and fully fitted most of the time, apartments inside each complex are usually laid out the same way, although there are typically some duplexes and triplexes on offer as well. Prices are absolutely ruinous thanks to both high rents and the massive management fees, for which there is no way to opt out, even if you don't use the facilities.

HOUSES

Lack of land makes it hard to justify building a standalone house for a single family, and the few that do exist are at the very top end of the market. Most are found in just a handful of more spacious districts, such as The Peak, Kowloon Tong, and Southside Hong Kong Island, and are universally luxurious. Again because of space, new homes are rare and only found in out-of-town developments. Most houses are older colonial homes, built for pampered British civil servants now departed, or more modern and ostentatious mansions inhabited by executives, directors, and lottery

New buildings are constantly being built and construction can cause noise and block views.

© MARTYNA SZMYTKOWSKA

traditional village townhouses near Sha Tin

winners. Despite their age, properties are kept in impeccable condition and will usually come fully fitted and fully furnished. Layouts vary, but two or three floors is standard. These houses include four or more bedrooms, including en suite marble bathrooms; separate dining room and lounge room; a maid's room; and garages. Given the neighborhoods in which houses are found, you will enjoy some space and sunlight away from the high rises, although townhouse developments are clumped together.

If you're lucky enough to have the cash to play in this price range, be demanding. Despite the paucity of houses, the rents they attract mean there is no shortage of them on the market, and considering the cost, extras—such as hot tubs and swimming pools—are by no means an extravagance.

VILLAGE HOUSES

Substantially cheaper houses are available in small villages in the New Territories and the Outlying Islands. Known as village houses, or legally, small houses, these can cost as little as HK$20,000, if you really get off the beaten track. Built by individual owners who are either residents in the area or have family connections, houses range from two-room huts with no running water and extremely low ceilings to modern, three-floor compounds. There are regulations limiting their size, although with the maximum set at 2,100 square feet, set over three floors of 700 square feet each, there will still be plenty to vacuum. The average village house will have a couple of bedrooms, a large kitchen, and bathroom set over no more than three floors.

Traditionally, villagers have had little money to spend on houses and they have been fairly barren, stone structures. Increasingly, however, property prices have risen in rural areas and houses are undergoing major renovations, boasting new kitchens and bathrooms and designer interiors catering to the growing exodus of city dwellers. Village house listings are becoming more common on rental websites and with real estate agents, but for many you'll still need to head to the village you're interested in and ask around. For long-term rentals and especially if you're buying, be sure to take a magnifying glass to the legal documents. Some houses are in violation of building codes and restrictions and may have added illegal extensions or built on land that they don't own.

TOWNHOUSES

Substantially cheaper than houses and as affordable as some of the apartments in swanky neighborhoods, townhouses are usually two or three floors of semi-detached or terraced houses in a street or dedicated development of identical properties. Lack of space has squeezed the majority out into the New Territories and Outlying Islands, where developments can range from 20 properties on a single street to sprawling estates.

The townhouse is a relatively new addition to Hong Kong real estate so most properties are fresh-faced with modern fixtures and fittings. Some, such as those in Tai Po's Beverly Hills development, are modeled on European architecture, although the design usually has all the finesse of Madame Tussaud's waxwork models. Each development will usually have a couple of basic floor plans to choose from and you can expect two, three, or more bedrooms, separate dining room and lounge, and a maid's room. Garages and gardens are not always included. Many of the bigger developments also offer communal amenities such as swimming pools and clubhouses, although these extras are reflected in the management charge. It's worth checking out the individual developments' websites for rentals.

BOATS

Boat make up a niche market, but a growing one. The lack of land and high prices for houses has seen an increasing number of people packing their sea legs and suitcases and setting up on the ocean waves in a houseboat. They have wooed many executives looking for an alternative to high-rise living. Houseboat converts say it's not only a property but a lifestyle within a close-knit community. Unfortunately, this isn't your chance to play Popeye. Most of the yachts and boats on offer require the crew of a small trawler to sail them safely, so you won't be able to commute to work in your floating palace. Instead, boats are anchored at marinas such as those in Discovery Bay and The Gold Coast, natural typhoon shelters that can withstand even the nastiest of storms that sweep through the area. This means the boat is usually cocooned from ocean swells and you shouldn't need to wear overalls every time you eat dinner. Most boats are luxury yachts with 3,000 square feet and upwards to roll around in. While they don't come cheap, you'll get more space for your money than in a luxury apartment. On top of rent you'll have to factor in the marina fee to rent your berth, as well as annual payments for insurance and maintenance.

FLOOR LEVELS AND VIEWS

Thanks to the sheer amount of high rises in Hong Kong the view from your window is usually limited to staring at the backside of another apartment block, or, if you're very unlucky, someone else's backside in the bathroom across the way. The higher up you go, the more chance you have of glimpsing blue skies, although prices will climb with you. Views on to the city or any sort of greenery attract premium prices and vistas over Victoria Harbour can easily double the price of an apartment. Possibly to preserve the dignity of their owners, Hong Kong apartments, particularly older ones, don't have a lot of windows, and lighting inside can be poor. Balconies are very rare and usually only found in older buildings or luxury apartments, although some buildings may offer communal roof access where you can hang-dry clothing, have a BBQ, and surface to enjoy the sun.

Also worth keeping in mind when choosing your floor is Hong Kong's creepy crawlies. Urban legend has it that the city's invincible cockroaches have no head for heights and you won't see them much above the 7th or 8th floor. I can personally dispel this firsthand and know they can both make it to the 26th floor and snuggle up with you in bed. Nevertheless, while well-kept apartments are unlikely to have a problem, the higher you go, the fewer cockroaches, mosquitoes, and other insects you're likely to find.

NUMBERS AND FENG SHUI

Superstition city means you might find your building has a few floors missing in action. The word four sounds like death in Cantonese, so developers often leave out the 4th floor and any other floors that end in the letter four. If they make it that high, some will skip the whole 40th floor. In a unique piece of racial equality, many developers have also give the 13th floor a miss for rabbit-foot carrying expats. If you don't mind tempting the fates, apartments on floors with the number four are always cheaper, sometimes substantially so. All this floor-skipping also allows developers to advertise their building as having 50 floors when a full climb up will reveal that a few physical floors are missing.

Hong Kong's reputation for feng shui is perhaps a little overblown. As soon as you get off the plane you'll notice the place could do with a good spring cleaning. And, while big commercial buildings such as HSBC have been designed with feng shui principles in mind, most residential properties don't have the space. That said, most people do believe in the power of good feng shui and buildings that are sea-facing and have water features and no pointed edges will be pricier.

DAILY LIFE

Renting a Home

Once you've picked yourself up off the floor after hearing the prices, the actual practical steps in renting an apartment are fairly easy. While it's certainly easier to let a real estate agent do the heavy lifting, the availability of English-language information makes it simple enough to browse yourself. In most cases, whether with an agent or not, the rental price listed is what the landlord would like to get, not what he will get. It's acceptable and expected to negotiate. When you first look at an apartment you may be forgiven for thinking that the quoted square footage has been mistaken for square inches. In fact the listed size of an apartment also factors in communal areas such as the lobby and even the elevator. Instead, you need to ask about usable area, which is the area of the actual apartment. Usable area can often be quoted as a percentage, such as 85 percent of the total square footage.

REAL ESTATE AGENTS
Few apartment rentals in Hong Kong are available on the open market, or rather they are but they aren't advertised, so you have no way of knowing about them. Instead, people employ a real estate agent to help them find a home. There are no shortage of real estate agents, so you can be fussy in who you choose. As ever, you'll find agents who will deliver exactly what you want, when you want it, and others who can't even locate the vacant real estate between their own ears. Either way, remember the agent isn't primarily out to make you happy but to make a profit, and they'll likely stretch the truth to get you to sign. They will also try and sell you on rentals that

are out of your price range, where they'll make more commission. Consider quoting them a price about 10 percent below what you're willing to pay.

Most real estate agents focus on just a couple of areas in the region where you will also find their office. Some are part of large companies, such as Century 21, while others are independent operators. There's no clear-cut difference between the two, although bigger companies may have preferential rates available on new developments and independent realtors are usually more willing to negotiate on their own payment. Realtors in expat areas, such as Happy Valley and Mid-Levels, will be used to expats and their particular requests and concerns, while those in Sheung Wan and North Point may find your need to have sunlight in the apartment somewhat peculiar. There are also a number of exclusive realtors who directly target expats. Most of the listings they have are at the very high end of the market and, although they may well be more familiar with expat needs, don't expect to get a deal on the price. They are expensive.

Before you go leaping from the airport to the real estate agent's office, do some legwork. Read our prime living location chapters and pick some areas you're interested in and visit them. There is no substitute for eyeballing an area. No matter what a real estate agent might claim, nobody knows better where you want to live than you. While it isn't the norm, fresh-off-the-boat expats may find both their naivety and their wallet taken advantage of by agents keen to exploit their unfamiliarity with the market. The solution to this is quantity. Be sure to see a lot of flats with at least a few agents, this will give you a good idea of who is giving you the expat special price. You'll often find three or four agents in the same neighborhood who will show you the same property at different prices.

Once you're in contact with an agency, they'll usually whisk you around a few properties in the first few days. Because agents don't charge a sign-up fee or hourly rate, they're a little like a two-year-old with a new toy: They'll soon get bored and move on if they haven't sold you on a place in the first week or two. Simply get a new agent. When you have picked a place, the standard agent's fee is half of a month's rent.

FINDING A PLACE ON YOUR OWN

While the pull of using a real estate agent proves irresistible for most expats, with English language listings in newspapers and on websites and many owners who speak English it's perfectly possible to find a home yourself.

www.gohome.com.hk is Hong Kong's most comprehensive property listing website and while most of the listings are through real estate agents, there are individual listings. The website lets you contact the landlord directly for free. The fortnightly Square Foot magazine is worth getting hold of for its insightful articles on the Hong Kong property market, and also listings. It can also be found online at www.squarefoot.com.hk. The South China Morning Post also runs a property section. For more informal listings, usually targeted at expats, try Hong Kong Magazine and forums such as geoexpat.com. You can also check craigslist.org, which is a good source for room shares, but be aware that scammers tend to target the site. In luxury apartment complexes or townhouse developments, the developer will usually have a website and you can approach them directly. For off the beaten track rentals in small villages, real estate agents aren't always much help. Instead, you'll need to visit the village and learn through word of mouth at the village shop what's available. The village shop is a good starting point. It's also worth checking out notice boards in Wellcome and Park N Shop supermarkets which often carry real estate listings in English in expat areas.

Remember the rental agreement in a private transaction is likely to be written to cater to the whims of the landlord. So unless you want weekly 6am Sunday inspections of the lint in the tumble drier, you'd be advised to pass it under the eyes of a solicitor. Landlords hold most of the cards in Hong Kong rental agreements, so it's important to know what's in your contract and be insistent if you want something changed.

RENTAL CONTRACTS AND WHAT TO EXPECT

Hong Kong's landlords have a tyrannical reputation and it's one that's somewhat justified. Raising rents, keeping security deposits, some people suspect they might be behind the JFK assassination. Nevertheless, while they may not be Hong Kong's most loved group of people, as long as you approach any contract as a business deal, which is what it is, you shouldn't have any problems.

Aside from serviced apartments, the minimum rental contract you'll come across in Hong Kong is for one year, with two years being the norm. Some landlords will offer discounts if you sign on for longer. Be careful, it's easier to break a voodoo curse than a Hong Kong rental agreement and you'll incur heavy penalties. If you suspect you won't be able to complete the full lease agreement, ask for a break clause. This typically allows either party to give two or three months notice that they want to leave once the first twelve months of the tenancy is completed. The break clause also allows for a correction on the rent in either direction depending on prevailing market conditions. Landlords are merciless in rising rents even on long term tenants, something which has been the ruin of many a good business. At the same time, if the market is depressed, you have the right to expect a reduction when it comes time to negotiate the rent. If you break your contract at other times, you will lose your security deposit and the landlord has the right to pursue you for the full rent over the whole life of the contract— although that rarely happens.

Make sure the tenancy agreement spells out not only the rent due but also who pays the government rates and management rates. Inclusive contracts will include these in the rent while exclusive contracts mean they are extra on top of the rent. The standard security deposit is for two months and is fully refundable at the end of the contract. Be sure to through the apartment from top to bottom with the landlord, security deposits have been deducted for the most innocuous reasons.

BUYING A HOUSE

Few expats buy an apartment in Hong Kong simply because the price for anything they would like to live in tends to be prohibitively expensive. The average square foot in Hong Kong sells for around HK$9,000, while Hong Kong Island prices level off around $12,000. The Peak has the highest square foot prices in the world. However, if you've got the dough, buying property is relatively painless and there are no restrictions on foreign ownership. You should, however, always seek legal advice to help you complete due diligence.

As to whether Hong Kong property is a good investment, it depends on who you ask and what graph they show you. Over the long term prices have certainly appreciated but there have also been some screaming cliff drop offs that have lasted substantial periods. All land in Hong Kong is leasehold so you will only own the property rather than the ground underneath.

You can buying with a browse at websites such as gohome.com.hk and move on to real estate agents when you're ready to get serious. Once you have found somewhere, it is the responsibility of the agent to assist you in carrying out due diligence. On top of the actual price of the house there are a number of other fees that you'll need to factor in. There will be soliciter and notary fees as well as a government stamp duty of up to 4.25 percent, depending on the price of the property. Real estate agents generally charge 1 percent, although this is negotiable no matter what fable of rules and regulations they may spin you. When the price and conditions have been ironed out, both parties will sign a Provisional Sale and Purchase Agreement which

© MAGDA HUECKEL & TOMASZ ŚLIWIŃSKI (MUZUNGU-ART)

DAILY LIFE

The humidity in Hong Kong causes buildings to lose their gloss quickly and older buildings can look like they've been under siege in the last few years.

outlines what deposit has to be paid to secure the property, when final payment is to be made and when the documents and keys are to be handed over as well as detailing who is set to pay which fees. When the PSPA is signed and the deposit paid, the only way out of the sale is to forfeit your deposit and pay all fees already incurred. The PSPA is followed by the Formal Sale and Purchase Agreement, signed a few weeks afterwards, where the property formally changes hands.

One possible hurdle on the path to property ownership is persuading a bank to offer you a mortgage. Loans are generally only offered to Hong Kong residents and while you may be one of them after a few short months, the bank will want to see a long term credit history in Hong Kong or from somewhere verifiable abroad. How much of a problem this is depends on your history. If you spent the last five years living in a beach hut in Botswana, the bank is likely to say no. If you spent the last five years diligently paying your bills and building up a credit history in Minneapolis, you shouldn't have a problem.

LANGUAGE AND EDUCATION

Ever since the British saddled a colony of Cantonese speakers with English as their sole official language, a situation somewhat ridiculously not remedied until 1974, the question of language has been a political hot potato in Hong Kong. Today, Cantonese, Mandarin, and English all vie for importance and who speaks what or, more importantly, who doesn't, still makes the headlines.

For 95 percent of the population Cantonese is their first language and the language of everyday use. Importantly, Cantonese does not mean Chinese, a fact that has tripped up many an overeager textbook linguist. While Chinese is listed as one of Hong Kong's official languages, Cantonese and Mandarin—the dialect which dominates in mainland China—are mutually unintelligible, despite the two sharing a common written language.

Crucially for prospective expats, English also continues to enjoy official status, although its use and cachet have declined since the British handover, as ties

© EMIL CHAN

and trade with mainland China encourage more and more Hong Kongers to instead focus on Mandarin as a second language. The quality of Hong Kong's English-language skills is far from fluent, but it's widely enough understood and spoken to mean the vast majority of expats survive here without ever uttering a word of Cantonese.

Language is also a consideration when it comes to choosing schools. Education is highly prized in Hong Kong and if you're bringing kids to the city, the Hong Kong education system is nothing short of first class. The bad news is tuition fees can unravel your finances faster than Bernie Madoff. Public schools, which are cheap, are taught in are Chinese medium, leaving English-speaking speakers parents with the choice of the partly partly-subsidized English Schools Foundation (ESF) and international schools which follow national curriculums. Both systems are excellent but both will leave your check book in a cold sweat. Whichever system you choose, your kids—and you—should be braced for somewhat of a cultural shift at school. Expect rigorous discipline, including uniforms, heavy workloads, and piles of homework.

The Languages of Hong Kong

ENGLISH

The inspiration for sacks of letters-to-the-editor in local newspapers and stirring speeches at over coffee in the mornings, Hong Kong's standard of English is a complex and emotive issue. Let's get the bad news out of the way first. While the city might promote itself as English speaking, those that come here expecting everybody to talk like they've eaten a Webster's dictionary will be disappointed; fluency remains far off. For most Hong Kongers, English remains a foreign language and the painful truth is that the majority have has only a basic working knowledge of English.

signs in both Chinese and English

© MARTYNA SZMYTKOWSKA

Nevertheless, for expats, the fact that English is an official language and that it remains the main language in many professional workplaces means you can comfortably live in Hong Kong without ever learning a word on of Cantonese. Street signs, public transport information, and official media outlets are bilingual. All government notices and information must appear in both languages and government officials, such as police officers and public heath employees, are required to have a certain level of English and usually do. On a more practical level, all major utility and service providers offer full English-language support, and realtors speak English, as do employees at many banks. Beyond that, the difference in English availability is geographical. In areas on Hong Kong Island, such as Central, Wan Chai, and Happy Valley, restaurants provide menus in English, shopkeepers hang bilingual signs and speak both languages, and even your hairdresser can chat about his vacation. Venture out to the far corners of Kowloon and you'll find none of the above.

It's somewhat of a misnomer to say that English is the language of business in Hong Kong, when much of it is obviously carried out in Cantonese, but international business, and the many, many Hong Kong firms who participate in it, is conducted in English. For employment purposes, companies that employ expats almost always have English-language work places, where group communication is in English and your local co-workers will have English fluency. Years of experience with expat employment means the expectation for you to speak Cantonese will be zero.

© INES YEH

In areas with a high concentration of expats, such as Discovery Bay, you'll find that English is the most widely spoken language.

WHAT'S IN A NAME?

It took an email demanding he only communicate with a single credit manager, rather than Mr. Kenneth Li and Mr. Li Wah-Ming, for my friend to realize that working out a Hong Konger's name can take a little bit of Sherlock Holmes deduction. The pair of credit managers were actually the same person masquerading under two names.

Because Chinese characters don't surrender many clues on how to pronounce someone's name, unless you read Chinese, Hong Kongers also have English or Romanized names. These are often straightforward transliterations of their Chinese name. Take, for example, Hong Kong director Wong Kar-wai. What you need to remember here is that the family name comes first in Chinese and in the transliteration, so Wong Kar-wai is Mr. Wong. Unfortunately, some bold and brave Hong Kongers have already reworked their Romanized name at home, swapping the family name into the Westernized second place. It sounds helpful, but it actually leaves you playing Guess Who and not knowing which name follows Mr. And that's just where the fun begins.

Some Hong Kongers choose their own, unrelated Western given name and stick it together with their family name; John Woo, the legendary action director, is one example.

Showing an untapped creative streak, many Hong Kongers are unconvinced by the middle-of-the-road names in the *Big Book of Baby Names* and instead cook up their own weird and wild monikers. Sticking with directors, Fruit Chan is a good example, but still fairly mundane when compared to others such as Crazy Lee, Morning Sun, and, in a local fast-food joint, none other than the Dark Crusader himself, Batman. These are sometimes related to the meaning of their Chinese names, which often have very direct meanings; other times they are inspired by TV, film, and apparently eating the sort of mushrooms not found in your local supermarket.

There's certainly no need to feel left out of the naming game and many expats also choose to take on a Chinese character name. For your family name you can simply choose a Chinese family name that sounds similar to yours. Your given name will probably have been transliterated already, although you're also free to pick and point at words in the dictionary; adjectives are popular. Obviously you'll want to avoid making the same mistake as Hong Kong's wannabe superheroes, so ask a few Cantonese-speaking friends to make sure the name isn't likely to have you banned from buying plane tickets.

CANTONESE

Hong Kong is one of the few places in the world where you can come to live and work and the locals are expected to know your language rather than the other way around——which is quite some privilege. But don't kid yourself that not speaking Cantonese isn't limiting. It is limiting, just less so than in other countries. If you want to really get to know the culture and people, just like everywhere else, you'll need to learn the language.

Cantonese is Hong Kong's mother tongue, spoken not only in the city but in

Guangdong Province next door, Macau, and, thanks to historic emigration, in Chinatowns around the world. And what a tongue it is. It's a tonal language, meaning it is based on the tone in which a word is pronounced. With up to nine variations on a single word, even language learners with the vocal chords of Tom Jones can find it a tricky song to sing. It can also provide a minefield of mistakes——hit the wrong note and instead of delivering a devastatingly charming comment on the cheesecake you'll tell your host just how tasty his wife looks. Progress for learners can be frustratingly low. The main problem is that text-based guides can't convey the tones, which are accented high, low, and seven places in between. It's essential to listen to learn. If you can train your tongue, it's worth knowing at least a few words of restaurant Cantonese so that you can avoid mystery meats in your dinner and meandering taxi rides. Stick with the language study and you'll open up a side of Hong Kong most expats rarely get to see.

Perhaps frustratingly for the increasing number of people who have learned Mandarin, or Putonghua as it's more commonly known here, Hong Kong is not the ideal place to try out your new language. Increasing business and ties with the mainland dictates that more and more Hong Kongers learn Mandarin, but it's not a situation that's relished. There is a growing concern that the influx of mainland workers, Hong Kong's dependency on the mainland, and, in recent years, active policy from Beijing is undermining Cantonese in the city. For a foreigner to speak to a Hong Konger in Mandarin is to cut them with the swords of a thousand insults. Firstly, they will assume you are either ignorant of the existence of Cantonese or resent the fact that you are aware, don't care, and assume they speak Mandarin. Secondly, by addressing them in Mandarin, you have committed the cardinal sin of making them lose face; not only have you assumed they can't speak English, your native language, but if they can't speak Mandarin, which is very possible, a *gweilo* (foreign devil) has just upstaged them in speaking the language of their own country. Always try English first.

WRITTEN CHINESE

If you were already confused about Chinese, this won't help. All Chinese speakers, whether Mandarin or Cantonese, use the same written language, known as Chinese. Each Chinese character has the same meaning for all readers of the language; it's just unrelated to its pronunciation. What makes Chinese so challenging to learn for foreigners—and even the natives don't find it easy—is the fact that there is no alphabet. Instead, individual characters represent whole words and syllables and convey meaning. Simple characters typically cover simple words and meaning such as 手 for hand and 目 for eye, which can be combined to create more complex characters such as look 看. Unfortunately few are quite this straight forward. Thankfully the number of characters is finite and most words are instead composed from two or more characters, which can be as straightforward as 二 for two and 手 for hand to create second-hand 二手. This means once you know a certain base number of characters, you will also start to recognize and understand more complex words.

So, how many characters do you need to know to read and write Chinese? Well, it depends on who you ask, but to understand a newspaper or magazine the most commonly quoted figure is between 3,000 and 4,000 characters and standard literacy on the mainland is set below that. Of course, even learning that amount of characters is no trivial task and illiteracy in China has historically been a problem. In an effort to improve literacy levels on the mainland, the Chinese government introduced Simplified Chinese characters. This reduced the number of brushstrokes used in many characters to make them easier to recognize and remember and attempted to standardize the many overlapping words and inconsistencies. The effort has met with mixed results and Hong Kong, Macau, and Taiwan all continue to use Traditional Chinese characters. This means those who have learned only Simplified Chinese characters can have difficulty in reading Traditional character text and if you want to learn Chinese characters for the purpose of reading and writing in Hong Kong, you will need to learn the Traditional characters.

Pinyin

The challenge with learning Chinese is that the characters don't give you any clue on how to say the word. Chinese effectively requires the learning of two separate languages, one spoken and one written. The bridge is pinyin. Pinyin is a phonetic transliteration of Chinese characters into the Latin alphabet, designed specifically for helping foreigners learn the Putonghua pronunciation of Chinese characters. So 你好 becomes *nǐ hǎo* or (hello) and while it can still be hit and miss, mostly miss on the tone, it does at least give you a sporting chance. Both Mandarin and Cantonese were originally transcribed in the 19th century by baffled foreigners and today each has their own official phonetic systems. If you're more eager to speak Cantonese, rather than write in Chinese, phonetics is ideal and many schools offer classes that only include pinyin, especially for beginners. However, if you want to learn written Chinese at the same time as learning either Cantonese or Mandarin, you'll need to find classes that offer teaching and textbooks with Chinese characters.

WHAT AND WHERE TO LEARN

With Cantonese and, Mandarin, and spoken or written Chinese all on offer, the first thing you need to do is decide exactly what it is you need or want to learn. Remember, Cantonese is spoken only in Hong Kong, Macau, and Guangdong Province, so if Hong Kong is just the first step on your China adventure, you might find Mandarin more useful. Many expats working for multinationals in Hong Kong who find they have to make frequent trips to the mainland, where English speakers are much scarcer, usually prefer Mandarin. It also has many, many more speakers than Cantonese and is one of the world's fastest growing second languages. Of course, if you're more interested in Hong Kong, then Cantonese should be your language of choice. Whether you learn just spoken Cantonese with Pinyin or have written Chinese included in lessons depends on what you want to use the language for; certainly for beginners it is far more gratifying to talk to someone on the street than read a few characters.

There are many Chinese schools in Hong Kong, most of which will offer courses in both languages. Most classes run in the evening, twice a week and start in September and January. Intensive courses are also offered periodically. Prices and quality vary, but you can usually come in for a trial lesson first. If possible, try to avoid Mandarin classes that include Cantonese speakers and vice versa; they, as well as Japanese and Korean speakers, tend to advance much quicker due to similarities between their languages and you can be left feeling like the class dunce. For lessons in your home country, before you leave, Mandarin is booming and classes should be easy

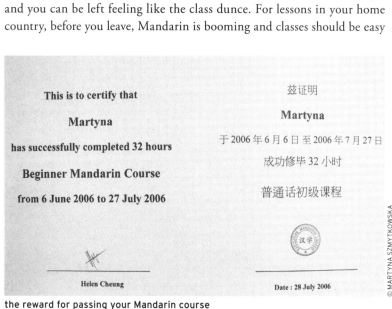

This is to certify that

Martyna

has successfully completed 32 hours

Beginner Mandarin Course

from 6 June 2006 to 27 July 2006

Helen Cheung

兹证明

Martyna

于 2006 年 6 月 6 日 至 2006 年 7 月 27 日

成功修毕 32 小时

普通话初级课程

Date : 28 July 2006

© MARTYNA SZMYTKOWSKA

the reward for passing your Mandarin course

to find. Cantonese could be more challenging, although most Chinatowns are Cantonese-dominated and their community centers and bulletin boards are good sources for information.

Education

Notoriously scrooge-like with its public coffers, education is the one area Hong Kong is willing to reach into its pocket and shell out a few coins. Education receives nearly a quarter of public spending. Alongside the public sector, there are a vast variety of private schools, non profit schools, and subsidized schools and just about every sort of public/private partnership in between. Choice certainly isn't a problem, although admission is by competition in both the private and public sectors, so placement can be tougher. Hong Kong universities are particularly well regarded and run the majority of their courses in English although places are thoroughly oversubscribed.

SCHOOLS

If you're bringing children to Hong Kong, finding and funding their education is likely to be one of your primary sources for of frustration during any transition. While standards at schools are high—very high—competition for places is ferocious and fees can be extravagant.

Hong Kong's recently reworked compulsory education system actually offers free and compulsory education from six years old, with three years of elementary school, three years of junior high school, and three years of senior high school, culminating in the HKDSE examinations which wins students access to university places. Most parents—more than 90 percent—also dispatch their children for three years of kindergarten from the age of three.

Unfortunately, Chinese is naturally the primary language of instruction in the majority of the city's well-regarded public schools, meaning they are only practical for children who already speak Cantonese or for young kids who can pick up the language easily in kindergarten. Almost all expats send their children to tuition-based international schools, where standards are as high as the yearly fees they command. An increasingly popular third way is to utilize the few public schools and Direct Subsidy System schools that offer English-language instruction in all subjects, but whose student body is mostly Cantonese-speaking.

Whichever system you plan on using, it's important to talk to your child and begin researching your options as early as possible. Certain schools only

KINGS, QUEENS, AND GODFATHERS AT TUITION CENTERS

Thanks to its unforgiving exam culture, Hong Kong has seen the rise of private tuition, or instruction, and it's estimated that more than one third of all high school students pay for a little insider knowledge at local tuition centers, known as cram schools. The majority of courses are specifically aimed at intense exam preparation and increasing the odds of your child ticking all the right boxes — many of the bigger tuition centers even employ crack teams of analysts who examine past papers, pour over textbooks, and gaze deeply into crystal balls to try and predict what to expect on next year's exams.

As a parent, the pressure to sign your child up for a tuition center can be immense, especially when all their friends have enrolled. In recent years, tutors have become local superstars, rivaling Cantopop singers and Hollywood heartthrobs. Tutors have coined monikers such as the Godfather of Science and King of English and are slickly and sometimes sexually marketed across billboards and TV. Accusations that some tutors spend more time looking in the mirror instead of at

books are rife. As with many things in Hong Kong, the clamor to send your child to the "best" center has become as much to do with throwing your cash around as education.

Nevertheless, tuition centers do deliver proven results in an exam culture that still focuses on the rote learning of facts and figures. For expats, most of the centers will be off-limits simply due to the fact that they only offer Cantonese instruction. But you aren't off the hook. English-language tuition centers do exist and are also popular. They tend to be smaller and offer one-to-one tutoring designed to raise grades rather than to pass a specific exam; although, there is coaching on passing entrance exams for British boarding schools, Ivy League universities, and other weighty educational establishments. Two of the more established and respected tuition centers are **ITS Tutorial School** (3rd Floor, Sun House, 181 Des Voeux Road Central, Sheung Wan, tel. 852/2116-3916, www.tuition.com.hk) and **Alpha Academy** (5/F Lyndhurst Tower 1, Lyndhurst Terrace, Central, tel. 852/3113-4276, www.alphaacademy.com.hk).

draw students from their neighborhood, which may affect your decision on where to live, while the prices of international schools may require a few more zeros be added on to your expected salary. Many schools, even back to kindergarten, are linked with preferential admittance for partner schools, so depending on how forward-looking you are, you may want to place your child in a certain kindergarten.

LOCAL SCHOOLS

Cantonese naturally rules the roost in local schools, the majority of which offer Chinese Medium Instruction (CMI) only. If your child is already of school age and doesn't speak Cantonese, you can't realistically consider the local CMI schools unless they continually kicked the back of your seat during the flight over.

For those whose children do speak Cantonese, the local CMI option is available and free and offers English and Mandarin lessons alongside Cantonese instruction in lessons. Expats with kids of kindergarten age may also consider placing them in a Cantonese-speaking kindergarten with an eye to enrolling them in a local school at the primary level. Kids of this age usually pick up languages easily and naturally, although it's important to take the long view. Kids who make their way through the local school system will emerge with fluent Cantonese and probably very decent Mandarin, invaluable skills they won't easily get at English-speaking international schools, however, CMI may impact their level of English, especially academically. The English-speaking parent may also find they are out of the school loop, unable to help with homework and that their child's interpretation and translation of their report card shows great creativity but little accuracy.

In recent years there has been much foot-stamping and angry letter-writing about the prohibitive cost of an English-language education in Hong Kong, not least of all by locals who still place a prestige on English-language knowledge. In answer to this, the Hong Kong government has allowed an increasing number of high schools to use English Medium Instruction (EMI). These schools can choose to use English for certain subjects or as the sole language of instruction, and the majority follow the Hong Kong curriculum. Most students who attend EMI schools are locals, so outside of lessons, students switch back to Cantonese—no matter what fairytales the school may spin you. This, however, can be a bonus for expat kids who get lessons in English but also exposure to local children and culture and will probably pick up Cantonese while at the school. Children enrolled at EMI schools who don't speak Cantonese will usually be offered extra instruction to help them learn the language.

Schools can only switch to EMI with government approval when they prove that the majority of their students are capable of learning in English and their staff capable of teaching in English. At least that's the theory. The primary drawback of EMI schools is the haphazard quality of the teachers' English skills. Supposedly fluent, some couldn't find their way from A to Z in the alphabet, let alone teach the ecosystem of the rainforest in English. Things have been improving and some schools are now regularly enroll expat children, but you still won't find a great number of native speakers on the staff. Direct Subsidy Schools charge smallish fees for enrollment and can afford to employ more native speaking teachers, although your best guide at any of these schools is probably how many expat children are enrolled.

State school–life can be somewhat of a cultural shift for expat kids, especially those from the United States who may feel they've been enrolled in a federal penitentiary. Many schools have a stringent uniform policy, a punishing homework schedule, and teachers that come across as aspiring prison wardens. Perhaps more worrying for potential parents, learning by rote is still popular, although it is mixed with more interactive teaching methods. It's not necessarily a fun experience, but Hong Kong's more traditional teaching methods do get results. Hong Kongers do well in tests and consistently place in the top three in global tests of student skills in math and science, the most revered subjects in the city.

Entry into primary schools is based on where you live and which primary net you fall into, although discretionary places are also available. For secondary schools you'll be thrown into the crowd vying for spots at the best schools, which are allocated on grades, location, and seemingly the phases of the moon. If your child misses out, he or she will be placed into the dreaded, lottery-like central allocation. EMI schools do have discretionary places available for expat children who only speak English. Class sizes have received a long overdue shave in recent years, and secondary school classes now average under 30 students; primary school classes around 25. School runs from Monday – Friday, starts between 8 and 9 A.M. and lasts until 3 or 4 P.M., followed by various after school activities that run on for another hour or so.

INTERNATIONAL SCHOOLS

With so many expats based in the city it's no surprise that Hong Kong is home to more than 50 international schools, including some with more than 100 years of schooling behind them. Students and staff at these schools are almost all native English speakers, or certainly fluent, and they provide an immersive English-language environment. The black-hole fees charged by the schools means they can attract high caliber staff from abroad, usually the United Kingdom and Australia, and maintain first-class facilities. Schools are split between the English Schools Foundation (ESF), which is partly subsidized by the government, and fully private international schools. The quality of education in both systems is excellent, but each one does have unique advantages.

The fully private international schools tend to follow the curriculum and work towards the exams of their home country. This can help minimize disruption to your child's studies, if they are already of school age, by letting them continue within the same structure they are familiar with.

It's also useful if you intend to return to your home country at some point and have them resume their education there. Most schools have historically followed the British curriculum, catering to British expatriate children, although the shift in expat demographics has seen a rise in the number of schools that follow an American curriculum, as well as schools offering Canadian and Australian curriculums. If a school follows the American or British curriculum, it does tend to attract kids from that country, but by no means exclusively.

The major drawback of international schools is the cost of tuition fees. On average you can expect to pay somewhere in the range of HK$70,000-100,000 per academic year. Some of the top schools charge far more, with a senior high school year at the highly respected Hong Kong International School costing a bank busting HK$158,600. And the pain doesn't stop there. On top of tuition fees, there are one-off reception fees, annual capital charges, and various other little hidden extras.

Despite the eye-popping prices, places at many, if not most, international schools are massively oversubscribed. Admission is competitive and based on each individual school's selection policy, which considers grades, overall school record, and occasionally gives preference to students from the school's mother country. Admission may also involve language testing and an entrance exam. Certainly the earlier you have your name down for a place at your chosen school, the better. One way around the nail-biting wait is to spring for a debenture. This is basically an interest-free loan you provide the school, repayable when your child leaves, and allows your child to skip the queue—some people might call it a bribe. Even debentures can be hard to secure and are also oversubscribed. Some of the major firms that employ expats have a certain number of corporate debentures reserved at certain schools each year.

The alternative to the private international schools are the schools of the subsidized and equally excellent English Schools Foundation (ESF). Including primary and secondary schools, the ESF system tends to attract longer term residents who plan to stay in Hong Kong and therefore don't need their children to follow curriculum from a home country. Like the private international schools, they attract an international selection of students and top quality native English-speaking staff.

Traditionally ESF schools have followed a British curriculum, including GCSEs at 16 and A-Levels at 18, but this is changing and many now offer the International Baccalaureate instead. Unlike the independent international schools, the ESF operates a non-selective policy where students are admitted based on geographical catchments areas and you can only apply to the elementary or secondary school in your zone. As with all the best schools, places are oversubscribed, but priority for admittance is given to children who don't speak Cantonese and the ESF tries to accommodate new arrivals in the city as far as possible. One catch is that you will first need your employment visa and a residential address in Hong Kong. As the ESF is partly subsidized by the government, it offers more affordable fees than independent, international schools, although at HK$61,000 for a year at elementary and HK$93,000 for high school they still won't make you smile.

COLLEGES AND UNIVERSITIES

Well respected in both the region and the world, Hong Kong's universities are regular stars on lists of the world's top institutions. Thanks to most degrees being offered in English and the fact that they are internationally recognized, the city is a popular destination for international students, and depending on where you're coming from, degree courses costing on average HK$90,000 per annum year can be surprisingly affordable. Many Hong Kong universities also have extensive exchange programs with individual institutions abroad and also offer associated degrees in partnership with universities in the United States and United Kingdom.

The university system remains relatively similar to the British system it was modeled on, with bachelor, masters, and doctorate studies offered, although three-year undergraduate programs are now being phased out in

the Hong Kong University of Science and Technology campus

favor of four-year ones. Semesters are split into fall and spring, with a break over Christmas and during the summer. Applications for study are generally accepted from November/December and onwards for admittance for the following fall. Standards required to win a place are specific to the university, but high school graduation alongside SAT scores for the United States, A Levels for the United Kingdom, as well as other national examinations, are applicable. Places at the city's top universities are massively oversubscribed and many locals actually end up studying overseas, particularly in the United Kingdom and United States. Luckily, Hong Kong universities are keen to maintain their multicultural and international mix of students, as well as their bank balance, so international applications are often considered favorably.

Most international students end up at one of the eight, government-funded universities. Almost a century old, the city's most prestigious institution is Hong Kong University (HKU), which was recently crowned the best university in Asia. HKU is trailed in the top five by Chinese University, and while other institutions offer their own specialties, the gap between the top and bottom universities is more of a gulf. While the list of degrees on offer is effectively endless, Hong Kong's business acumen means business and finance degrees are particularly well regarded, alongside programs in cultural studies, communication, computer sciences, and medicine.

Undergraduate tuition fees are usually fixed by the university and range from HK$80,000 to HK$120,000 per academic year, while postgraduate degree prices vary depending on the program. If you're already living in Hong Kong and are considering a university degree or postgraduate studies, you'll be charged lower local fees. All universities offer a wide range of generous academic and financially based scholarships and funds. On top of tuition fees, students who want to stay on campus will have to pay for their hall, or hostel as they are sometimes known. Fees range from HK$8000 to HK$20,000 per year and reflect the range of accommodation options available, from rare single rooms to dorms to multi-occupancy flats.

All international students who want to study in Hong Kong must apply for a student visa. This is done after you have been accepted into a full time study program at a Hong Kong university. The student visa has become more generous in recent years and now allows international students to take up to 20 hours of paid, part-time employment on campus and full employment on and off campus during the summer months. One attraction of studying in Hong Kong is non-local students who graduate in the city can return to work without an offer of employment for a certain period of time.

DAILY LIFE

HEALTH

With the world's second-highest life expectancy, it's fair to say that Hong Kong is in fighting fit form. Locals take their wellbeing seriously and visits to the family doctor, pharmacist, and Chinese herbalist tend to be proactive rather than reactive. The local diet is healthy, featuring a wide variety of fresh vegetables and seafood, and people aren't afraid to take the wrapping off their muscles and try them out once in a while.

Of course the city's elastic life span is also thanks to the miracles of modern medicine. Hong Kong has a first-class healthcare system and facilities and hospitals are second to none in the region, fitted out with cutting-edge equipment and staffed by doctors who stick their stethoscopes on all the right places. Incredibly, it's also heavily subsidized and very cheap for Hong Kong residents. Alternatively, there are a number of private, and pricey, hospitals in the city lauded for their luxurious hotel surroundings. Those worried about getting a glass full of boiled rhino horn rather than antibiotics, or acupuncture instead of anesthetic, should know that while traditional Chinese medicine

© RORY BOLAND

is an important part of many locals' healthcare, it is only used in the doctor's office as an alternative or an addition; it's never a substitute.

Despite good general health and healthcare facilities, the city is not without its problems. Air pollution has become a major issue in recent years and the gloomy haze that clings to the city can be more than a minor annoyance for asthmatics and those with respiratory diseases. Hong Kong has also proved a hotbed for communicable diseases, although lessons learned in the SARS epidemic of 2003 and small-scale Avian Flu infections means authorities are watchful and experienced in dealing with any outbreaks.

Hospitals and Clinics

Hong Kong's outstanding hospitals are world class. Split into public and private sectors, the hospitals provide the standard of healthcare you're accustomed to at home, if not better. Many expats will splurge on private healthcare, but in truth, although equipment and staff do vary from hospital to hospital, there is no great public/private divide, and hospitals in both sectors have their respective specialties.

It's worth mentioning that it can, at first, be difficult to differentiate between public and private hospitals. Private hospitals can have very public sounding names, such as Hong Kong Central Hospital, or look like a major public hospital, such as the grand, Victorian-style Matilda Hospital, so be sure to check before they hand you the bill.

PUBLIC HOSPITALS

Run by the Hong Kong Hospital Authority, there are over 41 hospitals and treatment centers in Hong Kong, 16 of which have accident and emergency rooms, meaning you are never far from an ambulance. The overall quality of hospitals in Hong Kong is excellent and you can

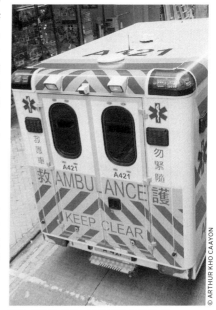

The city is well served by a fleet of ambulances.

expect state-of-the-art equipment and access to the newest treatments and best drugs. Contrary to the whispers at expat coffee mornings, public hospitals aren't staffed by cleaver-wielding butchers and are, in fact, home to some of the city's most talented doctors.

Of course, not everything is perfect. Don't expect a warm chat about your last vacation; doctors tend to be all business and have the bedside manner of a wardrobe. Patient input is not encouraged and communication with your parade of doctors is often reduced to them prodding you to see what sort of noise you make. While the treatment in the public health system is generally excellent, wait times for outpatient treatment or non-emergency surgery can be long. You'll also have to deal with the noodles-with-everything food, although this is easily supplemented by visitors, and a lack of privacy on wards of 4–8 people. For expats, the biggest grumble about public hospitals is the inferior English-language service. Although the vast majority of doctors and nurses have a good grasp of English, some people feel more relaxed having a native-speaking expat at a private hospital treat them.

For anybody with a Hong Kong identity card (HKID), treatment in the public healthcare system is heavily subsidized. Fees are standardized across the system and with a ward bed priced at HK$60–100 per day and an injection and dressing costing as little as HK$17, the prices make injuring yourself a little less painful. Conversely, if you have not yet obtained an ID card or are simply here as a tourist, expect to get shaken down. Prices jump to HK$70 for a shot in the arm and a dressing and HK$2,000–4,000 for a day in bed, although services at this price are supposed to include private rooms and better food.

PRIVATE HOSPITALS

If you like your hospitals like your hotels, with fresh flowers on arrival, five-star food, and a fluffy pillow, then Hong Kong's dozen or so private hospitals are for you. From en suite rooms and balcony views to English-language cable TV and Wi-Fi, each hospital offers its own little luxuries. However, while these added extras are attractive, the real appeal of private hospitals is choice. While the public system picks your hospital, doctor, and dates, private hospitals give you the luxury of choosing all three. This can be tempting for scheduled treatments and surgeries that have lengthy waiting lists in the public sector.

The level of medical care you receive doesn't differ greatly between public and private hospitals, although staff at private hospitals do generally have less work and more time to listen and are often more willing to take into consideration your input when choosing a course of treatment. Staff and patients at private hospitals also tend to be more international and most will employ at least a handful of expat doctors.

Unless you've robbed a bank—a big one—paying by cash for private health insurance is effectively out of the question; prices are extortionate. Almost everybody who uses private hospitals has private medical insurance. If you expect to use the system, be sure your employer offers medical insurance and research and find out what it covers, or price taking out a plan privately.

MATERNITY AND GIVING BIRTH

From bump to baby, maternity care is first class in Hong Kong, reflected in one of the lowest infant mortality rates in the world. Maternity units at public hospitals generally garner positive reviews from mothers, with the Queen Mary considered one of the best. Unfortunately, public patients don't get to choose where they give birth, and instead the hospital is assigned based on where you live, although under certain circumstances you can get reassigned. Giving birth is effectively free, bar minor costs for ward stays.

Prenatal and postnatal care is also free, including all tests and scans, and is carried out at your local Maternal and Child Health Centre (MCHC). While staff are well qualified and the service professional, waiting times at clinics can be frustratingly long and as a result some locals supplement their antenatal care with a visit to a private OB/GYN.

If you choose to use private healthcare, you'll be able to pick your hospital, enjoy a more personalized standard of care, and relax in hotel surroundings. Most private hospitals offer a maternity package, although prices vary depending on everything from what sort of room you book to the drugs you use—you can even book an auspicious time to have your baby delivered by C-section, for a price. Rates are not cheap and with a 3–5 day maternal stay costing from HK$20,000 for standard ward beds to HK$50,000 and upwards for first-class, private rooms, it's important to find out what your insurance provider does and does not cover. Despite the eye-watering prices, deliveries at private hospitals are oversubscribed, so you'll need to attend a private OB/GYN and book your expected delivery date at your chosen hospital as soon as possible.

Abortion is legal in Hong Kong and can be carried out at certain private and public hospitals.

DAILY LIFE

Family Doctors

For sniffles and general aches and pains your first point of contact is likely to be a family doctor, known as GP (General Practitioner) in Hong Kong. Doctors are generally as competent as their counterparts in the United States or Europe but, just like at home, standards do vary. Informally, doctors are split into three categories: locally born, locally trained; locally born, foreign trained; and foreign born, foreign trained. All these categories guarantee is a heavier price tag; there are experts and mediocre doctors in all three categories. Broadly speaking, rather than a better standard of medical care, foreign-trained doc-

© ROSS TALBOT

For true hypochondriacs, the Museum of Medical Sciences documents the city's well-being, past and present.

tors, often with degrees from the United Kingdom or Australia, offer a more Westernized approach to patient care and will also speak better English. The same goes for expat doctors, although at HK$300–700 for an appointment, they can be twice as expensive as a local doctor trained at the same university. Ask around to get a specific recommendation. It's a shopper's market, so if you aren't happy, try another doc.

If you're using the public healthcare system, you generally won't have a choice of doctors and will be assigned to a doctor at your local outpatient clinic. While long waits aren't really the norm, you may be left in the waiting room for up to an hour before being called inside, given the nightclub-bouncer frisk, having a prescription thrown at you, and shown the door. Most clinics work 9 A.M.–5 P.M. during the week and a half day on Saturday, while a handful have daily evening clinics. Appointments must be made in advance and cost a standard HK$45.

DENTISTS

Aside from emergency treatment, all dental care in Hong Kong is private and you'll need to ensure you're covered by your health insurance plan or alternatively pay in cash. Dentist surgeries can be found at most major hospitals as well as at private practices across the city. Decent dentistry work tends to be expensive and although there are cheap dentists around, don't expect them to speak English or be surprised when they give you a toothy grin and take out the whiskey and the pliers. As with doctors, many dentists have been trained in the United Kingdom and Australia and there are also a number of expat dentist offices. If you're new to the city and can't get a recommendation, be sure to visit the dental practice to ensure it's clean and modern and meet the dentist who will be treating you before agreeing to an appointment.

Prescriptions and Insurance

Hong Kong's doctors have an itchy finger for prescriptions and everything from a common cold to mysterious aches and pains tends to be attacked first with a battery of pills. Many doctor's offices, particularly in hospitals, have private pharmacies; otherwise your doctor will usually direct you to one nearby. Major drug stores include Mannings and Watsons, which have pharmacies in certain stores and should be able to offer English-language advice at stores in Central and other expat areas. Both brands also sell a range of over-the-counter medicine, although anything stronger than an aspirin tends to require a prescription. For a wider selection and more specific brands, try locally- and family-owned drug stores, although it's advisable to bring a Cantonese speaker.

Anybody with a Hong Kong Identity Card has access to the public health system at a heavily subsidized rate, including foreign residents on employment visas and dependent visas and just about everybody else bar tourists. Entitlement is automatic and essentially without restriction; all you need is your Hong Kong Identity Card. Charges and fees are extremely cheap and are paid at the point of delivery.

Private healthcare costs, however, are some of the highest in the world, comparable to those in the United States. As a result, many multinationals and major firms in Hong Kong offer a standard healthcare package as part of their employment offer, however, it's important to investigate the fine print as these can often cover little more than a band-aid for a scraped knee. If you aren't happy with your employer's coverage or they don't offer any, you'll need to take out your own healthcare insurance and there are a large number of both international and local suppliers. Local firms offer plans tailored specifically to the Hong Kong healthcare market, offering more flexibility in finding coverage that suits your health needs. They also tend to be more competitively priced. International firms can be a good bet, if you plan to travel a lot, especially to China, as they can offer universal, global coverage—at a price. Major firms include BUPA and AIA as well as banks in Hong Kong, such as HSBC, and these are a good place to price plans before shopping around.

Preventive Measures and Disease

VACCINATIONS

There are no required immunizations for entering Hong Kong and moving here is no more dangerous to your health than moving to New York or London. That said, The Centre for Disease Control suggests visitors to Hong Kong get vaccinations for Hepatitis A, Hepatitis B, and Typhoid. Although none of these diseases are prevalent in Hong Kong, the vaccinations are useful if you plan on travelling around China or the South East Asia region.

MOSQUITOES

While they don't enjoy the ferocious reputation of their brethren in the rest of Asia, it's still not uncommon to wake up in Hong Kong and find mosquitoes have held an all-you-can-eat buffet under your pajamas. Luckily, mosquitoes aren't prevalent in urban areas and if you keep your windows closed during high humidity periods with the air-conditioning on, you should only have to swat the odd intruder. However, if you're going out into rural areas, particularly after a rainfall or near dusk, consider yourself a picnic on a stick. Although rare, with less than 10 cases a year, mosquito-borne diseases such as Dengue Fever and the more serious Japanese Encephalitis are potentially fatal and it's advisable to wear long sleeves or trousers or marinate yourself in repellent to prevent bites.

AVIAN FLU AND INFECTIOUS DISEASES

With seven million people squashed in shoulder-to-shoulder and a hot, humid climate, Hong Kong has proved Mother Nature's incubator, a fertile breeding ground for the spread of infectious diseases. The most famous was the SARS (Severe Acute Respiratory Syndrome) outbreak of 2003 that killed nearly 300 people, put the city under quarantine, and dealt a serious blow to confidence in Hong Kong. Thankfully SARS is believed to be fully contained, with no reported cases since 2003. More menacing is Avian Influenza and its many strains. The disease made the jump from bird to human in Hong Kong in 1997 when it killed six people, and since then has made sporadic returns to the city each year, occasionally infecting humans and very rarely causing deaths. Chickens imported from Southern China, where hygiene and sanitation regulations are less strictly enforced, were the cause of recent outbreaks. Hong Kong is likely to continue to be on the frontline of outbreaks.

So, should you avoid moving to Hong Kong because of the bird flu? Absolutely not. Ultimately, any epidemic that kicks off in Hong Kong will, as in the past, quickly spread around the world. Hong Kong has experience with infectious diseases and is adept at bringing outbreaks under control quickly.

This history of exposure to infectious diseases does mean locals are sensitive about hygiene and sickness. Close-quarters living and the recycled air from air-conditioning means disease spreads quickly here and coughing and sneezing in public, particularly in elevators, on public transport, or in other confined public spaces, is frowned upon. Most Hong Kongers who have even the suggestion of a sniffle will stay at home, and those that have to venture out will often don a surgical mask. You'll also notice escalator handles and elevator buttons regularly getting swabbed clean to prevent the spread of disease.

Traditional Chinese Medicine

Alongside the wonders of modern medicine, many Hong Kongers are also firm believers in the benefits of traditional Chinese medicine (TCM) in both combating minor ailments, such as colds or skin diseases, to maintaining general good health. Cooked up by trained herbalists, medicines are usually tailored to an individuals needs, based on questions about diet, lifestyle, and health. Ingredients include herbs, roots, and other things swept off the forest floor, but also a wide variety of dried animal parts, such as fish swim bladders and deer antlers, as well as parts that are as illegal as they are stomach churning, including

© RORY BOLAND

Dried seafood is used to make Chinese medicine.

DAILY LIFE

rhino horn and tiger bone. Served in tea or soup form, they smell foul and taste worse.

But do they work? It depends. Gunshot wound or dose of influenza? For that a cup of tea laced with ground ginger isn't really going to help. However, for nonspecific problems, where no one disease or cause can be identified, such as digestion trouble or lethargy, you may be surprised how much better TCM can make you feel. Words like Qi, Ying, and Yang can make TCM sound like hocus-pocus, but many of the active ingredients included in the medicines have been proven to have positive health benefits. If you do decide to try, go to a registered practitioner and stay away from remedies that include parts lopped off endangered species.

Environmental Factors

AIR QUALITY

Standing on the streets of Central on a hot, windless day is not unlike being sandwiched between Marge Simpson's chain-smoking sisters inside a telephone booth while chewing on a briquette of coal. Air pollution is a chronic problem in Hong Kong and one which the government seems unable or unwilling to get a handle on, instead they wag their fingers at the smoke-belching factories across the border in Guangdong. The pollution is most visible in the haze that frequently blankets the city, occasionally blocking the view across Victoria Harbour. Far more worrying, it has also been blamed for a rise in respiratory diseases. As a result, an incredible one-fifth of the city's residents have considered packing their bags and their lungs and leaving for cleaner climes, according to a recent survey.

So, should you stay away? It depends. Generally the pollution is little more than an unpleasant taste and smell at certain times, its long-term effects, while undoubtedly negative, are unproven and Hong Kongers still boast one of the world's longest life expectancies. If, however, you have asthma or any other respiratory disease, the pollution in Hong Kong is likely to aggravate your problem and you may wish to speak to a doctor before making the move.

Naturally, urban areas have much higher levels of pollution than the New Territories or Outlying Islands and certain days, depending on wind speed and rain, are worse. The Hong Kong Government produces a daily API rating which measures the pollution, although the results are based on a dated standard and are little more than propaganda. Instead, check the Greenpeace

API rating, which bases its advice on the WHO pollution index and gives a more accurate, if depressing, picture. When the index is severe, try and restrict the time you spend choking fumes at street level, especially during rush hour—advice that is easier to give than follow, admittedly.

WATER QUALITY

Treated, filtered, and constantly tested, Hong Kong's tap water is drinkable—at least in theory. While the water that leaves the plant is clean, the poor state of old pipes in individual buildings means that what actually spills out looks like it passed through a rusty exhaust and tastes about the same. Although you're unlikely to catch anything nasty, especially if you boil water first, most locals tend to purchase distilled or mineral water. In restaurants you will almost always be offered bottled water, although ice, especially that used by fruit juice sellers on the street, will likely have come from the tap.

FOOD QUALITY

Food safety standards are reasonably high in Hong Kong and you're unlikely to come down with anything nasty as long as you employ a little common sense. Famously lazy with a mop and bucket, Hong Kong restaurants have become substantially more conscientious about hygiene since the SARS outbreak, although if you demand kitchens blitzed in bleach and dishes dunked in thermonuclear water it's probably best not to peek behind kitchen curtains. Thanks to Cantonese cuisine's insistence on freshness, seafood and poultry tend to be murdered on request at market. Meat, while freshly cut from the bone, can often be left hanging unrefrigerated in the humidity all day and some people prefer the packaged meat, often sourced outside of China, stocked in supermarkets. Fruit and vegetables, whether bought at the market or supermarket, should always be washed carefully as they are usually imported from China where pesticide use is heavy-handed.

SMOKING

Following in the footsteps of other world cities, Hong Kong recently implemented a smoking ban which stops smokers from lighting up in public places, from shopping malls to beaches to restaurants and bars. Unlike other cities, however, Hong Kong levies fines on the smoker rather than the owner, and therefore some bars and restaurants have turned a blind eye. If you're caught flouting the ban by one of the city's tobacco control officers, you'll win an on-the-spot fine of HK$1,500.

Disabled Access

While disabled access to public buildings and public transportation has improved in recent years, the city remains a daunting prospect for disabled travelers, especially wheelchair users. Simply getting around the sheer mass of people clumped together on the narrow sidewalks can be a major challenge and requires patience, demon-driving skills, and a willingness to roll over a few toes to get where you're going. You'll also face steep inclines and an assault course of ramps and lifts connecting subways and overhead walkways. Access to newer buildings tends to be wheelchair- and, occasionally, visually-impaired–friendly, but older buildings often consider wheelchair access covered by a working elevator, no matter how many steps you have to climb to get there. Public transport is somewhat easier and most MTR stations now offer wheelchair access thanks to step lifts, or in some cases a pair of on-call strong arms, as well as tactile maps and tactile paving. Buses and many ferries also offer wheelchair access. Aside from the Peak Tram, trams are not wheelchair accessible.

Safety

CRIME

Those accustomed to creeping around the streets of New York or Los Angeles with one hand on their mace spray and the other fumbling for the small hand cannon in their bag are likely to find Hong Kong a breath of fresh air. Hong Kong's crime rates are very low, with violent crime, gun crime, and street crime all but nonexistent. While the police enjoy pinning badges on each other in celebration of the low crime rates, in truth much of it has to do with the density of the city and the 24-hour lifestyle—if you sneak a penny candy in Hong Kong, 37 people will witness the crime. This feeling of safety invariably ranks as one of the top reasons expats enjoy living in the city and women in particular feel much freer here, where it's perfectly safe to walk home at night in all but a handful of sketchy neighborhoods. Similarly, the subway, railway stations, and other areas where hoodlums usually hold court are well lit, clean, and safe.

Still, it's not all picnics and rainbows. As immortalized by John Woo, Hong Kong's Triads (secret societies) present a serious organized-crime problem. Thankfully, unless you're involved in illegal gambling, counterfeit goods, or prostitution, you're as unlikely to meet a triad in Hong Kong as a wise guy in New York.

A problem that you're more likely to encounter is petty crime and the bustling streets with thousands of people squeezed together are the perfect playground for nimble-fingered pickpockets. Be sure to keep your handbag close and your wallet closer, particularly on the MTR at rush hour and at night markets. Those arriving from the United States may be surprised by the amount of public drunkenness on weekends, when expats and locals alike hit the bars of Wan Chai and Lan Kwai Fong to drink, dance, and fall over. Arguably the worst culprit is the U.S. Navy; when a ship docks in town, you may want to steer clear of the bars in Wan Chai, where the horseplay can occasionally get out of hand.

Police

Decked out in blue uniforms and armed, the Hong Kong police maintain a high-visibility but low-key presence on the city streets. Professional and polite, police are approachable and helpful. Although officers are supposed to speak English, in reality the quality varies and you may have to wait for an English-speaking officer to be dispatched to you. The police do have limited stop and search powers and always have the right to demand your ID (passport or ID card), which you should carry at all time. Racial profiling is less of a hot button issue in Hong Kong than in other parts of the world and if you look South East Asian, Middle Eastern, or like you're from the subcontinent, you're more likely to be stopped by officers looking for immigration offences rather than something else.

In general, the police are a tolerant bunch and if you're caught breaking a minor misdemeanor law, commonsense usually prevails with a slap on the wrist. If, however, you're caught with your nose in something naughtier, don't expect your consular officer to ride to your rescue on a white horse. You'll likely be handed a list of lawyers and sternly told to not call again at silly hours of the night.

NATURAL DISASTERS

At least a couple of typhoons sideswipe Hong Kong between May and October, dumping buckets of rain and turning umbrellas inside out. While all the wind and water can look dramatic, Hong Kong is well prepared for typhoons and, once everything is tied down, they cause only the minimum of disruption. Occasionally, rarely more than once a season, a typhoon will roll right up to the city's doorstep, closing businesses, stopping transportation, and causing limited destruction. While it's essential to stay up-to-date on warnings posted on the TV, radio, and around the city and take necessary precautions—typhoons in full flow are incredibly dangerous—the city is generally back on its feet in less than 24 hours.

EMPLOYMENT

Once upon a time you only needed the right size mustache or the ability to swing a cricket bat to walk into a job in Hong Kong. Expats employed expats and, with no visa restrictions, expats found work doing just about anything, from banks to bars. Things have changed. Not only have the screws on work visas been tightened, but there is massive competition both from local and mainland candidates for jobs. English speaking, trained and experienced in both local and foreign working culture, they can do everything an expat can do, but don't need all the enticing incentives. In short, it's more difficult than ever to find work here.

But don't let that put you off. Hong Kong still has many unique advantages over working in other foreign cities. While many expats who move abroad are restricted to teaching or appearing in hair commercials, English remains the dominant language in many Hong Kong workplaces, allowing you to compete on a relatively equal footing with the locals. And, although banking and finance are the most prominent industries, expats still work in a wide variety of professions and careers. Sadly, the demise of the expat package means fewer

and fewer people can expect a laundry list of perks and pillowcases of cash, although local salaries for professionals are still very generous. Just be prepared to work for your money. Hong Kongers put in hours that would make an Egyptian pharaoh weep and you will be expected to do the same.

Relocating

Many of the expats who find themselves packing a suitcase for Hong Kong are being dispatched by their company to work at a regional or head office. While these transfers were previously restricted to more senior personnel within the company, who often had considerable experience, these days firms are keener then ever to give all their staff international exposure. Relocating as part of a company is usually a fairly stress-free process and the company will hold your hand through the visa application and help you find, and, if you're lucky, fund an apartment. They should also cover any costs associated with the move. While the glory days may be behind us, expats being relocated can expect a bump in salary and at the very least a housing allowance.

CONTRACTS

Before you put pen to paper on a transfer, you need to look under the bonnet and see how it works. First of all, find out who will pay you. If you continue to be paid from the company at home, into a U.S. bank account, you need to investigate how that will affect your tax situation. You'll almost certainly have to pay Hong Kong taxes anyway and they are far more generous. What happens if you break the contract? There is often a misconception amongst many expats that if they don't like Hong Kong, they can simply hotfoot it home and pick up where they left off. It's often not quite that simple and in a worse case scenario, if you quit Hong Kong, you may well have to quit the company. You should also be clear on what guarantees you have about returning to your former position and the possibility of promotion in Hong Kong or afterwards when you return home.

SPOUSES

Considering that most of the expats who are relocated to Hong Kong are of the senior executive vintage, it's not surprising that many are joined by Mrs. or Mr. Senior Executive. Once your partner has his or her visa, spouses are automatically entitled to a dependent visa, and unlike in previous years when the spouse was under effective house arrest, dependent visas now allow spouses to work in Hong Kong effectively without restrictions.

Expat wives, traditionally, had somewhat of a storied and ignoble reputation in Hong Kong. Known as ladies who lunch, or *Tai Tais* (women with lots of free time and even more money thanks to wealthy husbands), they were derided as gossips mostly concerned with shopping, drinking coffee, and worrying about which parties they haven't been invited too. Today, expat wives and husbands also tend to be at the center of the expat community, exhaustless organizers and a major force in raising funds for charity.

Traditionally, with their partner usually strapped to their desk round the clock, expat spouses had the harder time adjusting to life here. With their wife or husband away and usually active socially through work, the spouse can quickly feel isolated and homesick, with no work, friends, or support network. It can be a trying time, but it's important to note that there are hundreds of others in a similar situation. Groups and clubs comprised of expat spouses are common and an easy way to meet new people in similar circumstances. For something less cliquey, try your clubhouse, sports group, or study group. More free time and usually more disposable income also means you can take up new hobbies, learn the language, or take classes. Now that spouses are allowed to work, they have many more options open to them.

The Job Hunt

For those on a solo job search, the tightening of visa laws over recent years and increasing competition from mainland immigrants has made finding employment markedly more difficult. While you once found expats sloshing pints out from behind the bar or counting change in shops, these jobs are effectively only available for residents. Instead, employment visas are aimed squarely at professionals. To earn a visa you'll probably need a degree, qualifications relevant to the job, and/or extensive experience. The job also needs to bring in a wage that the immigration department considers substantial enough to attract a bona fide expert and reflects the role you'll be taking on. This figure depends on your profession, but the expat rumor mill has it that HK$20,000 is around the absolute minimum figure immigration wants to see.

All this immigration doom and gloom can make it sound like it would be easier to get work selling ice creams in Pyongyang, but in reality there are thousands of companies here that have expats on their books; over 1,400 U.S. firms operate in Hong Kong alone. Some of the major areas where expats have historically hung their hat are banking, finance, IT, media, marketing, and hospitality, although there are openings in just about every industry for suitably-qualified, English-

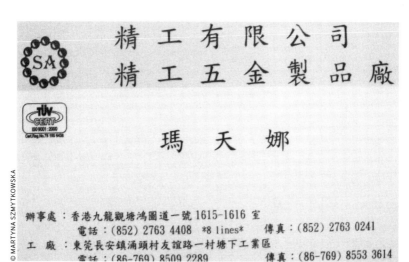

精 工 有 限 公 司
精 工 五 金 製 品 廠

瑪 天 娜

辦事處 ：香港九龍觀塘鴻圖道一號 1615-1616 室
電話 ：(852) 2763 4408　*8 lines*　傳真 ：(852) 2763 0241
工　廠 ：東莞長安鎮涌頭村友誼路一村塘下工業區
電話 ：(86-769) 8509 2289　傳真 ：(86-769) 8553 3614

You can't do business without a business card, preferably a bilingual one.

speaking candidates. Work can also be found providing services to other expats and the local community, most notably in teaching, but also there are opportunities for everyone from doctors and lawyers to sports coaches and veterinarians.

In theory, you are supposed to obtain an employment visa before you move to the city. In reality, unless you're relocated here by your company, you'll need to get your boots on the ground and your CV under a few noses before you start attracting some interest. Relocating shows you're serious about moving to Hong Kong and lets you attend interviews. Once you've found an employer, they will apply for your visa.

WHAT EMPLOYERS WANT

The ability to speak English has lost some of its cachet in recent years, but a great many white-collar companies try to maintain an English-speaking workplace and a Western approach to work. Employing expats is an essential component. Companies still take out job advertisements that specifically target expats because they consider speaking English, as a native, an essential skill. But English skills alone won't sew up any job interview. You'll often be up against British- or American-born Chinese, who also speak English, or mainlanders educated abroad, who know both Chinese and English. Just like a normal interview process, you'll need the qualifications and experience that proves you can do the job better than the next guy. Although there are exceptions, Hong Kong isn't really the place to kick start your career, most jobs on offer to expats are at least junior level and more often senior.

Previous international experience is often considered favorably by employers.

International companies prefer employees who've been exposed to other countries as much as possible, but perhaps more importantly, they don't want to employ someone who will pull the emergency handle and run home after a few weeks. Adjusting to living abroad involves a certain amount of adaptability and determination, among other things, and although previous stints in foreign countries are by no means essential, they prove a track record in making the transition success. No matter how little international business and travel you've been exposed to, anything you have done is worth a little elaboration. Turn that weekend in Canada into a show-stopping story.

WHERE TO LOOK

The *South China Morning Post*'s (SCMP) *Classified Post* is the de facto expat job center. All the jobs listed are specifically aimed at English speakers, although many still require Cantonese, Mandarin, or both. The *Post* comes out each Saturday and you can also browse and apply for jobs through the *SCMP Classified Post* website. Also online, the Jobsdb.com Hong Kong site has pages of jobs listing, all in English, although not all specifically targeted at expats. Monster.com.hk and recruitonline.com offer similar services. Gumtree.com.hk has less ambitious job postings and, as most are part-time, they won't solve your need for a visa. Senior postings and positions are sometimes filled by headhunters and you can certainly put yourself on their radar by contacting a headhunting firm and setting up an interview.

You can also try and leverage some good old-fashioned *guanxi* (relationships) when looking for jobs. The explanation of *guanxi* can often be overly complex, involving giving and receiving face, who has *guanxi* with who, when to give gifts, and what to give. It can be like reading smoke signals. While often conducted differently, it is broadly similar to the idea of networking and integral to Chinese culture, particularly business practice. Of course, new arrivals won't have a bagful of *guanxi* to dip into. Instead, you'll need to build up

job listings in the *South China Morning Post*

your contacts. Have some business cards made up in both English and Chinese and start handing them out like confetti. Get in touch with your chamber of commerce and the chambers of commerce from other countries where you speak the language. They regularly hold conferences, lunches, and meet and greets, which can be a great opportunity to shake the right hands. Also, look out for conferences and exhibitions held in your field. The more people you meet, the better.

CONTRACTS AND SALARIES

As compensation for leaving loved ones and moving across the globe, relocated expats have traditionally been plied with a Santa's sack full of goodies. On top of handsome wages, there were housing allowances, school allowances, free flights home, car and driver, and contract completion bonuses. Today, Hong Kong is far from a hardship posting and there are usually employees lined up, willing to shovel each other over the head for the opportunity to work here. Employers simply don't need to sweeten the deal anymore—at least not too much. That being said, relocation to Hong Kong will almost certainly mean a considerably fatter pay check and housing allowance and flight allowance home are still a fairly standard part of any package.

Job hunters are less likely to be offered the red carpet expat package, although international companies often have a standard employment package for expats, regardless of whether they're transferred or recruited. Most people are offered a local contract, meaning local pay and terms. If you're offered a local contract, it's certainly not the end of the world. Hong Kong salaries are very competitive and often include a standard bonus at the end of the year, as well as various other incentives.

Once your contract is signed, you're still not supposed to start work until your visa has been approved—which can take a couple of months. In reality, many firms are so experienced with employment visas that they approach them as a formality and may ask you to start work immediately, while they wait for your visa, and pay you cash in hand. It's a widespread practice that immigration generally turns a blind eye to, but you will, nevertheless, be breaking the law. Unfortunately, the company may not be willing to wait two months for you to start work.

Almost anybody working in Hong Kong needs to contribute to the MPF (Mandatory Provident Fund). This government run retirement plan requires your employer to siphon off 5 percent of your salary for the fund and to also kick in 5 percent themselves. You can be exempt from the scheme, if you have a retirement plan that you contribute to in your home country. If you do pay MPF, the money is refundable when you leave Hong Kong and have surrendered your employment visa, or, when you retire.

Teaching

With nearly 60 international schools operating in Hong Kong, most of which use English as the medium of instruction, the teaching industry is a major source of expat employment. Here, instead of being limited to TEFL (Teaching English as a Foreign Language), international schools recruit native speakers across all subjects, from history to gym. However, unlike in some other countries, the ability to string a sentence together in English and use a pen doesn't qualify you as a teacher in Hong Kong. Competition for jobs is stern and requires an impressive résumé. The reward is lucrative pay and conditions.

International schools are split into the state supported ESF (English Schools Foundation) and wholly independent schools. The exact qualifications required vary from school to school, but as a minimum you will need a bachelor's degree and a teaching qualification equivalent to the U.K. PGCE and at least a year's teaching experience, often more. Most schools prefer to draw upon teachers that are either from or familiar with the curriculum they follow. The ESF recruits around 100 teachers each year with annual recruitment in January for work the following September. Their recruitment procedure often includes regional interviews in the United Kingdom and United States. Independent international schools may start their recruitment process as early as October of the preceding year, although January is also more usual. Again, some schools may run regional interviews and attend international recruitment fairs and all will post openings on their websites and through the *SCMP* newspaper.

An alternate route into teaching is the government run NET (Native-speaking English Teacher) Scheme that recruits native-speaking English teachers to teach English as a second language in Chinese medium primary and secondary schools and also help in training teachers in the use of English.

Ideally, applicants for secondary positions should have a bachelor's degree in English language or literature, education, or modern languages; a postgraduate teaching degree; TEFL certification; and experience in teaching English as a foreign language. In reality, not too many applicants have collected that bag of certificates. At the very least, you need a degree in English language or literature, a TEFL certificate, and at least one year on the frontline. Salary is dependent on your credentials, but is in the HK$20,000–50,000 range, and you'll also be eligible for relocation and medical and housing allowances. Requirements for primary school nets are a little more relaxed and those simply with a recognized teacher's certificate may find work, although pay and conditions are leaner.

One problem with the NET Scheme is that it can be a bit of a lottery. While it's the EDB (Education Bureau) that does the interviewing and accepts you, after that it's blind date time. Your CV will be sent out to schools looking for NETs, who then choose the candidates they want to interview, usually by phone. If you can, choose your school carefully and don't accept the first suitor that turns up with flowers. There are some great government schools in Hong Kong and there are also some awful ones, unfortunately the awful ones tend to have a higher turn over of NETs. Research your school carefully and ask to talk to previous NETs, before you put pen to paper.

Partly thanks to the success of the NET Scheme, private TEFL-teaching is not the big business in Hong Kong as it is in other Asian countries. There are jobs available, but there are relatively few established schools who will be willing to act as a sponsor for your visa. Instead, many TEFL teachers are reduced to picking up hours at a couple of different schools and dodging the immigration authorities.

Self-Employment

If you fancy yourself as a future fat cat, a budding Bill Gates, what better place to begin spinning your fortune than in the world's freest economy? Entrepreneurship and hard work is massively admired in Hong Kong and setting up a business is the goal, or at least dream, for most Hong Kongers. The government encourages this enthusiasm and has streamlined bureaucracy and wrapped up the red tape to make establishing a new business as painless as possible. Once you've secured your visa, you are subject to roughly the same rules and regulations as locals.

Hong Kong is an incredibly dynamic place to do business and is designed to help people stick their pickax into the oil well. The city comes out second in both rankings of world competitiveness and access to capital and according to *Forbes* magazine is the second best place in the world to do business, somehow beaten to the champagne by the Danes. Another major attraction for those considering opening a business here is the possibility of expansion into China, where Hong Kong enjoys preferred access. Tax rates are also some of the best in the world with no capital gains tax or dividends tax and a maximum corporate tax of 16.5 percent. You can file all your official documents in English and find English-speaking accountants, lawyers, and just about any other professional service you might need.

BUSINESS POSSIBILITIES

Red tape–free or not, very few expats who first move to Hong Kong are here to set up a business. This is not surprising. Setting up a new business in an area or region you know nothing about is a suicidal business plan and it would be quicker to simply flush the money down the toilet. Most expats who open up a business have been in Hong Kong for a few years, know the local market, and most importantly have made contacts. An Aladdin's lamp filled with *guanxi* is essential in establishing a successful venture. Like opportunities for employment in Hong Kong, the businesses expats can and do get involved in is almost limitless. Bars and restaurants are popular ventures, but I've seen expats operating everything from a realty office to a garage, from wine distribution to a publishing house. There really is no limitation on what you can achieve, bar your own skills, knowledge, and how much cash you have to plunge into the project.

HOW TO START A BUSINESS

The first task to tackle when setting up a business in Hong Kong is getting a visa. You have two options. If you have HK$10 million stashed in a shoebox, flash your assets at the folks in immigration and you'll win an investment visa under the Capital Investment Entrant Scheme, no questions asked. While this visa allows you residency, you can only invest in companies in Hong Kong, not set up your own business. For this, you'll need an investment visa. The process for which is a little backwards. You'll first need either an individual or company to act as your sponsor, which is easy enough if you're involved in setting up said company. You'll need to show proof of financing, the viability of your business plan, and, crucially, how you will contribute to the Hong Kong economy, usually by employing local residents. Be warned, immigration will go through your business plan like a cranky Donald Trump, so make sure it is as watertight as possible and expect questions.

Labor Laws

While not quite as drastic as until-death-do-us-part, once you've signed up with an employer who has sponsored your employment visa, the two of you are stuck together like newlyweds. If you want to swap employers, you'll need to reapply at immigration for a new visa. Barring exceptional circumstances, such as bankruptcy or layoffs, immigration doesn't usually take kindly to new arrivals hot swapping through jobs. If you resign or are sacked, your employer is duty-bound to cancel your visa and you'll only have a few weeks to get out of Dodge.

While certainly a naughty offence in the eyes of immigration, many expats, particularly teachers, students, and those involved in publishing, do moonlight. By paying cash in hand, this practice usually goes unnoticed, although if you start sticking an extra HK$5,000 in the bank each week, the tax auditor may invite you in for a coffee. Ads on gumtree.com.hk, *Hong Kong Magazine,* and on student notice boards often feature short-term or part-time work.

Business Culture and Working Conditions

One location you are likely to encounter culture shock is in the workplace, where business culture tends to be distinctly different to that in the United States or Europe. Reflecting the culture of society as a whole, offices tend to be hierarchical, less democratic, and there is more distance between managers and employees. How much you'll be exposed to this depends on where you work, how many local employees there are, and whether your boss is Chinese or not. One of the reasons international companies employ expats and staff with international experience is specifically to foster a more Westernized workplace and business culture. Nevertheless, they are often swimming against the tide if the company has a massive number of local employees, and it's important to be aware of and sensitive to local business culture.

WORKPLACE CULTURE AND ETIQUETTE

Hong Kong workplaces usually have a well defined chain of command and stepping outside of the chain is rare and frowned upon.

© RORY BOLAND

Office staff dress well and dress expensively. Hong Kong is the city where the bow tie never died.

EXPAT INTERVIEW: JC CORTEZ

Originally attracted to Hong Kong as a classic career-climber expat, Los Angeles native JC Cortez spent her first few years working for an international hospitality design firm, putting pencil to paper on designs for some of the city's swankiest properties. In 2009, she opened her own interior design business, GreyZone, where she fulfills the wallpaper fantasies and gold-trimming whims of both expats and locals alike.

Tell us the story behind your move to Hong Kong.

I ended up in Hong Kong by an accident of fate, rather than by grand design. I went for a job interview at a large Los Angeles-based design firm, hoping to get a position there and was offered a job in their Hong Kong office instead. For someone straight out of school it was an amazing opportunity and I jumped at the chance. I hadn't been to Hong Kong before, but it's a city which you read about, see on the screen, and it has a certain international allure.

Why is Hong Kong a great place to set up a small business?

Hong Kong is great for a small business because so much of the advertising and marketing is by word of mouth. There's no point in spilling out tons of money on advertising here because the strength of personal recommendation is so persuasive. This encourages businesses to work hard on customer satisfaction, instead of making idle boasts on TV ads. I also like that it's so simple to set up and run a business. There is little bureaucracy and you can be up and running very quickly.

What are some of the challenges of setting up a business in Hong Kong?

Like everywhere, competition is the biggest challenge. With such a large expat community come a lot of ideas specifically aimed at that community, and competition is stiff. Chances are you are not the only one doing what you do. It is also incredibly hard to tap into the local market if you are not Chinese and don't speak the language. The expat population is big enough and wealthy enough to be lucrative, but ultimately it has its limits. For a con-

While Western expats may be used to voicing their concerns, doubts, and downright disagreement with ideas and plans, when the boss speaks in Chinese companies, employees listen—no matter how crackpot the boss's schemes may be. If the sergeant major says you're going over the top, you'll jolly well jog over there, no questions asked. The urge to speak up can be overwhelming, but even if the point you make is correct or acknowledged, you will likely make more trouble for yourself in causing the boss to lose face in front of the staff. Disagree in front of clients and you may as well walk across and slap your boss in the face with a wet fish before bundling it down his or her trousers.

This deference for superiors and elders owes much to Confucianism and

DAILY LIFE

sistent stream of customers, you need to tap the local population, which can be very difficult.

How does it compare to business practices in the United States?

Well, if you're an expat, you're working in a far more concentrated community. You can fail quicker here. If word gets out that your place is overpriced or just poor quality, you can be dead in a week. But it's also a great place for entrepreneurial spirit, for encouraging, fostering, and encouraging you to breed ideas. Hong Kongers feel like they have the right to have a dream and the right to try and fulfill that dream, much more so than even in America.

What do you love about Hong Kong?

Well it's probably the best place in the world to fulfill your potential. It certainly has been for me. In more practical terms, I love the convenience. This is truly a 24-hour city, where you can shop late, eat around the clock, and have anything delivered at anytime. Domestic help is easily affordable and it can save you an incredible amount of time, letting you do things you want to do rather than have to do. They may sound like relatively small things, but they become essentials that you couldn't imagine living without. I'm a traveler, so for me Hong Kong is also a great location to do some more exploring. It's close to plenty of great destinations and you can see a lot of Asia during your time here.

What advice would you give to expats considering a move to HK?

I would say come and check out the city for a few days and see if it's right for you. What you see is what you get with Hong Kong, so if you don't like it in a few days, chances are it is not for you. Most people love it and the buzz and lifestyle can be addictive. Really, there has never been a better time to come. Aside from the many, many business opportunities, most things are manufactured in China, where the economy is booming and experience with that market is only going to be an amazing asset.

dictates that there should be a certain distance between employees and the boss, and relationships will likely be far less casual than you are used to. Positions also tend to be well defined and employees have a keen sense of where they stand in the office hierarchy. Unless they feel they are being lined up for a promotion, employees will resent being asked to pitch in on other projects they see as below them or outside their job title.

Above all else, it's important to avoid confrontation. Like an invisible line that must be followed at all times, the concept of face is one of the most pervasive in Hong Kong society and giving and receiving face is essential both in the workplace and in building up *guanxi* in business. In the office, disagreements and disputes are usually dealt with gently, or, more often, ignored, in order to save face for the parties involved. Obviously, if you have a junior member of staff you're unhappy with, for whatever reason, you need to take action. However, the discussion should be couched in the language of how they should improve, rather than what they've done wrong—at least at first—otherwise they will lose face. Public scolding is the equivalent of pulling your employee's pants down in front of the class. Almost never acceptable, it will reflect as badly on you as it does on the offender.

Perhaps the most frustrating aspect of face for foreigners working in Hong Kong is the unwillingness of just about anyone you work with professionally to say no. While this can happen in the workplace, it is particularly true of business meetings and negotiations. Directly saying no causes both parties to lose face and is generally avoided. Instead, you'll be met with silence, a battery of maybes, buts, and possibly, and some minor objection that you probably feel can be solved easily. These are all polite ways of saying no, but new expats can often find themselves on the wrong end of an understanding. It is worth noting that business meetings and banquets are somewhat stage-managed. Who pays the bill, who gives which gifts when, who walks through the door first can all affect face and the possible success of a business deal.

No matter how frustrating or downright wrong you feel any of this is, and it's important to note that Hong Kong business has done pretty well for itself, when you break the unwritten rules of the workplace you make other employees feel uncomfortable. There is a lot of leniency afforded to expats in Hong Kong and you certainly aren't expected to know all the rules, but no one will appreciate it if you're constantly slapping their face.

LATE NIGHTS AND LONG HOURS

Pack a lunchbox and order a pizza, Hong Kong's working hours are long and laborious. While it may say 9-to-5 on the door, many Hong Kong office workers routinely stay well beyond advertised office hours, usually working at their desk for an extra couple of hours. This may suggest that the miserly grouch with the purse strings is too mean to hire enough staff and everybody is incredibly overworked. In fact, it has little to do with workload, and most of this extra time is whiled away in do-or-die eBay battles or improving one's solitaire skills. It's not that Hong Kong employees are lazy, far from it, they are some of the most productive staff in the world. This after-hours culture has little do with their workload. Instead, it's a show for the boss to prove how hard you work and how important you are

THE LEGENDARY 5.5-DAY WORK WEEK

As you crash, yards from the coffee dispenser, at the tail end of another working week, look no further than Hong Kong's 5.5-day work week as the culprit for your inhumane working hours. Unlike just about every other developed economy on earth, Hong Kong has for decades resisted the move to a five-day work week, with companies forcing resentful employees to sweat their way to work on a Saturday from 9 A.M. to 1 P.M. to stare at a computer screen while they dream of rainbows.

Belatedly, in 2006, the government began a concerted effort to encourage the adoption of a five-day work week, officially "to reduce work pressure and to improve the quality of family life." Local legend has it that it was actually done to halt the seemingly terminal decline in Hong Kong's birthrate and encourage locals to take a tumble beneath the bed sheets a little more often. Progress on the initiative was initially glacial and coincidentally only seemed to affect government workers themselves, who all got Saturday off while the rest of Hong Kong continued to toil. But the idea has slowly caught on and many companies and businesses, especially in the professional sector, have now abandoned Saturdays as a work day and more are expected to follow. While Hong Kong's current average working week, estimated at 48.7 hours, may not sound like a picnic, it's down considerably from the eye watering 55.2 hours recorded in 2004, mostly thanks to the shift over to five working days.

Unfortunately, that's where the fun statistics stop. An estimated quarter of a million workers book in more than 60 hours at work a week, while one in four, presumably sleepy security guards, log a back-breaking 72 hours at their station. Many multinationals and business firms actually beat the government to the two-day weekend by contracting staff to stay an extra hour on weekdays. More, if not most, simply expect you to stay at your desk, regardless of the fairytale hours they agreed to in your contract. Meanwhile, Saturday working refuses to die. Despite trying to gently usher business in the right direction of healthy working hours, the Hong Kong government fears legislating a standard working week will affect the city's precious competitiveness. Somewhat of a crackpot theory considering Hong Kong keeps company with those "kings of commerce," North Korea and Burma, as the only country in Asia not to introduce a mandated working week. So the fight for more human working hours continues. Until then, try and make it to the coffee dispenser.

to the company. Unfortunately, it's so widespread that it's now become the norm to stay beyond your working hours regardless of how much work you actually have. Expats are somewhat excused, bosses expect them to take off early. Although, if there is genuinely work to do, they will expect that to come first before any home commitments.

The importance of *guanxi* to business means you may be required to attend a busy calendar of banquets, parties, and opening nights or entertain clients after work. This is seen as an extension of your job, although you'll

© ROSS TALBOT

Work and pleasure often go hand in hand in Hong Kong. Parties, balls, and dinners are all part of greasing the wheels of *guanxi*.

rarely see a matching extension to your salary to make up for the extra hours. While it's possible to dodge the odd event, the expectation is that you'll attend the majority, and not doing so will suggest a lack of dedication to your job and the company.

FINANCE

Making money is what drives Hong Kong, and banks, bonds, and stock markets are a way of life in the city. This is after all the world's "freest economy," a major center for international banking that has grown rich off the back of world trade. Hong Kong's stock market is the seventh biggest in the world—astounding when you consider Hong Kong is a city, not a state. The boom years brought buckets of wealth to Hong Kong and its GDP, based on purchasing power parity, weighs in at a hefty $43,000, the seventh highest in the world and a number that has increased over 80 fold since the 1960s. Professional salaries are high, roughly on par with the United States and Europe and taxes are some of the lowest in the world, with no sales tax or capital gains tax. Personal income tax brackets are also very favorable and remain one of the major draws for foreigners considering a move to the city.

Yet, while salaries and taxes may make it easy to amass a small fortune, it's just as easy to squander one. Hong Kong is geared towards luxury and the cost of living can be eye popping, especially on housing, wining and dining,

© MARTYNA SZMYTKOWSKA

and private education. Most expats do manage to both live quite comfortably and stash a decent pile under their mattress, but it's important to be aware of the costs before you agree to your salary. As a major international banking center, you'll have no problem opening an account with one of the many local or foreign banks in the city, nor accessing credit systems or making international currency transfers.

Cost of Living

No matter where they try and hide the measuring stick, Hong Kong consistently finds itself at the wrong end of various lists measuring the world's most expensive cities. And, while there are plenty of ifs, buts, and maybes, depending on your lifestyle, the short answer to whether Hong Kong is an expensive place to live is yes. Yet, happily, Hong Kong also sits proudly at the right end of world GDP and PPP rankings and wages are high, something that is particularly true for expats considering the professions and positions where they usually find employment. When they pull out the calculator at the end of the month, most expats find they naturally earn a decent amount more than they spend and Hong Kong can be a good place to have a good time and save.

Hong Kong does allow for a variety of budgets and lifestyles, so the fact that you're not being posted out as a fat cat executive shouldn't necessarily foil your move here. If you plan to come out job hunting, be ruthless when estimating your expected bankroll. Setting up in a city is always a drain on finances; eating out every night while you don't have a kitchen, staying in hotels or hostels, and paying for all the fees related to renting a place can quickly eat into a piggy bank that doesn't have a wage bill replenishing its reserves.

MONTHLY EXPENSES

Once you're living here, Hong Kong really is as expensive as you make it. Not a very useful statement, but a true one. Certainly compared to New York or London, there is far more potential to live very cheaply or spend lots of money and the gap in between is substantial. The key is expectations. Attempts to recreate your two-bedroom house, four-door car, and steak-and-wine-for-dinner lifestyle will be punished with high prices. Throw in international school for the kids, a domestic helper, a few vacations a year, and a cocktail habit and your monthly budget can easily start tipping towards HK$200,000 and over. More realistically, the average expat lifestyle, which is one of substantial comfort, can be bought for around HK$30,000–40,000. This would allow you to rent a fairly decent one-bedroom apartment in a neighborhood on Hong Kong Island, do Westernized shopping at a standard supermarket, eat out a couple of times a week at modest Western restaurants, including the occasional blowout, and conduct a thorough investigation of the bars in Lan Kwai Fong. In all honesty, although most expats would consider it a lowball offer, it's perfectly possible to live in reasonable comfort on HK$20,000, a figure still above the city's median income.

Any salaries below HK$20,000 are likely to attract attention at immigration, although there are expats who live on less. Move out to a less salubrious neighborhood into a flat the size of your old bedroom, eat only at local restaurants, shop in wet markets and buy their own brand of groceries, live on secondhand books, and Pearl TV and you could probably make it by on as little as HK$15,000. While all this is possible, you need to ask yourself whether it would be enjoyable. You certainly don't need a maid, a house on the hill, and club membership in Hong Kong to have a good time, you don't even need a great deal of money, but you do need some money. It's not fun to be poor in any place, but Hong Kong is particularly merciless to the financially-challenged expat. Not being able to go out to restaurants and bars or join sports clubs will cut you off from your fellow expats, an important, some would say essential, support network for fitting in and feeling comfortable. Moving to a new country is stressful enough and a severe lack of funds probably causes more gray hairs than one person should have to handle.

HOUSING AND UTILITIES

The nuclear bomb in your budget is almost certainly going to be housing, which is universally expensive and given the ridiculously small amount of square feet you get for your rent, akin to theft. For a one-bedroom apartment in a swanky expat neighborhood like Mid-Levels, expect to pay anywhere from HK$10,000 to HK$15,000; move down to Kennedy Town and you'll get a pair of rooms for the same price or a one-bedroom for HK$6,000–8,000. Moving farther off the island will slash your rental costs, and on the fringes of Kowloon or the New Towns in the New Territories and Lantau you can find one-bedroom apartments below HK$5,000. You and your luggage just won't be able to be inside at the same time.

Getting set up in an apartment is when you will really leak money. You'll need extra cash for a security deposit, advanced rent payments, and agent's fees.

Utilities are thankfully more straightforward. For gas, electricity, and water you should budget about HK$1,000 a month. The only real variable here is your electricity bills. If you're working at home or have a partner at home

HIRING A DOMESTIC HELPER

Even for those accustomed to regular seats at the opera and their champagne by the bottle, domestic help is often a luxury. That's not the case in Hong Kong. Here, employing a domestic helper is seen as a necessity – even by the aspiring middle classes – and many, if not most, of the expats you meet will have a fulltime, live-in *amah* (maid). Many claim the popularity of domestic helpers in Hong Kong has to do with the city's hectic working culture. It's an excellent excuse, but that's all it is. Highflying New Yorkers and Londoners spend a similar amount of time chained to their desk and they still work a washing machine. The real reason is money. Domestic help is incredibly affordable in Hong Kong, with the minimum wage for a domestic helper fixed by the government at HK$3,580 per month. That gets you a helper who can look after your kids, cook your meals, and clean your house six days a week, all for less than you'd pay for a single night in a five-star hotel, an absolute bargain when measured against the wages of the city's professionals.

Despite the widespread appeal of domestic helpers in Hong Kong, new expat arrivals often feel uneasy about the idea of someone working for them fulltime, someone who is, essentially, when all the politically correct clouds are swept away, a servant. It's a definitive cultural shift, made all the stranger by the fact that expats you meet, often from your own country, treat the issue with complete nonchalance. It may raise questions of equality, class, and race (most domestic helpers are from the Philippines or Indonesia) as well as good old-fashioned guilt about someone else doing the chores you think you should be getting your hands dirty with. Riddled with guilt, one

expat I knew said he always sent his domestic helper on vacation when his mother came to visit; he just couldn't face telling her that he didn't do his own housework. Debates and arguments about the rights and wrongs of employing a domestic helper are complex and often passionate, but heard less frequently than you would imagine. When they do hit the news it's usually because of some despotic employer who has exploited or abused his domestic helper. Poor treatment of domestic workers is sadly common and some are treated like the family car, or worse; I once met a woman who proudly boasted that she allowed her six-year-old to direct her domestic helper in cleaning up the child's bedroom. But this isn't the norm. Most domestic helpers are treated as employees, fulfilling their duties and tasks for the day before clocking off; some even come to be considered extended members of the family. Ultimately, the question of whether you'll be comfortable with employing a domestic helper lies with you and your family, but there are certainly a few things to consider.

Life with a domestic helper is considerably easier, less stressful, and leaves you with much more time to do the things you want, whether that's focusing on your career or on the yoga mat. However, there are some tradeoffs. Legally, all domestic helpers are fulltime and live-in, and you act as their sole employer. And while there are domestic-helper shares and other ways to find part-time help, the majority of people do live with their domestic helper. As part of the terms of employment you must provide accommodation within your own house, not in rented accommodations elsewhere, so you'll surrender a lot of privacy. On top of paying wages, you are also responsible for providing food and medical insurance, and as almost all domestic helpers are from the Philippines or Indonesia, you will act as sponsor for their visa, usually for a two-year period. If you decide the arrangement isn't working out or have cause to fire your domestic helper, the immigration department only allows them two weeks to find an alternate employer, before cancelling their visa. It can be an awful lot of responsibility, especially if you expect your financial or geographic circumstances to change quickly. The Hong Kong Labour Department has a blow-by-blow guide to the rules, regulations, and red tape you'll need to know before you employ someone.

Ideally, once you've decided to employ a domestic helper, you'll be able to find one that has a glowing recommendation from an expat family leaving the city. In reality, it's rarely that straightforward. Many people prefer to hire a Filipino or Indonesian domestic helper who is already in Hong Kong but out of contract with their previous employer; these are known as local hires. The advantage of hiring someone locally is that you can interview them face to face, check their references, and will have to wade through considerably less bureaucracy in getting their visas transferred. To find local hires directly, head to employment agencies on Sundays, the traditional day off for domestic helpers, when you'll find them camped outside looking for employment. Alternatively, you'll find a much larger pool of potential domestic helpers through dedicated agencies. These are overseas hires, direct from the Philippines or Indonesia, and the agency will try to match your expectations with the candidate's expertise, although it's

very much a hit and miss experience and you shouldn't always expect everything the agency tells you to be the whole truth and nothing but the truth. It's also possible, with a little legwork and much paperwork, to direct hire someone from overseas using websites such as www.amah-net.com.

Whichever route you take, make sure you give a thorough interview and talk to a number of candidates; you'll be inviting them into your home and spending a considerable amount of time with them, so it's essential that you're able to strike up at least a professional relationship. It's also important to be upfront with any potential employee on what's expected of them. Telling them they'll only need to do some light dusting and throw a salad together from time to time, before proceeding to unveil a pair of grinning teenagers on day one is a recipe for a screaming match. Consider their background as well. Some domestic workers are helping support a whole family back home with remittances and may have a husband and kids; others are free, single, and fresh from domestic helper school at home.

Most importantly of all, and this can't be stressed enough, don't be *that* guy. Every expat in Hong Kong knows someone who treats their domestic helper like a slave whose sole purpose in life is to carry their briefcase, 30 pounds of shopping, and a four-year-old up the steps to Mid-Levels, while they swish past in a taxi, arriving home first to scream that dinner isn't piping hot on the table. Respect domestic helpers as employees and humans, give them their free time, personal space, and pay them on time, every time, and you should have a happy employee who will help lighten the load.

DAILY LIFE

all day, air-conditioning can and will put a little kick in your bill. On top of these basic utilities, you can probably factor in broadband, cable TV, and a mobile phone plan that lets you phone your parents at least a couple of times a month. This can add another HK$600 to your outgoing calls, more if your parents like to talk.

GROCERIES AND EATING OUT

Eating out is one of Hong Kong's great bargains, and many locals who don't have time to shop or room in their flat for more than a pair of hot plates, will often eat all their meals out. Of course, to eat cheaply you'll need to eat Cantonese, although other Chinese cuisines and Indian food can be very cheap as well. Thankfully, cheap doesn't mean bad in Hong Kong—Tim Ho Wan, the world's cheapest Michelin-starred restaurant with pork buns for around HK$10 is in Hong Kong. A tasty meal of rice and meat will set you back as little as HK$30–40 at a neighborhood restaurant. Hitting Western restaurants can, on the other hand, dent your budget. A sandwich at lunchtime will run about HK$50, while a meal in a modest Western restaurant costs around HK$150, fancier places upwards of HK$300, and for a meal from one of the superstar celebrity chefs, a cool grand.

Depending on where you decide to shop, grocery prices are reasonably in line with those of a major city in the United States. In expat areas, the standard Park N Shop and Wellcome supermarkets stock just about all the home comfort goods you'll want. See the grocery store prices for an idea of how much

Most of Hong Kong's biggest deals are struck over group dinners.

© ROSS TALBOT

HAPPY HOUR, TEA SETS, AND MORE WAYS TO SAVE MONEY

If you took one look at the prices in Lan Kwai Fong and decided the only Western food you'd be seeing in Hong Kong are stacks of 7-Eleven sandwiches and cans of Blue Girl beer, there is a solution for your stomach and your wallet. Somewhat of a Hong Kong institution, tea sets have been partnering cash-strapped gourmands with their favorite food for decades. Essentially set menus, tea sets offer a choice of two main courses, along with a desert or starter, and a drink; the total cost is usually somewhere close to the price of the single, main course dish, sometimes less. Originally offered by small, neighborhood Cantonese restaurants trying to get a few customers in seats during the 2:30-5 P.M. post-lunch lull, tea sets these days have spread to cuisines of every color and include such goodies as soup and curry pairings and beer and burger combos. Most restaurants will have a different tea set each working day and some swap out the whole menu each week; as such, it's impossible to list the best ones on offer. Instead, look for the menus posted outside restaurants just after lunch or check out *Hong Kong Magazine* and *Time Out* for some of the more upmarket tea sets.

Those that like to drink beer probably won't like Hong Kong – at least not the prices. Drinking is a pricey pastime here with a draft beer costing HK$50-60 at pubs in Lan Kwai Fong and Wan Chai. It can make for a sobering surprise when you pry free the wedge of receipts shoveled into all four trouser pockets the morning after. For a little more liquid for a lot less dollar, take advantage of the generous Happy Hours that run at almost every bar in town. The range of offers is endless, although the boilerplate promotion is buy one, get one free or half-price beers, usually from late afternoon until 7 or 8 P.M. Increasingly popular is Crazy Hour, usually held sometime after midnight and aimed at encouraging those already facing serious time bent over the toilet to splash out on evil-looking shots and truly ignite the volcano lurking in their belly. Best avoided. Women who like their drinks speared with an umbrella should look out for Ladies Nights at bars and clubs on Wednesday and Thursday nights, where you'll find free mixed drinks, even champagne, some nibbles, and hordes of drooling men. Again, offers change week to week and bar to bar. Look out for promotions posted in bars or in the listings section of *Time Out* and *Hong Kong Magazine*.

you'll pay. There are also several supermarkets aimed specifically at expats, with an endless range of products and a broader range of brands. In return, you'll be robbed with prices that are two or three times as expensive as a standard supermarket. These supermarkets are best used for the odd sinful pleasure, rather than buying rice from the foothills of the Himalayas and organic oranges picked only by koala bears. Many locals still shop at the ubiquitous wet markets found in each neighborhood, where you can pick up fresh meat, vegetables, and fruit. Wet markets are often touted as being cheaper than supermarkets, but in reality there is little difference in the prices.

MEDICAL EXPENSES

The choices here are fairly straightforward, if drastically different. If you're happy enough using the generally excellent public healthcare service, medical expenses won't be a concern as prices are very low. Conversely, private healthcare costs are enough to put you in the hospital. If you can, try and squeeze coverage out of your employer.

EDUCATION

Bringing kids to Hong Kong can be a deal breaker. Unless they speak Cantonese, you'll need to enroll them at an English-speaking school and those don't come cheap. Fees for international schools are horrendous and while the government-supported ESF program is often a little cheaper, tuition fees are still crippling at HK$93,000 per year for high schools.

TRAVEL AND TRANSPORTATION

Stick to the superb public transport system and you'll save yourself a lot of stress and money. How much you'll need to spend monthly will depend on the distance of your commute, but as an idea, a round-trip across the harbor between Central and TST costs HK$16 and a round-trip on the Lamma ferry about HK$30. Those who will only have their car keys pried from their cold, dead hands, may well get the opportunity to kick the bucket when they see the cost of parking and gasoline. If you're lucky enough to have a parking space at your residential building, which is far from a given, you'll still need to rent a space near your work, which in Central can set you back as much as HK$4,000 for a monthly plan. Gasoline comes in at around HK$15 a liter, although given there aren't a great many places to drive, a full tank should last a while.

As a regional and international travel hub, Hong Kong is a great city to get away from and you'll find a slew of destinations within a few hours' flight. Package vacations that combine flights and hotels are very popular with expats and locals alike and weekend getaways to Thailand, Taiwan, Japan, and the Philippines can start from as little as HK$2,000.

ENTERTAINMENT

How much you spend on entertainment is very much under your control. Many of Hong Kong's favorite pastimes, such as hiking around the New Territories, Tai Chi, and window-shopping at mega malls, are free. Of course, if you can't stay

THE GREAT ESCAPE

Hong Kong might be a great city, but it is also a great city to escape from. Much of Asia sits within easy reach of Hong Kong's doorstep and on weekends and holidays locals and expats grab their toothbrush and a spare pair of underwear and jet off to Asia's best bars, beaches, and shopping. This weekend break culture has blossomed thanks to Hong Kong's status as the parking garage for Asia's biggest fleet of planes, keeping prices low and destination choices high. Weekend getaways are big business and travel agents and online web portals are locked in a spiral of deepening discounts to win customers.

While there are several budget airlines operating in Hong Kong, such as DragonAir, Air Asia, and Jetstar, the best and most popular deals come courtesy of two-night, three-day packages that combine flights and hotel. The frequent-flier destinations are Bangkok, Shanghai, Taipei, and the beaches of the Philippines, which are just a couple of hours away, and packages can cost as little as HK$3,000. Farther afield, the sun, sea, and sand of Bali and shopping streets of Tokyo can be bagged for HK$4,500. Prices are often based on the quality of hotel you want – from five-star luxury to cockroach conventions. As ever, the key to getting the best deal is to shop around with different agents. One of the biggest travel agent chains is Travel Expert, although many Hong Kongers have long-term, personal relationships with individual agents who will alert them to deals when they come onto the market. In recent years, the cheapest deals have come from Zuji.com, an Asia-based booking website that's part of the Travelocity group. Their prices on weekend breaks and long-haul flights have become very hard to beat.

on the right side of the window, Hong Kong's shops can quickly max out your credit cards. Socializing is an important part of the expat lifestyle and much of it is done while gripping a drink that has too many umbrellas and a heavy price tag. A draft beer will come in at around HK$50–60 with Hawaiian-inspired concoctions topping HK$100. Cinema tickets cost HK$60–80 and a ticket to an international rock concert will set you back HK$500–1,000.

Shopping

To say shopping is a passion in Hong Kong doesn't quite do justice to the fervent following it has among the population. I can't remember the amount of times I asked a co-worker about their hobbies and got the reply *shopping;* a focused list only occasionally expanded to include both markets and malls. The city's reputation as a world-class destination is fully justified and living here just gives you more time to explore it all.

© MARTYNA SZMYTKOWSKA

Cheap clothes, shoes, and handbags can be found at the city's many markets.

There are more shops in Hong Kong than blades of grass. Not strictly or factually correct, but it can certainly feel like it when you find yourself in a district like Causeway Bay or Mongkok, barricaded by shops. The city has dozens of serious-size malls, even more markets, luxury stores, computer and electronic centers, outlet streets, and whole areas dedicated to a certain type of product—from birds to wedding cards. On top of all this, there are also your basic, straightforward shops, which are pretty much wedged in everywhere. The selection of goods on offer can be overwhelming and, alongside the thousands of independent retailers, you'll find many of your favorite retailers from home have a store in the city.

Unfortunately, the time of jaw-dropping prices in Hong Kong has long since passed and the bargains have certainly bolted to the basement. That said, Hong Kong is still a cheap place to shop and there are good deals available, particularly on clothing and electronics. Stick to the small, independent retailers or markets and buy brand-less clothing stitched together—not always convincingly—across the border in the workshop of the world, Guangdong, and you'll find deep, deep discounts. If, however, you prefer major chains and international brand names, you won't find much difference between the prices here and at home. For some, luxury brands are the only brands worth talking about and the lust for expensive Louis Vuitton bags and the newest Steve Jobs brainwave is relentless. Many European retailers will base their first and sometimes only Asian outlet in Hong Kong, and Central is stacked with luxury boutiques. Selection, however, doesn't equal cheap and prices are similar to other major world cities.

WHERE TO SHOP FOR WHAT

Seemingly the start and end of most Hong Kong conversations—the hunt for the best prices for the best goods—is a serious sport and after a few months in town even the most squeamish shopper will fall into water-cooler banter over the best place to buy a new flatscreen TV or whether Gladys got a bargain buying her new suit.

Alongside education, electricity, and water, Hong Kongers see it as their fundamental human right to have a mall on their doorstep. This is no better illustrated than in the new towns, where a mall is usually thrown up before a library, theater, and just about anything else. Most malls have a fairly identical mix of international brands, although malls in upscale areas, such as The Landmark in Central, have upscale shops and those in more modest neighborhoods, such as the Dragon Centre in Sham Shui Po, have more modest stores.

Sadly, Hong Kong's atmospheric street markets are starting to lose their sparkle as an increasing number are lost to cheap chopsticks, chessboards, and other tourist souvenirs made across the border in Shenzhen. Markets are still a solid and popular choice for food, fresh vegetables, and meat, and you'll find at least one indoor wet market in every district. Other markets are usually dedicated to a certain type of product; Mongkok, for example, is home to the Goldfish Market, Bird Market, and Ladies Market, the latter stocking clothes rather than ladies. Local markets in less central neighborhoods tend to feature a wide variety of goods and are still a cheap place to shop.

Nothing sets local hearts beating faster than the arrival of a new piece of technology in town. Regardless of whether they actually need a phone that can simultaneously connect to video calls in 14 different countries, monitor the movement of the moons around Jupiter, and breathe fire, most Hong Kongers are early adapters and demand the newest, fastest piece of kit. As a result, laptops and cellphones are swapped out and upgraded before most people have even made it through the instruction manual. This can be great news for those of us who can manage with monitoring only one of Jupiter's moons, because there is an absolute slew of secondhand cellphones and laptops on the market that are only a few years or months old, in good condition, and at great prices. These can be found at the city's computer markets: Wan Chai Computer Centre, Mongkok Computer Centre, and the Golden Shopping Arcade. Geek heaven, the secondhand and new software, hardware, and assorted cables are stacked floor to ceiling, and prices can be very good. Major electronics and computer retailers are Broadway and Fortress, which are, at the very least, a good place to price goods.

Other useful retailers you'll find in town are Japan Home Store and Pricerite, which both offer cheap house-ware products. Decorator to the world, IKEA is the cheap solution to home furnishings. Hong Kong has a pair of homegrown department stores, the upscale Lane Crawford and the more modest and middle-aged Wing-On. The Japanese department store SOGO has a branch in Causeway Bay, where it is both a city landmark and a popular place to shop.

HONG CONNING

The pirates may have chased out of town centuries ago, but Hong Kong still has somewhat of a shifty reputation as a station for crooks and conmen looking to swell their swag bag. It's a reputation that's hugely exaggerated, but unfortunately fresh-off-the-boat tourists and expats are the primary target of the city's fraudsters, and, if you're naive enough, there will always be someone willing to sell you some magic beans.

Unlike China, the brains behind the world's most creative scams, Hong Kong con artists are kept reasonably in check by the police and most of the city's scams involve bending the law rather than breaking it, a situation helped by very light consumer protection. You won't encounter any trouble in chains, brand stores, and major malls, nor will you at the majority of independent retailers, but there is a small and unscrupulous minority ready to pull a swindle. Most are concentrated along Nathan Road and in Tsim Sha Tsui. The typical scam relies on forceful and verbally aggressive sales techniques designed to pressure you into the sale. Forget the "Have a Nice Day" shopping of home; sales staff here aren't afraid to put the truth on a bungee cord to make a sale. It's important not to be squeamish and ensure that you make it clear exactly what you want and how much you're willing to pay. It's also worth noting that while you should always report any rip-off to the **Consumer Council** (tel. 852/2929-2222, www.consumer.org.hk) or the police, once you've handed over your money and walked out of the shop, there is usually little anyone can do for you but wipe away your tears.

BAIT AND SWITCH
Hong Kong's most enduring scam, bait and switch, basically boils down to you viewing a certain electrical item in the shop, agreeing to buy it, but leaving the store with a far inferior item that is vastly overpriced. There are a couple of ways this can happen. The classic routine was for the salesperson to disappear with your Sony Focus 500 camera into the stockroom, emerge with the Sony Focus 500 box, only for you to discover the box actually contains the Sony Focus 400 when you got home. The store has a no returns policy, naturally. Few people fall for this as they simply look inside the box, but there are some variations. Currently in vogue is disappearing into the stock room

BARGAINING AND SHOPPING CULTURE

Where once you had to bargain for the price of your bus fare, today set prices are the norm. Just like at home, try to bargain in main street stores and chain shops and you'll be met with a finger pointing at the price tag, although on bigger and multiple purchases, you should still get a few extras thrown in.

Smaller, independent stores are fair game for bargaining, although fewer and fewer are staffed by family members, and employees are only allowed to drop the price so far. The only place left where you can lock horns with a true opponent is at the city's markets. Prices here are a suggestion rather

for 20 minutes, reappearing, and claiming they don't have the Sony Focus 500 in stock but that they do have the Canon 6100, which is exactly the same if not better, and you can have it for the same price. Sounds great, right? Wrong, the alternate model may look similar and have lots of nice numbers on the end, but you'll be lucky if it takes color photos. Another special routine for tourists is claiming Sony is sold under the Suny name in Hong Kong so the Suny Focus 500 is the product they're looking for. It's not. It's probably the union of a pin hole camera and supersized lashings of superglue.

GETTING ACCESSORIZED

Another scam that primarily targets electronics, the accessories con again relies on you not peeking inside your box. After you've paid for the product, the salesperson will inquire if you want to purchase some accessories, unfortunately, these "accessories" are actually items essential to the running of the product that have been removed, such as a lens cap for a camera or a cell phone's battery. The worst case I heard about was a particularly ruthless seller who had removed the keys from a laptop computer.

The accessories will be offered to you at an extortionate price that explains the great steal you got on the price of the product. Depending on what's missing, the fact that the seller doesn't specify what was included in the sale makes this a legal gray area.

THE MYSTERIOUS MING VASE

It's hard to class this as a scam as it just involves the seller telling a full deck of barefaced lies about the age of a product, but it's still one of the most popular ways for tourists to find they've poured their money down the drain. There seems to be a common misconception that everything in China is old; it's not, in fact Mao managed to take a hammer to much of the best stuff. Yet, when normally savvy buyers are told by a Hong Kong seller that the $2 Jade Buddha they are selling is 400 years old and was gifted to the Emperor by his long lost child bride while he lay on his deathbed, they think that they've found the world's last bargain. They haven't. What they have found is a piece of green modelling clay from Shenzhen. Sellers are smart, and if something seems too good to be true, it almost certainly is.

than a rule and both seller and buyer expect to bargain to reach a fair price. If you're speaking English and are Caucasian, the seller probably sees you as a walking wallet that needs to be emptied and it can be a challenge to wrestle the price back to local levels. If you live here, mention it, and even if you speak a few words of Cantonese, unleash them. Tourist prices are targeted at tourists, if the seller thinks you live here, he'll know you know the prices.

Although pussycats compared to what you'll experience in other countries in Asia, Hong Kong sellers can come across as pushy and assertive. Like the locals, be sure to give back as good as you get and stay firm on your price. Scams are rare and mostly confined to tourist areas such as Tsim Sha Tsui. Unfortunately, there is relatively little consumer protection, so make sure you're absolutely clear on what you're buying, what the terms of return are, and what are the exact warranties. Once you walk out of independent stores with your product you basically leave any rights behind.

Banking

Since Hong Kong is a major international banking center, you'll never be more than a few feet from a bank. Aside from homegrown favorites such as HSBC and Hang Seng, 70 of the world's 100 largest banks can be found here, although some are business-only branches. While having a branch of your local bank here can be useful for receiving payments from home, in practical terms it's probably easier to open an account with a local bank. It's straightforward to set up an account and expats have access to credit cards almost instantly.

OPENING AN ACCOUNT

Opening a bank account in Hong Kong couldn't be simpler. If you have just arrived, all you'll need is your passport or driver's license and proof of your home address in the form of utility bills or official government letters that have both your name and address. Once you have your HKID you can update your registration to reflect your resident status, giving you access to a fuller range of services, including credit cards and mortgages. If you don't have proof of your Hong Kong address, some banks will mail you a letter that you can then return as proof of address. Banks usually require a small deposit to activate the account and there is often a monthly charge for the account, although this is sometimes waived if you maintain a minimum balance. Alternatively, if you don't think you'll need the services of a cashier, you can open an Internet-only account. These are generally free and let you move money around via the Internet or phone, as well as with automated teller machines. All accounts come with an ATM card.

Basic accounts are very much the same wherever you bank, but if you have specific needs, you'll find an endless list of extras and services. Particularly useful to expats is the ability to open foreign currency accounts in a number of world currencies, as well as combine several currencies in a single multicurrency account. This can make transferring money across the world much cheaper. All banks operate English-language websites and those with Internet banking will also have an English option. In the branch, you will always find an English-speaking teller, especially in Central. Many expats use HSBC, simply because their ATMs are the easiest to find and they have representation in so many countries.

CURRENCY

The Hong Kong dollar is a major international currency that is traded and sold with no restrictions. Pegged to the U.S. dollar at a fixed rate of HK$7.80, a situation that is unlikely to change, at least in the near future, notes are issued in HK$10, HK$20, HK$50, HK$100, HK$500, and HK$1,000 denominations. In addition there are HK$10, HK$5, HK$2, HK$1, 50 cents, 20 cents, and 10 cents coins. The smaller cent coins are not widely used, at least by shopkeepers who are often too lazy to bother fishing them out from their cash register. Prices in Hong Kong are listed with just the dollar sign before them, the HK prefix is only added if there is cause for the price or information to be confused with the U.S. dollar.

© MARTYNA SZMYTKOWSKA

the Hong Kong dollar

One odd thing you'll notice is that because Hong Kong's notes are issued by three separate banks, the design on their reverse side differs. On the coins, inspect the reverse side and you may find a stony-faced picture of the Queen looking back at you. Dating from colonial times, they are still legal tender.

CREDIT CARDS

You can pretty much swipe your way through a shopping trip in Hong Kong with only the smallest grocery shops and markets declining plastic. Visa and MasterCard are the most widely used cards, while American Express is more limited. It's easy enough for foreigners to get a credit card from a Hong Kong bank, assuming their monthly wage meets a bank's requirements. To obtain a card you'll need your HKID employment contract; some banks also require proof of income in Hong Kong over at least three months.

ATM

The number of banks in Hong Kong is only surpassed by the number of ATMs, and unless you're in the backwoods of the New Territories, you'll never be far from one. The most widespread network is the JETCO ATMs. These allow customers of several participating banks to use the machines for free. Hang Seng and HSBC customers can use each other's ATMs for free and they're conveniently placed in all MTR stations and most malls. Both the JETCO and HSBC machines accept foreign ATM cards as part of the Cirrus system and there is also good coverage for PLUS cards via several banks, such as Citibank. ATMs always display their information in English.

Most ATM cards from major banks can also be used with the EPS (Electronic Payment Services). This allows you to use the card for payment in the thousands of shops that display the EPS logo, withdraw cash from shops when paying, and even pay your utility bills over the counter at certain locations, such as Circle K stores.

Taxes

Barring far-flung Caribbean Islands and countries the size of a soccer field, Hong Kong has the world's lowest tax rates and the city's taxation—or lack of it—is some people's main motivation for relocating here. The headline attraction is the 17-percent salary tax, which is the top limit for people on incomes over HK$120,000—which is many expats. Below this, an income of HK$80,000–120,000 attracts a rate of 12 percent; HK$40,000–80,000, 7 percent; and HK$40,000 and below, 2 percent. There is no capital gains tax for companies and no sales tax.

Tax deductions are not carried out by employers, but due at the end of the tax year in April. As employers report earnings to Inland Revenue, there is little opportunity to spin a fairytale to authorities. Only income sourced in Hong Kong is taxable. Based on your employer's report, the Inland Revenue Department will issue a demand for payment that can be amended, if necessary. As tax returns go, it's all remarkably clear-cut. You can pay with your credit card over the phone or on the Web, with your ATM card at certain EPS points, or in cash, in person. Your tax status is linked to your immigration status, so any misadventures on your tax form and you're likely to have your visa revoked. It's also impossible to skip out of town without paying, as your employer is bound to withhold your last month's salary and any bonuses until you've settled your account with the tax collector.

One potential source of confusion is the taxation of any housing allowance you're issued. Broadly speaking, these allowances are considered part of your income but are subject to separate and lower taxation. Theoretically, as long as your employer only pays you the exact rental amount, you should be subject to the lower rates, but it's also dependent on your employer's reporting methods and relationship with the tax collector. This is certainly something you should ask about when negotiating your employment contract and pay.

U.S. INCOME TAX

Just because you're out the country doesn't mean Uncle Sam doesn't have his eye on you. As well as their Hong Kong tax return, all U.S. citizens must file a U.S. tax return, although you may not be liable to pay any tax. You can exclude a maximum of $91,500 of your income under the foreign-earned income exclusion, which means you won't pay any tax if you earn $91,500 or less, but will pay tax on any income you earn above that. So if you get paid $100,000, you won't pay tax on the first $91,500, but will pay tax on the extra $8,500. To qualify you need to have spent one full year as a resident in a foreign country or have been physically present in a foreign country for a minimum of 330 days in any 12-month period.

Your first year can be particularly messy as you won't yet meet the residency or physical presence requirements to qualify for double taxation relief. Essentially, you'll have both governments rifling through your pockets. One way around this can be to file for an extension, which might help you meet the residency or physical presence requirements. The U.S. Embassy maintains a useful list of U.S. tax consultants with offices in Hong Kong.

Investing

If you've always aspired to play Warren Buffet, you'll find no better place than Hong Kong to live out your stock market dreams. Not only is Hong Kong one of the world's most important stock exchanges, but it's also considered the safest way to tap into the swelling wealth of China.

Rather than being confined to companies and bankers, many average Hong Kongers do sink modest amounts of money into the stock market. Expats in Hong Kong can also get involved and most banks will provide straightforward trading services to help you dip your toes in the pool. Of course, it's highly advisable to take professional advice—and there are no shortage of brokers to choose from—before you dump the family fortune into a tip you overheard at the racecourse. One of the most popular ways for the armchair investor to get involved

The Bank of China is not only a landmark building, it is one of the biggest financial movers and shakers in the city.

and not lose their trousers is through mutual funds. These are packages of shares in a number of companies that are collected by type, such as technology, or by region, such as China or Asia. While different packages have different returns and risks, investing in a spread of shares is considered less risky and your portfolio should rise and fall with the region or sector.

For U.S. citizens, trading can be difficult. While legally permitted to do so, brokers and banks are often unwilling to take U.S. citizens on as clients because of the bureaucratic bomb of paperwork required by the IRS. The way around this is to use a U.S. broker based in the city who will be familiar and comfortable with the reporting process.

COMMUNICATIONS

In a city so thoroughly obsessed with getting ahead and staying ahead, the need to know what's going on all the time everywhere, from the next office to the next continent, is insatiable. This desire has turned Hong Kong into one of Asia's prime media hubs and fuelled a cutting-edge and dirt-cheap telecommunications industry. The undoubted king of communication in the city is the cell phone. As the ultimate tool for making sure you're always up to date, always on top of the next big deal, and always available to tell people you're on the bus, cell phone ownership in Hong Kong has reached a staggering 160 percent, meaning the average Hong Konger has two cell phones in his pocket. Savage competition between network providers and regular promotions has made tariffs incredibly cheap and it's an easy city to develop a trampoline jaw. It's also helped launch 3G, with cell phone Internet access and even streaming TV, into the mainstream. Internet access is similarly impressive and comes at space-age speeds unheard of in the West. With cell phones barnacled to their ears and fingers cemented to their keyboard, Hong Kongers also have

© MARTYNA SZMYTKOWSKA

music director
d conductor of
he Hong Kong
Sinfonietta,
campaigning
r a permanent
home for the
chestra, writes
Tim Metcalfe

an appetite for the newest, fastest, and shiniest technology, all of which is available at reduced cost.

Although access and availability to communications is excellent, customer service is downright lousy and if you do encounter a problem, expect to spend plenty of time being told no one on the hotline speaks English, then be put on hold, and then hear the line go dead. Don't take it personally, the service for Cantonese speakers is no better, but do be prepared to show a lot of patience. Contracts can be equally challenging with enough caveats, restrictions, and qualifications to keep the Harvard law class behind after the bell.

Telephone Service

Having a cell phone in Hong Kong is essential, as is answering it no matter where you are—the only valid excuses are being unconscious or dead. The cinema, hospital, and library are all perfect places to strike up a loud and lasting conversation about what you had for dinner or what Gloria in the office was up to today. Given that Hong Kongers are almost never at home and their mobile phone is generally glued to the side of their face, it's surprising how many of them still maintain landlines. Whether you'll want a landline depends on how much calling you're going to do, especially at home.

LANDLINES

Almost all apartments are fitted out with a landline connection, although depending on how long the property has been empty, the landlord may have deactivated the service. If the line has to be reactivated, there will be a small fee, although this is usually waved when you sign up for a service plan. The main attraction of a landline in Hong Kong is that you only pay for the line rental; all calls to Hong Kong numbers, including cell phones are then free. For expats it also means your family and friends can call you from home without incurring the highway robbery charges attached to calling a cell phone. The major telecommunications provider is PCCW, followed by HGC, both of whom have basic landline rental packages starting around HK$100.

IDD AND CALLING HOME

If you want to phone home from Hong Kong, you'll need to sign up for an IDD (International Direct Dial) package or buy a pay-as-you-go IDD card. The former is recommended if you plan on picking up the phone a lot, the latter if it's for birthdays only. IDD packages are independent of your landline provider, so while you may have PCCW providing your landline, you can have HGC as your IDD provider, with packages attached to your landline, cell phone, or both. The choice of providers is dazzling, including most cell phone network operators, and although many expats go with PCCW or HGC out of convenience, if you shop around, you'll likely find more competitive prices. Companies worth looking up include New World Telecom IDD 009, IDD1609, and IDD1529. Some providers offer a full contract service, paid monthly, while others just require you to register the phone number you plan to call from and pay only for the minutes you use. If you're signing a contract, look for flat rates, rather than peak charges; fixed rates for the period of your contract; and free minutes, especially when signing up for longer periods. Prices and promotions bounce around, but rates for calls to the United States should be somewhere between HK$0.20 and HK$0.40. If you're not much of a talker, you'll probably find it easier to pick up an IDD phone card. Available at most 7-Eleven stores, some of the cheapest are found in the kiosks at Worldwide House in Central. Most cards are tailored to certain destinations, so unless you only want cheap calls to Sri Lanka, check the call rates for your country first.

CELLULAR PHONES

We actually knew a woman who always carried four phones in her purse; one for personal calls, one for work calls, one fitted with a Canadian sim card for calls from abroad, and the other was, well, just a back up in case one broke. Telling a Hong Konger that you don't have a cell phone is a little like admitting you still aren't eating solid foods, only more shocking, and you'll want to get a local number as quickly as possible.

Certainly one of the great draws of cell phones in Hong Kong is the incredibly competitive tariffs, with rates far cheaper than those in the United States or Europe. Keeping in mind that free minutes to users on the same network tend to be more generous, Hong Kong's biggest network operator is 3, followed by CSL, under the One2Free and 1010 brands, then PCCW, SmarTone, and China Mobile. All are in cutthroat competition with each other, so pricing and promotions tend to be aggressive. Basic plans start at around HK$100 a month and include roughly 1,000 free minutes to local numbers and a handful of free sms and mms messages. Premium plans can cost as much as HK$500, which will win you around 5,000–10,000 free minutes, reduced price video calls, and occasionally a free rice cooker. On top are an endless list of negotiable extras and bundles, including IDD minutes and broadband access, as well as free or reduced price handsets. 3G has become incredibly popular in recent years and you'll often see Hong Kong commuters using their phone to watch videos or keeping dedicated Facebook followers abreast of all the gripping events on their journey home. Plans that include free access to videos and limited TV stations and extensive Internet data usage are available at less than HK$200.

If you aren't yet able to get a contract or want to keep costs to a minimum, consider using one of the pay-as-you-go services offered by all of the major network providers. Starter packs containing a local sim card and a number of free minutes can be found in providers' stores or at 7-Eleven. Once your credit has run down, add more using your credit card or with a stored value card.

Internet

SETTING UP INTERNET ACCESS

Most Hong Kong apartments are already hooked up and Internet-ready, although you may have to reactivate the service. If you're moving into an older building, it's conceivable that you'll need to have wires installed, but once you've signed on with a provider, installation is usually free and happens in less than a week. Connection speeds are bolt-lightning fast, with the average connection clocking in at just under 10mbps. Many service providers are already offering Star Trek speeds of 50mbps, 1,000mbps, and even 1gbps, however, unless your plotting to download Guiding Light's whole back catalogue or hack into NASA, 10mpbs is more than generous.

The major Internet service provider (ISP) is PCCW and their netvigator service, trailed by I-Cable HGC, and 3, who may or may not be available in your building. Most ISP's bundle cable TV packages with their broadband deals—useful if you want cable, less useful if you don't—and they will attempt to tie you into an endless list of extras when you sign up. Dial-up is dead, at least in Hong Kong, and at this point almost

Hong Kong's public phonebooths are Wi-Fi hotspot-enabled.

DAILY LIFE

all home Internet plans cover unlimited usage. For a basic plan with somewhere between 10 and 20mpbs connection, expect to pay HK$200–300 per month. If you can't or won't take out a long-term contract, PCCW offers pay-in-advance monthly deals, although they will empty your pockets for the privilege.

Alternatively or in addition, if you have a laptop and plan on using it outside of the home and office often, you can try the mobile anywhere Wi-Fi packages. These allow you access to the Internet in cafés, shopping malls, and various other hotspots around the city via your laptop. Again PCCW has the most coverage with more than 7,000 hotspots, the only drawback being that many of the hotspots are next to useless: 7-Eleven is a great place to grab a Slurpee, but it's not the best location to check your email. PCCW offers both monthly usage plans and pay-as-you-go services payable by credit card.

If logging in while hiding behind the frozen food aisle at Marks and Spencer's doesn't sound ideal, and it isn't, you can instead spring for a USB modem stick, known as a dongle. Lower speed and dropped connections can make dongles a poor substitute for home Internet, but they do let you connect anywhere in the city, making them a better value than the hotspot plans. Most of the cell phone network operators have mobile broadband connection plans, including pay-as-you-go plans for the contract-shy. Unlimited usage packages start at around HK$200, although you'll also need to rent or buy your own dongle.

PUBLIC INTERNET

One drawback of almost universal coverage in individual homes is that the number of Internet cafés has started to decline and unless you're willing to share your space with sleep-deprived, deodorant-free teenagers, they are best avoided. The good news is that Hong Kong is quickly descending under a Wi-Fi cloud and free Wi-Fi access is available to anyone with a laptop at a number of locations, including libraries, parks, ferry terminals, and most government buildings, with no registration. You can find a full list at www.gov.hk. If you don't have a

Send emails, Skype friends, and blow up bad guys at a Hong Kong internet café.

laptop and don't want to brave the Internet cafés, you can also find free computers with Internet at certain libraries, including Central Library, and at selected branches of Pacific Coffee.

Postal Services

Hong Kong Post is cheap and efficient and can be relied upon not to lose your letters and packages. With the rise and rise of email and online payments, it's unlikely you'll be posting too many letters within the city, if you do, postage is HK$1.40 and post is delivered the next day. Hong Kong Post also offers a courier service via CourierPost.

International airmail is split into two zones: Zone 1 covers Asia and costs HK$1.90 for a letter; Zone 2 covers Japan and the rest of the world and costs HK$2.50. Hong Kong Post also offers a standard air package and surface package delivery; the latter can be cost effective in shipping back non-urgent items before you leave the city. Items are registered and can be tracked online, however, Hong Kong Post can only track them until they reach the often-slippery hands of local postal providers. Postage is priced by weight and must be weighed at your local post office, where you will also be given a customs declaration form. For speedier deliveries, you can try SpeedPost, an international express mail service run by Hong Kong Post, which offers full tracking and insurance options. While your package or letter is sure to turn up safely, SpeedPost has limited reach and its reliance on local postal partners in other countries makes it less reliable than global competitors such as FedEx, UPS, or DHL. DHL has handy drop-off points for packages at several MTR stations, including Central and Causeway Bay.

Television and Cable TV

Hong Kong has four free-to-air terrestrial stations: TVB Jade and ATV Home broadcast almost wholly in Cantonese; ATV World and TVB Pearl broadcast in English. However, if you like to play couch potato from time to time, these two English channels are unlikely to sate your appetite. While Pearl does run a handful of recent U.S. series and recent movies, prime time on World can amount to reacquainting yourself with Bill Cosby and 1980s New York or documentaries on making butter. Most expats usually splash out on cable deals, which are cheap and include more channels than your fingers can flick through. The

Individual TV screens at a restaurant mean never having to miss your favorite show.

majority of Internet providers offer cable TV bundles, including the two biggest, PCCW's NOWTV and I-Cable's CABLE TV. These bundles will typically offer a couple of dedicated English-language channels, such as AXN and BBC Entertainment, as well as their own brand channels that will feature your favorite shows, although not necessarily from last week. You'll also find English-language news, including CNN and BBC, and movie channels such as HBO and TCM. Sports events and leagues tend to be exclusive to one provider or another, so be sure to check out the schedules, lest you get stuck with the Nigerian Falconry League rather than the National Football League. Typically, you'll need to pay for line rental, rental of the decoder box, and installation, although some of these fees are waived if you also sign up for Internet with the same provider. As with anywhere, the more channels you want, the more you have to pay, but also the more you can negotiate. For the best deals, try the salespeople standing by their desks at computer centers, such as the one in Wan Chai.

If you absolutely can't stand not knowing who Horatio Caine is slapping the handcuffs on this week, there are a couple of options. With the speed of Internet connections in Hong Kong many locals simply download the most recent episodes of current shows and hook their computer up to their TV. Alternatively, if your conscience or the police prevent you from downloading, you can set up a slingbox. These set top boxes are hooked up to your TV in your home country, or that of a willing friend, from where it slings the live signal across the Internet to your computer, which can be hooked up to a TV—it's simpler than it sounds. You'll be able to view any channels that are available at your home location.

Media

Unlike their cousins to the north, Hong Kong is censorship free, as reflected by the number of international media organizations that have a regional base here, such as CNN and the *Wall Street Journal*. Books banned in China are available in the city, and Google results for sensitive Chinese topics such as Falun Gong and Tibet appear unmolested. However, while critics of the government won't be whisked away in black sedans by men with oversized sunglasses, there is an increasing problem with self-censorship. Soft pressure by the powerful pro-Beijing business lobby and the advertising they control has led to some newspapers and individual journalists moderating their articles and toning down their criticisms of the Beijing government and issues important to them in Hong Kong.

NEWSPAPERS

The *South China Morning Post* (SCMP) is Hong Kong's major English-language daily with a history dating back to 1903. The quality of the reporting, which focuses on local, Chinese, and international issues, can rival that of broadsheets in the United States and the United Kingdom, although its kowtowing to a pro-China editorial line can be heavy-handed and does attract criticism. It also runs a number of weekly supplements, including the useful *Classified Post* which contains English-language job listings, as well as an online subscription website. The paper can be picked up at most newsstands around the city. Its only English-language competitor is *The Standard,* a lightweight, free publication given away five days a week at metro stations and on the street. For a taste of local news before you come, *The Standard* can be found online for free. International newspapers such as the *International Herald Tribune, Financial Times,* and *USA Today* are available at select newspaper stands around the city, particularly in Central. British newspapers can also be found in supermarkets and shops near expat enclaves, such as Park N Shop and Great in Central, although they will usually be a day or two late and attract a premium price tag. If real news upsets you, try the *China Daily's* Hong Kong edition. The official mouthpiece of the Chinese Communist Party, it paints a picture of a utopian Chinese society where farm girls plait each others hair, workers hold hands, and communist party officials give out candy bars.

MAGAZINES

Hong Kong is swamped by local English-language magazines, although the bulk are little more than glorified advertising leaflets. Exceptions include *Hong Kong Magazine,* a weekly listings magazine that includes lighthearted and occasionally casuistic articles on local politics, culture, and life. It can be picked up for free at restaurants and bars in Wan Chai, Lan Kwai Fong, and SoHo and its Thursday delivery is much anticipated by many expats. *Time Out* also has a branch in Hong Kong, replicating the finger-on-the-button listings that have made it popular the world over. The monthly *Peak Magazine* is aimed at the Armani crowd, with profiles of moguls, fat cats, and in-depth articles on fast cars and shiny things. Also monthly, if you're newly arrived, try *CityLife* magazine, which focuses on the city's sights as well as culture and history.

Foreign English-language magazines are widely available from newsstands in popular expat districts, particularly Central. Supermarkets such as Park N Shop and Great in the same areas stock a broader selection of mostly British publications, including magazines aimed at teenagers, kids, and pricy glossies. Usually a week or so late, they're handsomely priced. For American publications visit the Fleet Arcade in Wan Chai. Leased to the U.S. Navy, you need to pay a yearly subscription to visit the mall, but inside you can buy magazines and newspapers at cover price. If you want to track down something specific, try some of the specialist magazine shops that can help you subscribe for a price.

BOOKS

Unlike most expats heading to far-flung destinations who are forced to subsist on a diet of Dickens and Shakespeare, Hong Kong has a number of English-language bookshops with a broad selection. The two biggest are Dymocks and Page One, both are chains that have stores throughout the city. Dymocks has a reputation for Sherlock Holmes–perseverance in tracking down obscure books, while Page One stores are usually bigger. Unfortunately, books don't come cheap and you will almost always pay the full cover price, with discounts few and far between. If you need a cheaper option to help fill your library, you'll find a small selection of secondhand books at Oxfam and the bookstore attached to St. John's Cathedral, while Flow, in SoHo, is an atmospheric secondhand bookstore bulging with books both new and old. Online shoppers should try local firm Paddyfields.com, which offers a wide variety of titles, while Amazon.com and Amazon.co.uk both ship to Hong Kong, although postage is pricy.

RADIO

If your morning tumble out of bed isn't complete without some music, weather reports, and gripes about the traffic, Hong Kong has a couple of English-language radio stations to point your antenna at. RTHK 3 is the

DAILY LIFE

government-run English-language radio station that offers a familiar mix of pop, news, and the usual breakfast-show banter, while its sister station, RTHK4, broadcasts a high-minded mix of Beethoven and Mozart and other classical heavyweights. Commercial station Metro Plus is aimed at Hong Kong's multicultural masses, featuring music and news from the Philippines, Pakistan, and the rest of the globe. Of course with any sort of decent Internet connection, you can simply stream radio from home on to your computer.

Contracts

While there are pay as you go deals available for most communications in Hong Kong, over the long term most expats find it easier and cheaper to sign up for a contract. Contracts are notoriously easy to come by, even for foreigners, and while a rental agreement, bank account, and HKID are usually required, we've known expats who have signed up with just their passport and a smile. All service providers offer a bilingual service, meaning your contract and bills will be in English, as should customer support, although trying to find someone at a call center who is both a competent English speaker and competent at their job will likely raise your blood pressure.

One of the problems/advantages of media companies in Hong Kong is that they have their finger in just about every pie. So, while you might walk into the shop looking to sign up for Internet services, you'll leave with contracts for cable TV, cell phone, and dog-trimming services for the dog you now need to buy. While it can be convenient to have everything bundled up with the same service provider, it can also lead to you being saddled with a substantial bill for a bunch of services you don't need. You certainly shouldn't expect impartial advice from sales staff; most have been trained at the Pinocchio center for customer service and will tell you your phone will work on the moon to make a sale. Make sure you have an idea of what you want and how much you're willing to pay, before you go into the shop: Check out websites; talk to friends; and shop around. It's also important to be demanding. Few things are set in stone, despite what the sales representative might tell you, and the more services you buy, especially for pricy packages, the more freebies and incentives you should demand in return. Contracts are usually set at around 18–24 months, although, again, sales staff will try and get you to sign up for the remainder of your natural life and sign over your first born son as well.

TRAVEL AND TRANSPORTATION

The rickshaw is dead. Once used to ferry the city's elite up and down the hilly terrain, Hong Kong's iconic rickshaws died many years ago, and today are replaced by a world-class public transportation system. Safe, cheap, and clockwork-efficient, the system is a bright red embarrassment to cities like London, New York, and, well, just about anywhere. Hong Kongers are not patient people and transport, particularity the MTR, tends to run with astounding frequency. Tellingly, even those that own a car tend to prefer public transport, simply because it's quicker and far less stressful.

The flagship is the MTR, a subway system that zips across just about every inch of the city and the New Territories, stretching as far as Shenzhen in China. The MTR is complemented by fleets of air-conditioned buses, the iconic Star Ferry and tram network, and even the world's longest outdoor escalator. Connections between different modes of transport are well planned and helped by

© PAWEL LOJ

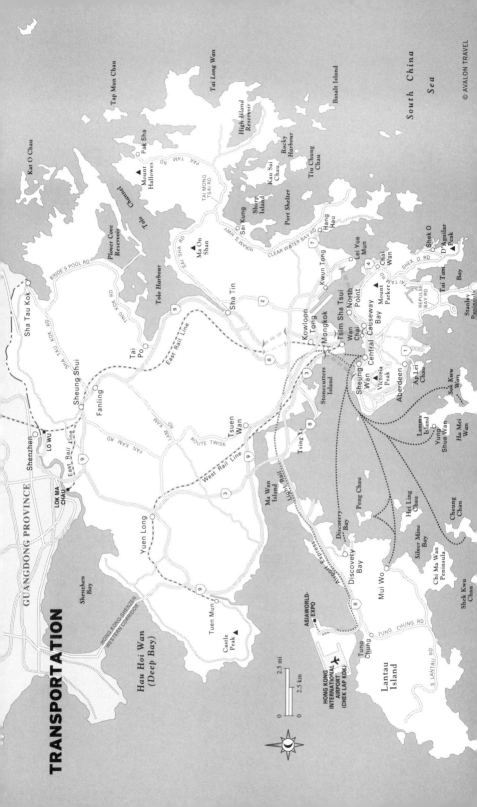

the ubiquitous Octopus Card, an electronic payment card first pioneered in Hong Kong and now copied around the world. Those that are in a rush can also call on one of the many cabs stalking the streets. Stringently regulated, they are ubiquitous, cheap, and a guilty pleasure that can be hard to avoid.

If there is something to grumble about, it's the sheer number of people who use public transport. During rush hour, gloved attendants hustle commuters onto packed MTR trains, and it can be almost impossible to disembark trams. Success requires sharp wits and sharper elbows.

One of the great pleasures of living in Hong Kong is leaving. Nearly half the world's population is just three or four hours away by flight. Weekend beach breaks to Thailand, the Philippines, and Vietnam, among others, are a popular activity.

By Air

The vast majority of travelers to Hong Kong are introduced to the country at Hong Kong International Airport, or Chek Lap Kok as it's also known, and what a wonderful introduction it is. Opened to great expense in 1998, passengers, airlines, and critics have spent the years since falling over each other to praise the airport and it regularly jostles with Singapore to be crowned the world's best. Over 50 million passengers pass through its doors each year and it carries more international passenger traffic than anywhere else in Asia. Yet, despite its size, it is incredibly well run and efficient. Forget clueless check-in staff and labyrinth layouts, the two terminals are spacious, well signposted, and never feel overcrowded. It's also well hooked up to the public transport network. Despite being out on Lantau Island, the Airport Express train offers a connection to Hong Kong Station in Central in 24 minutes, where selected airlines let you check your bag up to 24 hours in advance. There are also coach services connecting to over 100 Chinese cities, and direct bonded ferries regularly travel to Macau and Shenzhen.

As a major international and regional hub, the airport boasts nearly 100 airlines serving more than 150 destinations, including almost all major cities in Asia, particularly China's Beijing, Shanghai, and Bangkok, and many European and Middle Eastern runways, including a conveyor belt of flights to London. Direct connections to the United States are less frequent, but destinations include San Francisco, Los Angles, New York (15 hours), Chicago, Detroit, and Vancouver. Hong Kong's unofficial flag carrier, Cathay Pacific, offers the most comprehensive international schedule and has a reputation for

© THIERRY MEURGUES

There aren't many places that Hong Kong International Airport can't fly you.

five-star service, while their subsidiary, Dragon Air, is the leading provider of flights to China, covering 17 cities with 400 weekly flights. More connections to China and substantially cheaper fares can be found at Shenzhen Bao'an Airport, just across the border, although the hassle of traveling there and the lack of English service often means the effort outweighs the savings.

Plane tickets can be bought online, either direct from the airline or from a travel portal, or from one of the cities travel agents, although the latter option is usually pricier. Hong Kong's role as an international and regional hub keeps ticket prices honest, and competition on many routes means there are regular and aggressive sales and promotions.

By Train

Hanging off the edge of the country's skirt in the very far south of the country, Hong Kong is a long way from anywhere in China and train travel is not really very practical. The most useful route is the connection to Guangzhou, which runs a dozen times a day, also stopping in Dongguan, and takes around two hours. All trains are air-conditioned and a standard ticket costs HK$190.

Traveling farther afield, a single train runs to Beijing and Shanghai on alternate days, although, at 24 hours and 19 hours respectively, you'll want to bring a good and biblical sized book. Aside from the time involved, long haul train travel to China can be a great adventure, an opportunity to meet locals and see the countryside, and it's also cheaper than standard air fares. As with all Chinese trains, there are a wide range of seats available, although all are sleepers: first class is Deluxe Soft Sleeper, which is two berth bunk beds and has a private bathroom; followed by Soft Sleeper, which is four birth bunk beds; and finally Hard Sleeper, which is a sort of an open plan dorm of six bunk beds. Apart from the number of people you'll be snoring with and the lack of a door in Hard Sleeper, there is little to choose between the classes. Bedding and hot water are universally provided and Chinese electrical sockets are increasingly available. Tickets to Beijing West are priced from HK$1,191 for a Deluxe Soft Sleeper to HK$574 for a Hard Sleeper, while the same classes to Shanghai Railway Station cost HK$1,039 and HK$508, respectively. Children get one-third off the ticket price, although bafflingly anyone over the age of 10 is considered an adult, and round-trip tickets often attract discounts of 10–20 percent. Tickets can be bought from Hung Hom Station, where all international trains depart, online, or from travel agents around town, such as China Travel Service (CTS).

By Bus or Boat

Given the distances involved, long-distance bus connections are infrequent from Hong Kong, and unless you want to lose the feeling in your ass and possibly the will to live, bus travel really should be a last resort.

Most available services travel to the Pearl River Delta and Southern China with regular services to several cities, including Jiangmen, Foshan, and Zhongshan, as well as Fujian and Shantau farther out. Hong Kong has no dedicated bus station, but most buses originate at Hong Kong International Airport, where you can buy tickets and check timetables. There are frequent bus connections to both Shenzhen and Guangzhou, but both of these destinations are better served by their subway and railway connections, respectively.

Set on the tip of the Pearl River Delta, one of the more enjoyable and often most efficient ways to travel around the region is by ferry. Hong Kong has regular ferry connections to Macau as well as to several nearby Chinese cities. The ferry is the most practical way to reach Macau, with sailings almost every 15 minutes during peak periods and taking a little over an hour. Tickets can be bought from travel agents or online. They are also usually available directly before the sailing at either the Hong Kong Macau

Ferry Terminal in Sheung Wan or the China Ferry Terminal in Tsim Sha Tsui and cost HK$130–180, depending on the day and time of the sailing. Shenzhen is also well served by ferries, although they serve the Shekou district rather than downtown Shenzhen. There are also bonded ferries to both Macau and Shenzhen, as well as Guangzhou and other Pearl River Delta cities, available from Hong Kong Airport's Sky Pier. These allow you to transit to your destination without passing through Hong Kong immigration. From the China Ferry Terminal there are also services of varying frequency to around 10 destinations on the Pearl River Delta, including the popular beaches of Zhuhai.

Ferries on all routes are either modern boats or slightly faster catamarans which have individual passenger seating, icy air-conditioning, and big screens constantly blasting advertisements about beauty products to ensure that you don't get a wink of sleep. Some have a small shop, but the journey is usually so short that by the time you sat down, it's almost time to leave again.

Public Transportation

If they have public transportation in heaven, it probably looks like this. There are few cities in the world that can truthfully claim that public transportation will get you to work quicker (every day) than your car and not turn your blood pressure into a telephone number at the same time. Hong Kong can, that's why the vast majority of residents commute on public transportation. Breathtaking in its scale, the public transportation system covers trams, buses, minibuses, ferries, the much-vaunted MTR (Mass Transit Railway) subway system, and even a near-kilometer-long system of outdoor escalators. Those living on north Hong Kong Island or in Kowloon will rarely be more than a block or two from an MTR stop, with the system also covering the New Territories and traveling as far north as Shenzhen in China. If you choose to live on the islands, you'll face a more ambitious commute, but ferry services are regular and reach even the smallest hamlets.

The crown jewel in all this movement is the Octopus Card. Much imitated in other world cities, this stored value card lets you stroll onto just about all forms of public transportation like Obi Wan Kenobi, waving your card over the card reader. Over 95 percent of the population are card carriers and it can be used for more than just transportation, such as paying at parking meters, buying your cinema tickets, or even picking up a late-night sandwich from 7-Eleven after a night in La Kwai Fong has turned your wallet upside down.

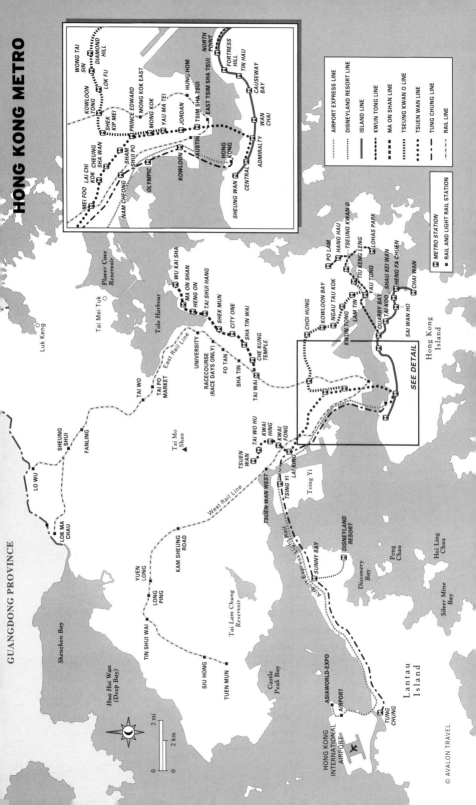

SUBWAY

Of all Hong Kong's many ways to get around, the MTR (Hong Kong's subway) is easily the most efficient and your daily commute to work will be substantially shorter if you can travel point to point by MTR. Covering around 175 kilometers of tracks on nine separate lines, the MTR is the most comprehensive and utilized form of public transport in Hong Kong. Its 82 stations are mostly centered on the north side of Hong Kong Island and Kowloon but also branch out along several lines into the New Territories, stretching as far as Shenzhen at the China border and to Hong Kong Disneyland on Lantau Island.

© RORY BOLAND

Hong Kong's MTR trains are cleaner than most hospitals.

If your experience of the subway is riding in creaking, graffiti-covered carriages while dodging passengers recently released from a federal penitentiary, the MTR will be a revelation. Service is fast and frequent, with trains at rush hour on the Island Line in a constant congo line of departure and waits of more than five minutes the exception on most main lines. Stations and trains are modern, air-conditioned, and cleaner than some hospitals. Riding the subway is also safe, even after dark, although watch for pickpockets on the prowl in rush hour. Announcements on the system are in Cantonese, Mandarin, and English and there are maps at each station directing you to the correct exit.

A victim of its own success, the only negative of the MTR are the massive crowds it attracts during rush hour. While it rarely takes long to get on a train, you'll almost certainly have to adopt the straightjacket position during your journey before coming out of your corner swinging to get through the crowds at your stop.

Most people navigate the MTR with their Octopus Card, which you wave at entry and exit barriers and which calculates and automatically deducts the fare for you. All stations also have automated ticket machines and machines for recharging your Octopus and most have staffed ticket booths. Fares for paper tickets or the Octopus Card are calculated on the length of your journey, with the Octopus Card attracting cheaper fares. The MTR starts running around 6 A.M. and winds down between midnight and 1:00 A.M.

BUSES

With well over 500 routes, Hong Kong's bus network can get you just about anywhere you want to go. Although the city's chronic traffic means it can't beat the MTR in a foot race, the bus network does cover far more destinations and is particularly useful for reaching Hong Kong Island west and south and the New Territories. Night buses are also the only practical way to move around the city and across the harbor after the MTR turns off its lights. The sheer number of routes can make the system seem impenetrable, particularly as it's run by several different companies. But, you will find route information, including stops, and the fare posted at bus stops. The fare is payable on entry to the bus, where it's also displayed, either by Octopus Card or with coins. Drivers carry no change and less patience and there is little point in asking questions about the route as most also do not speak English. Fares can range from under HK$2 for short hops to around HK$50 for an airport trip, with cross harbor journeys and night buses attracting higher fares. Timetables are displayed by frequency, with many urban routes enjoying a service every 5 or 10 minutes.

Public Light Buses

Public light buses, or PLB, are 16-seater minibuses that often offer quicker connections thanks to the Indy 500 drivers sitting behind the steering wheels. There are two breeds of minibuses, green and red. Green-roofed minibuses have a fixed route and timetable and are usually a more direct alternative to the city buses for destinations in the New Territories. The destination is usually displayed in both Chinese and English on the front of the bus, although the route information on the side is often only in Chinese. You pay when you board the bus by dumping the correct fare, which will be displayed, into the cash box; Octopus Cards are also widely accepted.

Red-roofed minibuses are less strictly regulated and usually compete with city buses on the most popular routes. While substantially quicker, they have no set stops and have to be flagged down from the street. Destination and, occasionally, route information is posted on the front, although the route to the destination can vary depending on the driver. You will need to indicate to the driver when you wish to alight and although most drivers don't speak English any sort of shout will usually result in a raise of the hand as an acknowledgment and a sharp swerve to the side of the road. Payment is also made when

© IOAN SAMELI

Death-defying driving aside, the city's public light buses are often the quickest way from point A to point B.

you alight and in theory drivers carry small change. Fares are unregulated on red minibuses and are regularly hiked up by drivers during rush hour, in bad weather, or if they backed a donkey at Happy Valley last night. Red minibus drivers have a reputation for regarding speed limits as more of a suggestion than a rule and their fleeing-bank-robber driving style can be too stomach churning for some people.

FERRY SERVICES

With 200 plus islands, ferries are an essential element in Hong Kong's public transport network and part of many people's daily commute. While it might seem romantic to float to work every morning, in practice you may find your daily life beholden to a timetable. While fares are cheap and ferries modern, you can add 30 minutes to an hour onto your commute. Mornings can be a constant battle to make the last ferry that will get you into work on time, while limited night services can mean you have to live like Cinderella. Sampan trips at 4 A.M. after a night out in Wan Chai are neither kind on the wallet or the stomach.

Cross Harbor Ferries

The flagship of Hong Kong's ferry fleet is the Star Ferry, which zigzags the waters of Victoria Harbour, connecting Wan Chai and Central on Hong Kong Island with Tsim Sha Tsui in Kowloon. Boasting over a century of history and boats with evocative names, such as the Celestial Star, the old-fashioned green and white ferries have become Hong Kong's blockbuster tourist

More than one hundred years old, the regal Star Ferry is still a workhorse of public transportation.

attraction, mostly thanks to the jaw-dropping views offered on the Tsim Sha Tsui-to-Central crossing. Yet, while commuter numbers have suffered since the opening of the MTR and several cross harbor tunnels, the Star Ferry's low fares and more relaxing ride means it still fills up with business suits during rush hour. Fares are as low as HK$2 for a lower-deck seat during weekdays between Tsim Sha Tsui to Central and can be paid with an Octopus Card or with a token bought from the booths on site. While the 10-minute crossing between Tsim Sha Tsui and Central is no match for the MTR, the Star Ferry service is by no means sleepy: Ferries run 6:30 A.M.–11:30 P.M., with services as often as every six minutes during peak times.

Outlying Islands

If you're planning on living out on one of Hong Kong's Outlying Islands, the frequency and price of your ferry service is something that is likely to have a direct bearing on your quality of life and your bank balance. Just how much you will be affected depends on whether you need to commute daily and which island you plan to live on. Bigger islands with major residential communities, such as Lamma and Lantau, benefit from frequent ferries which can run as often as every 20 minutes, while far-flung islands, such as Po Toi, may only see a ferry every few days. The smallest islands and settlements are served only by kaidos, smaller ferries with an irregular service often limited to weekends and holidays.

Most ferries from the Outlying Islands go from destination A to destination B with no intermediary stops. The hub is the Central Ferry Piers found in the heart of Central, next to Hong Kong Station, although there are also less frequent inter-island ferries. While fares are not particularly expensive, a one-way ticket from Central to Lamma is HK$14.50 during weekdays, HK$20 on Sundays; those commuting two times a day, five times a week should consider a monthly ticket which offers unlimited travel for a fixed fee.

Like the rest of Hong Kong's public transport, ferries generally run on time and although inclement weather can occasionally make for delayed crossings, cancellations are rare unless a typhoon is in town. Ferries serving Lamma, Lantau, and Cheung Chau are sturdy vessels that can hold 300–500 people on two decks, have impeccable safety records, and are reasonably immune from the swelling South China Sea. Inside, they have padded seats, toilets, and, on some ferries, small shops selling snacks and drinks. There are generally two types of ferries, ordinary and fast, with the latter knocking roughly a third off the journey time, but on the Lantau and Cheung Chau routes the price doubles.

TRAMS

Adding a little Victorian spirit to the streets of Hong Kong, the city's double-decker trams, turned out in their distinctive green livery, have been rattling along the north of Hong Kong Island since 1904. As with the Star Ferry, trams are one of the more enjoyable and leisurely ways to travel around the city, offering bird's-eye views of the bustling streets below from their upper deck. Unfortunately, because they run at street level, they often have the top speed of a bicycle and can come clattering to a complete halt during rush hour. Despite the sluggish speeds, trams are popular with commuters thanks to their HK$2 flat fee—one of the city's great bargains—and are useful for short hops in the city center. The line runs between Shau Kei Wan and Kennedy Town, with a branch line to Happy Valley; stops in downtown are often less than 500 meters apart. Board the tram through the

Hong Kong's trams ply north Hong Kong Island and are packed with commuters during rush hours.

turnstiles at the back of the tram and pay with exact change or an Octopus Card when disembarking at the front. Be careful when boarding at rush hour as queuing tends to descend into mob rule and I've seen a number of people pitched into an unplanned somersault over the turnstiles.

The other tram system operating in Hong Kong is the Peak Tram, which, while popular with tourists for its death-defying crawl up Victoria Peak, is too expensive at HK$25 a pop for commuting. Besides, if you can afford to live on the Peak, you probably don't know what public transport is anyway.

TAXIS

When even walking to the nearest bus stop is too much effort, you'll rarely be more than a couple of seconds away from a Hong Kong taxi. Each day the city's 20,000 odd cabs carry an estimated one million passengers, an indication of just how cheap fares are in Hong Kong. Unlike New York and London, taxi rides in Hong Kong are not reserved for birthdays and lottery wins and the low fares, HK$18 for the first two kilometers and HK$1.80 for every subsequent 200 meters, mean locals make everyday use of them.

Prices are fixed no matter what the time, no matter what the weather and in comparison to many of their cowboy comrades around the world, Hong Kong drivers are flawlessly honest and will almost always flip the meter on. Some drivers, arguably a minority, speak English, and if you're heading to a major landmark or street, they'll usually recognize the English word. If not, they'll simply raise someone at base who speaks English on the radio to translate for them. Those that are available for hire will have their taxi light lit; but they are not permitted to stop on yellow lines or crossings.

In general, you'll only ever deal with red taxis, which serve Hong Kong Island and Kowloon, but can

Taxis are relatively cheap in Hong Kong and are a popular way to cover short distances.

© MARTYNA SZMYTKOWSKA

DAILY LIFE

go anywhere in Hong Kong. Green taxis are restricted to the New Territories and blue taxis are solely for Lantau. Red taxi drivers will often refuse to cross the harbor, usually because they don't know the street layout well enough on the other side, although the lure of a juicy fare can be enough encouragement for them to get you both lost. If you do take a cross-harbor trip, you'll need to pay the tunnel toll, twice—once for the way over, once for the driver to get back—on top of the fare. You can avoid this by using the unofficial cross-harbor cab stands, where you'll find cab drivers looking to return to their own side who will only charge for the single toll. Some cabs sitting around with their not-for-hire sign displayed in the front window are also waiting for a cross-harbor fare.

Driving

If you like sitting in your car, you'll like Hong Kong, because that's pretty much all drivers here get to do, sit, while forlornly turning the radio dial to try to find a traffic report that doesn't predict doom. With 285 vehicles for every kilometer of road, the city has some of the worst traffic density figures in the world and downtown Hong Kong Island and Kowloon are in various states of gridlock throughout the day. Space is the main problem. Hong Kong doesn't have much of it and once off the main arteries, roads, through built-up districts, quickly slim down to dual- and single-lane affairs, where you'll be pitched into battles against steely-eyed bus drivers and the city's swarm of taxis. Lack of space also means parking spaces are like gold dust and monthly parking charges border on extortion. Of course, there are also advantages to owning a car. Many Hong Kong motorists don't actually commute in their cars, instead dusting them off on weekends to enjoy the relatively open roads of the New Territories. And, while fuel and maintenance costs are relatively high, used cars can be picked up cheaply thanks to the high turnover of both company cars and departing expats.

RENTING A CAR

As few tourists bother to rent a car when visiting the city, rates tend to be somewhat high. Before you splash out, ask your firm if they have a car available; some maintain a car pool and you'll often get a driver thrown in for free. Rental rates at international car rental firms, such as Hertz and Avis, start at around HK$700, rising to HK$1,800 for something fancy. Local firms are a little cheaper and longer rentals usually attract discounts. HAWK Jubilee International Tour Company offers day rates for their cheapest cars for HK$500 and seven-day rentals from HK$2,500.

BUYING A CAR

New car sales are one the few areas where Hong Kong suffers from a lack of competition and as a result prices are stubbornly high. The sticker price on a cozy Ford Fiesta is HK$169,000; Hong Kong's favorite car, the Toyota Corolla comes in at HK$190,000; and a lush and leathery S-Class Mercedes is just over HK$1 million. These is certainly wiggle room in these prices, particularly for extras, but don't expect the price to fall off a cliff. Dealers for just about every brand in the world can be found along the waterfront of Wan Chai and Causeway Bay.

As with anywhere in the world, tread carefully when buying a used car in Hong Kong; tales of chop shops and hotwired cars from China are legion, if usually overblown. The good news is prices are very fair and the turnover of cars is high. There are several dedicated used-car dealerships, such as Vin's Motors and Vincent Motors, who will also accept trade-ins on your old car. You'll find cheaper prices if you buy direct from a seller, and expats leaving with little time to wait for the right price often offer cars at rock bottom prices. You'll find listings in the trading post on expat website forums and posted on the notice boards of supermarkets in popular expat areas. As there isn't much road to drive around, mileage tends to be low on used cars, but the use of poor quality gasoline, brought in from China, is widespread and it's always worthwhile having someone who knows a spark plug from a steering wheel nose around the engine.

The actual process of buying a car is reasonably straightforward, although you'll first need a HKID and a local license. If purchasing a new car, you'll need to pay for the vehicle to be registered by the Transport Department and get a license. These costs can often be haggled into the price of the car, which also means the dealer will handle the paperwork. Licenses for all cars must be renewed yearly; certain models that meet environmental standards and smaller cylinder cars receive tax breaks and incentives. For used cars, you should apply for a Certificate of Clearance from the Transport Department that states that there are no outstanding debts associated with the vehicle. Both seller and buyer must submit a Notice of Transfer, which legalizes the transfer of ownership once accepted. Cars that have passed their sixth birthday are required to submit to annual road-worthiness examinations. These are organized by the Transport Department and appointments can be booked up to four months before your current certificate expires. Before you take to the road, you're required to have at least third party insurance.

Aside from buying and maintaining the car, it's important to keep in mind the price of parking. There is effectively no free parking in Hong Kong and parking meters, if you can find a free space, will deplete the credit on your Octopus Card in a matter of minutes. Instead, most people rent a space monthly or annually at a parking garage, which, while also pricy, is much cheaper than the hourly and day rates. If you are planning on using your car in Hong Kong, try to rent an apartment building that also has parking spaces for residents, and many don't, and ask if there is parking space allocated at your workplace. The worse case scenario, and I've known several people who did this, is that you are commuting between two parking garages and paying for both.

DRIVER'S LICENSES

Those with driving licenses from the United States, United Kingdom, Australia, and most European countries can obtain a Hong Kong license without passing a test. Your license needs to be valid or not expired for more than three years and you need to have a passport from the country where the license was issued. To get your freebie, bring your HKID card, proof of address, passport, and license, along with a medical certificate, to the Licensing Office and expect to receive your Hong Kong License in a couple of weeks.

RULES OF THE ROAD

For those coming from the United States, the most noticeable change will be driving on the left-hand side of the road in a right-sided vehicle, a system inherited from the British. Apart from that, driving in Hong Kong holds few surprises. Seat belts must be on; mobile phones should be turned off or at least no talking while driving. Overtake on the right and give way to traffic when turning right. Hong Kong drivers have the big bad bully reputation associated with drivers in most big cities, but, while there is certainly a lot of honking, their bark is worse than their bite and most people do adhere to the rules of the road. You will find that constant tailing and traffic means that when the opportunity arises to use the accelerator, many people find they have developed an anvil foot. Beware: Traffic cops are everywhere and are ticket happy. You should also expect a few dents. Thanks to the cramped and often climbing roads, small fender benders and scratches are a way of life in Hong Kong. Few people have heard of a no-claims bonus on their insurance.

PRIME LIVING LOCATIONS

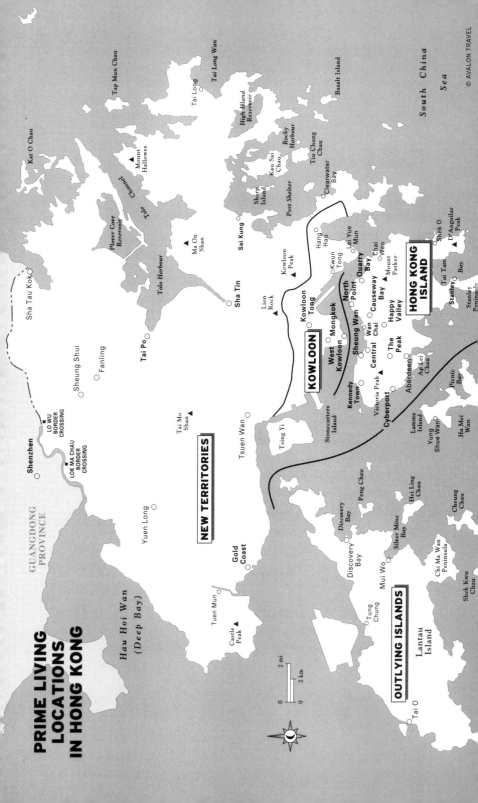

PRIME LIVING LOCATIONS IN HONG KONG

GUANGDONG PROVINCE

Shenzhen

LO WU BORDER CROSSING

LOK MA CHAU BORDER CROSSING

Sha Tau Kok

Hau Hoi Wan
(Deep Bay)

Yuen Long

Sheung Shui

Fanling

Tuen Mun

Castle Peak ▲

Gold Coast

Tsuen Wan

Tai Mo Shan ▲

NEW TERRITORIES

Tai Po

Tolo Harbour

Plover Cove Reservoir

Tao Channel

Ma On Shan ▲

Sha Tin

Kar O Chau

Tap Mun Chau

Tai Long Wan

Tai Long

Mount Hallowes ▲

High Island Reservoir

Sai Kung

Sharp Island

Kau Sai Chau

Port Shelter

Rocky Harbour

Tiu Chung Chau

Basalt Island

Clearwater Bay

South China Sea

© AVALON TRAVEL

Tung Chung

Tai O

Lantau Island

OUTLYING ISLANDS

Mui Wo

Silver Mine Bay

Discovery Bay

Peng Chau

Hei Ling Chau

Chi Ma Wan Peninsula

Shek Kwu Chau

Cheung Chau

Yung Shue Wan

Ha Mei Wan

Lamma Island

Cyberport

Stonecutters Island

Tsing Yi

Kennedy Town

Victoria Peak ▲

Aberdeen

Ap Lei Chau

Picnic Bay

KOWLOON

West Kowloon

Mongkok

Sheung Wan

Central

Wan Chai

The Peak

Kowloon Tong

Lion Rock ▲

Kowloon Peak ▲

Kwun Tong

North Point

Causeway Bay

Happy Valley

Hang Hau

Lei Yue Mun

Chai Wan

Mount Parker ▲

Quarry Bay

HONG KONG ISLAND

Shek O

D'Aguilar Peak ▲

Tai Tam

Stanley Bay

Stanley

Stanley Peninsula

2 mi

2 km

0

0

N

OVERVIEW

There may be 1,104 square kilometers in Hong Kong, but for most expats coming here the only 81 square kilometers that matter are those of Hong Kong Island. Few expats moving to the region ever consider living off the island, some consider a trip to Kowloon an "out of town" trip requiring a packed lunch and a flashlight, and a handful of others still suspect access to Kowloon requires a passport. Hong Kong Island's hold over expats is mostly due to its cosmopolitan, expat-friendly neighborhoods. From private hospitals and international schools to hamburger joints and English pubs, all delivered in English—if you want to forget you're living in China, nowhere in Hong Kong is more convincing. For most expats, it's love at first sight.

The hype of Hong Kong Island means the rest of Hong Kong is often overlooked, somewhat criminally. Few people realize it, but Hong Kong is an incredibly diverse region of mountains, islands, beachside fishing villages, and bustling market towns. There is a wide range of accommodation on offer beyond the boxy high-rises and at prices that don't have to break the bank.

This section covers the most popular places for expats to place their hats, both on the island and off. These areas include Hong Kong Island, Kowloon, the Outlying Islands, and the New Territories, with coverage of individual neighborhoods, towns, villages, and in some cases, islands. If you find a major neighborhood missing, such as Central, it's because, as with Central, it's an area that is primarily commercial rather than residential.

HONG KONG ISLAND

If you've come to Hong Kong to live in one of the world's greatest cities, you've come to the right place. Hong Kong Island is the home of modern Hong Kong and amongst its skyscraper-lined streets, you'll find the city at its most urbane, most ambitious, and most frantic. The city's financial muscle, business brains, and government are all crowded onto the north shore as are the most and best restaurants, the swanky shopping, round-the-clock social life and the finest cultural stages in town. If it's happening in Hong Kong, chances are it's happening here.

This is also the natural habitat of the expat. Major multinational and financial firms have always been headquartered on Hong Kong Island and expats working in Hong Kong will almost without exception find themselves in an office in this area. As a result, several nearby neighborhoods have been closely associated with expat settlement for the best part of a century and remain hubs for the community. With such a concentration of foreign residents, it's no surprise that English is effectively the first language in many of these areas and widely understood in others. This is very much part of the attraction, as is the availability of expat-orientated services and apartments styled towards western sensibilities. Quite simply put, if you're an expat, this is the easiest place to live, where you'll suffer the least culture shock and face the fewest difficulties. But, there is also more to Hong Kong Island than skyscrapers. On the island's south side are some of the most sought after beachside addresses in town, and sumptuous mansions that would make a Saudi Prince blush. Away from the playboys and champagne, there are also more traditional, local neighborhoods where wet markets and street-side food predominates.

The common theme wherever you're renting on the island is price. Hong Kong Island rent prices are top dollar and include some of the priciest per foot real estate in the world. Whether you're looking at marble floored mansion or a room where you and your luggage don't fit at the same time, rates are the highest the city has on offer. There are also other drawbacks. The pollution is Dickensian and likely to leave you feeling like the Marlboro Man at the end of the day and the crowds and noise can seem relentless.

KOWLOON

Overcrowded and somewhat unattractive, what Kowloon lacks in beauty it makes up for in character. Distinctly and visibly more Chinese in character than Hong Kong Island, the cramped quarters living means much of life here still takes place on the street corner and revolves around commerce. Family-owned shops spill out on the sidewalk and street markets clog the streets, while the area's humble Cantonese restaurants are the most mouthwatering in Hong Kong. With barely room to breathe, there is an enjoyable urgency and energy to life that is at times both invigorating and exhausting. Rent prices here are dramatically reduced and while buildings are run down, it's still sage. Links to Triads are notorious and legitimate, but like the rest of Hong Kong there is no feeling of menace even after dark. Beyond the seething streets at its center, Kowloon does have a softer side and several neighborhoods with leafy streets, international schools, and a suburban pace that's popular with expats.

NEW TERRITORIES

For those unimpressed by skyscrapers and high octane living, Hong Kong's rural hinterland in the New Territories is the ideal alternative. Ignoring the ugly new town developments that have now swallowed up more than half of Hong Kong's population, much of the area is unspoiled wilderness, wetlands, and soaring mountains.

The remoteness of New Territories compared to Hong Kong Island is now what attracts an increasing number of professionals and expats to relocate out here. Its bustling market towns and small villages offer not only a respite from the suffocating, pollution-clogged streets, but a completely different, simpler, quieter and more community-based lifestyle. Village life is particularly distinct and despite the proximity to the modernity and internationalism of the city, life and customs in these small villages has stubbornly weathered the changes of a hundred years and are grounded in Chinese values and tradition. Yes, there are satellite dishes poking out from the close-knit streets and Hello Kitty t-shirts hanging from the clothes line, but many inhabitants still hail from the same clan, the ancestral hall remains the focus of city celebrations, and the village elder, rather than local government, is the true master of village bureaucracy. Of course the classic drawback to country living applies—there is very little work out here even for locals and virtually nothing for expats, so you'll need to commute. While the public transportation network for access to the bigger market towns, where you'll find services and malls, is excellent, living in the smaller villages requires a car. You'll also be plunged into the world of village politics, where disputes over parking spaces, illegal construction, and land are legendary, and you'll want to do as much research into your neighbor as the property.

OUTLYING ISLANDS

Scattered throughout the South China Sea, Hong Kong has over 200 Outlying Islands, although less than a dozen are inhabited and of these only Lantau and Lamma support substantial populations and frequent transportation. Most of the inhabited islands have traditionally been host to fishing communities, but as the local fishing industry has dried up so has the money—and, the drift of younger people to the city to look for work has proved a fatal blow to many. In the opposite direction have come professionals, and a not insubstantial number of expats, looking to parachute out of the rat race—at least after work.

On the islands themselves the major draw is undoubtedly natural beauty and the sort of laidback lifestyle that lets you enjoy the surroundings. Aside from northeastern Lantau, which has been the scene of some ferocious development in recent years, and is the location of the airport and Hong Kong Disneyland, the islands remain largely undeveloped. Covered in lush greenery and surrounded by long strips of golden sands, you can choose between life in a sleepy fishing village or complete isolation buried beneath the greenery. Property also tends to be far cheaper and the availability of generously sized village houses, many of which have now been renovated and restyled for the more demanding professional immigrants, is a major attraction.

Of course complete isolation means just that, isolation, and you'll need to compromise substantially on access to amenities. You'll still get internet and satellite TV, find a handful of shops and a bar in the nearest village, as well as the best seafood restaurants in Hong Kong but that's about it. Depending on where you live, public transportation may be basic or non existent. Getting to work, and if you have kids, getting them to an international school will mean joining the ferry commute and although none of the islands are more than an hour from the city, the morning and evening float remains a major gripe for island inhabitants.

HONG KONG ISLAND

When people around the world talk about Hong Kong, they mean Hong Kong Island. All those glossy pictures splashed across the front of weighty travel books and snapshots plastered on movie posters are of the island's awe-inspiring cityscape. At the heart of this is Central, which, as the name suggests, is the city's business and administrative nerve center. If you've come to Hong Kong to make millions, this is where they print the money. You only need to look up to find proof of its success; blanketing the island's north shore are the offices of multinationals, the best restaurants and nightlife, luxury shopping malls, and the city's cultural hub. For some, the island is Hong Kong.

Expats are mostly drawn to the island because it offers Western restaurants and food, is served well by international schools and private hospitals, and most importantly English is widely understood. It's also where most expats work. Residential options are broad, although rarely cheap and almost never spacious. Most expats plump for one of the centrally located

© MARTYNA SZMYTKOWSKA

bedroom communities, which offer an easy commute to Central. There are also a number of more traditional districts that offer substantially cheaper rents. On the south side of the island, residents enjoy rare access to green spaces and beaches in luxury, low-rise apartments and houses set among small fishing villages, and towns like Stanley.

If there's a downside to living on the island, apart from the rents, it's the lifestyle. The relentless pace of life, while exhilarating, can also be exhausting. People put in long hours both at work and on their bar stools and it's hard not to do the same. But, if you want to experience Hong Kong head on, at its breakneck best, it's the only place to be.

LAY OF THE LAND

Just 80 square kilometers in size and containing less than 7 percent of Hong Kong's total area, Hong Kong Island is home to more than 1.3 million people. Much of the population is squeezed along the length of the northern seashore, facing Kowloon, from Kennedy Town in the east to Chai Wan in the west. The hubs, from west to east, are the downtown districts of Sheung Wan, Central, Wan Chai, and Causeway Bay. These are mostly commercial districts rather than residential. The amount of people and the pace drops off in the neighborhoods in Island East and Island West on either side.

Dwarfing the skyscrapers of the north shore is Victoria Peak, whose slopes are home to residential districts such as Mid-Levels and Pok Fu Lam and, at its crown, the swanky Peak neighborhood. Crouched beneath The Peak and Tai Tam Country Park on the west of the island is Happy Valley, the gateway to the south side. Hong Kong Island's personal pocket of countryside, the rugged hills of the south side have minimized development to small communities and villages on the seafront, such as Deepwater Bay, Repulse Bay, Shek O, and, the hub for the area, the seaside town of Stanley.

Where to Live

CENTRAL AND MID-LEVELS

With all the relentless PR painting Central as skyscraper city, many people feel Central is the only place to unpack their boxes. In fact, this is about the only place in the city where you can't live. As Hong Kong's flagship financial district, all the space here is office space and downtown Central doesn't really have much to offer apartment seekers. Those that exist are found on the start

Slopes are part of life in Hong Kong and you'll often be faced with an Everest-like climb to get to where you're going.

of the slope towards the Peak, behind the bar headquarters of Lan Kwai Fong and along Hollywood Road.

Most people who want to live near Central end up in Mid-Levels, a smart strip of residential property half way up the Peak. This classy bedroom community has long been Hong Kong's favorite expat enclave. Not unlike taking the Chinatown concept and turning it upside down, you'll find little local culture here; instead there are international schools, private hospitals, and supermarkets laden with home comforts all geared towards English-speaking expats. For some, this is a little too much like Hong Kong–lite; for others, it's the only place in the city they would consider living.

Too expat or not, Mid-Levels feels clean, quiet, and private, despite being almost wholly high rise, and is enjoyably crowd-free. Its short distance yet massive difference to the sardine streets of Central mean many residents feel they can strike a good balance between life and work by living here. One of the major attractions of the neighborhood is a near one-kilometer-long system of outdoor escalators which run from Des Vouex Road in Central to Conduit Road in Mid-Levels and shuttle commuters down the hill in the morning and back up the rest of the day. It's Hong Kong's easiest walk to work. The area is also well served by minibuses to destinations all over Hong Kong Island.

Running parallel to the coastline, all the way from Sheung Wan to Happy Valley, Mid-Levels is a big neighborhood that is commonly split into Mid-Levels East, Mid-Levels Central, and Mid-Levels West, although there are no definitive lines between the three. Its location and executive residents mean demanding rents. You'll find more luxury apartment complexes fitted with clubhouses, swimming pools, and other Hollywood luxuries than anywhere else in Hong Kong. But prices and quality are not uniform and although there aren't any bona fide budget areas, there are cheaper streets.

Most of the highest priced apartments are clustered around the east side of the escalator in Mid-Levels Central, perched directly above Central and SoHo. Even a basic one bedroom in this area comes in somewhere around HK$20,000–25,000 and higher. Move farther east towards Hong Kong Park and Magazine Gap Road and you'll find newer, more luxurious pads with clubhouses, penthouses, and harbor views with hefty prices. Three or four bedrooms can easily threaten HK$100,000. If you want to live in Mid-Levels for access to the city rather than for the luxury accommodations, apartments farther down the hill, closer to the city, tend to be older, smaller, and considerably cheaper. The far end of the district, perched above Sheung Wan, is the original Mid-Levels, now Mid-Levels West. Apartments here are squashed in a little closer and are more mature in years, but still offer the benefits of Mid-Levels' quieter surroundings and access to the city. A one bedroom here can usually be found below HK$20,000, occasionally as low as HK$15,000. Wherever you're shopping for real estate in Mid-Levels, remember there is a lot of real estate available, so take your time in finding something that balances what you want with a budget you're happy with.

WAN CHAI

Rarely advertised as a residential area, Wan Chai is more closely associated with pubs, nightclubs, and sex workers, and while you can certainly find all three, that's just a handful of streets in a large neighborhood. Less talked about is the fact that it's second only to Central for skyscrapers and business. It also has an excellent selection of mid-range and budget apartment options.

Sandwiched between the sheen of Central and the shopping malls of Causeway Bay, Wan Chai does more than any other neighborhood to capture Hong Kong's East-meets-West reputation. With high rises and high density, the streets are some of the oldest in Hong Kong and crammed with family-run shops, blue-collar restaurants, and, despite repeated government evictions, various street markets. This traditional face shares the stage with a string of British pubs, streets full of international restaurants, and Italian delis that rub shoulders with Chinese medicine shops. The streets are combatively busy with people and ideal for those who want to live downtown.

In all honesty, Wan Chai could also do with a lick of paint. Much of the housing stock is older and often in less than pristine condition, although newer buildings are springing up and there are a lot of options in size and quality. The rents are very competitive. A designer one bedroom on swanky Star Street could cost as little as HK$15,000, while a pokier and older apartment in the midst of the district will rarely climb above HK$10,000.

For the young, single, and thirsty, Wan Chai is home to arguably Hong Kong's best bar and club scene on Lockhart Road and the surrounding streets. Although, be warned, while it might be fun to drink in a bar, it's less fun to live above one. The late-night noise of revelers screaming at sports, taxi drivers honking horns, and *mama-sans* (sex workers) catcalling to potential punters makes the intersection of Lockhart Road and Luard Road, as well as streets nearby, well worth avoiding. The north of the district is mostly commercial, while the majority of the residential property is clustered around the south side.

© MARTYNA SZMYTKOWSKA

You'll need a head for heights if you live on the island. Views out your window can make you weak at the knees.

HAPPY VALLEY

One of Hong Kong's most appealing neighborhoods and sought-after addresses, Happy Valley owes its appeal to an enviable location, away from the congested districts on the shoreline, that has allowed it to develop its own distinct, village-like community character. While still busy with high rises and just 10 minutes away from Causeway Bay, the neighborhood's setting around Sing Woo High Street with local bakeries, cafés, and shops feels more settled and less chaotic than downtown, without sacrificing any vibrancy or cosmopolitan allure. The area has been an established expat stronghold since the British carved out a racecourse here back in the 19th century—though unlike Mid-Levels, it doesn't feel exclusively or overwhelmingly expat.

Happy Valley is rightly regarded as an upscale neighborhood and although there are a variety of properties, from older low rises through newer high rises to luxury complexes, rent at all levels tends to be expensive. People pay for the location and it's not a neighborhood in which you would find a bargain. The average rent for a one bedroom is HK$17,000–19,000, more, if you want to rent something brand new or with racecourse views. While some of the older buildings may look a little weathered on the outside, they are usually well kept inside, roomier than more modern flats, and often offer communal roof access.

Happy Valley has a fairly settled community and when properties do become available they are often snapped up quickly, meaning there is little room for shopping around. Aside from the normal real estate agent route, it's worth checking out the notice board at the local Wellcome and asking around at The Jockey and The Chapel pubs.

There are a couple of drawbacks to living in Happy Valley. There is no MTR, so your commute options are reduced to chugging along on the tram, which is a less regular branch service, or getting snarled in traffic on the bus. And, while the Happy Valley races are one of Happy Valley's great attractions, especially if you have a racecourse view, they can be less than happy when you're trying to make an emergency diaper run to the local pharmacy only to find the roads crammed with trams, buses, and cars—as happens on most Wednesday evenings.

THE PEAK

Effectively separating the men with mustaches from their Chinese subjects, the Peak was originally carved out by Hong Kong's colonial elite as a refuge from the sweltering summer heat and the hungry mosquitoes. They built luxury mansions and villas, were ferried around by sedan chair, and presumably sat around plotting to turn more of the map red. Back then the Chinese were banned from living on the Peak. Today the only obstacle is the depth of your pockets as the neighborhood has lost none of its prestige. Stomping ground for tai pans (top business executives), Cantopop stars, and the boardroom of HSBC, the Peak is not only the most exclusive address in the city, but the real estate here is, per foot, the most expensive in the world.

Aside from dodging the dastardly mosquitoes and nudging the temperatures down a notch or two, much of the Peak's pull is simply the status of having an address here. It's also the only place on northern Hong Kong Island where you can find low rise, low density housing. The detached houses and small villa complexes sit down secluded driveways or on small streets surrounded by greenery. Its hilltop location also means breathtaking views of Victoria Harbour and the South China Sea and a little less smog drifting in over your morning cornflakes. Despite the prices, or because of the prices, there is usually no shortage of properties available on the Peak—so long as you're prepared to pay. Renting a luxurious, three-bedroom or more house won't leave you much change from HK$300,000, but you will get a rooftop terrace, swimming pool, and other tasty extras. For slightly cheaper prices, consider looking at the apartment complexes farther down the hill, towards Mid-Levels, or on the backside of the Peak, although there is little around for below HK$50,000.

Apart from the rents, Peak living does have a couple of disadvantages. Its location means public transport is not fantastic by Hong Kong's demanding standards. The Peak Tram is an efficient drop to Central in 15 minutes, but is not particularly frequent and is prohibitively expensive, while the more regular bus services can often find themselves snarled in traffic along the Peak's slender roads. There are schools, hospitals, shops, and a Park N Shop supermarket in The Peak Galleria shopping mall, although residents grumble that goods seem to attract a premium price.

NORTH POINT, QUARRY BAY, AND ISLAND EAST

Critics dismiss Island West as living out in the sticks, but with excellent connections to downtown, some of Hong Kong Island's cheapest rents and in Quarry Bay one of the city's most rapidly developing districts, it's hard not to consider it as a place to live.

Settled by mainland refugees in the 1950s and 1960s, North Point is very much a traditional neighborhood and considers itself a bastion for Chinese culture. Busy, but not mobbed, it feels like part of downtown but more Chinese in character. If you came to Hong Kong to experience another culture rather than find shadows of your own, then the wet markets, cha chen cheengs (inexpensive neighborhood diners that serve their idea of Western food), and nose-curdling smells of North Point are an excellent base. This is also one of the cheapest areas on Hong Kong Island, and although the district is older and feels more than a little beat up, there are well-maintained apartments available if you scratch around a little. The bill for your very own box—with separate bedroom—should be HK$8,000–9,000, heading towards HK$10,000–12,000 for something that's been painted since Woodstock.

Just up the road, Quarry Bay has quenched Hong Kong's thirst for more office space, slotting in sparkling skyscrapers and smart, residential high rises. It feels modern and considerably less crowded when compared to Central and the favorable rents have seen some of Hong Kong's blockbuster companies, such as the SCMP, relocate out here. Hot on their heels have come the massive Cityplaza shopping mall and many outlets of Lan Kwai Fong bars and restaurants, centered around the Taikoo Place commercial property and the Taikoo Place residential estate, served by their own Tai Koo MTR station. While the brand new apartment complexes here have fewer gimmicks than comparative properties in Mid-Levels, they offer a lot more floor space for your dollar and have proved a hit with middle-class Hong Kongers looking for a more sensible living space at a more sensible price. Modest apartments that have just a few amenities but room to breathe start at around HK$10,000 for a one bedroom and go up to HK$30,000 for four bedrooms.

KENNEDY TOWN, CYBERPORT, AND ISLAND WEST

While it may not have the cachet of Central or Mid-Levels, it also doesn't have the sky-high rents: In recent years Island West, particularly Kennedy Town, has become an increasingly popular neighborhood for expats of more modest means.

Off the MTR line, Kennedy Town was historically derided as little more than a sleepy suburb. But residents here value the more peaceful, less clogged streets and harbor-side location. It's also shoulder to shoulder with Central, meaning commutes can be as little as 15 minutes, a little more during rush hour. While Kennedy Town is almost wholly residential, there are local restaurants, expat-orientated supermarkets, and all other amenities in the district, including the University of Hong Kong and the community that surrounds academic life. Housing in Kennedy Town is all high rise and reasonably high density and the majority of apartments are middle-aged and mid-range, a combination that delivers very affordable rents. Studios and one bedrooms sometimes go for as little as HK$8,000 and two bedrooms for HK$10,000–12,000. For something more upscale, one-bedroom apartments in the popular Merton building can be had for HK$15,000.

Be warned, with the slated extension of the MTR into Kennedy Town more upmarket residential apartments have started to appear, bringing more expats, more Western restaurants and bars, and higher rents.

Farther west from Kennedy Town is Pok Fu Lam and the futuristicly-named Cyberport. Rural Pok Fu Lam enjoys an enviable setting, nestled at the foot of the Peak as it slopes off into the South China Sea. It's popular for its low-rise apartment blocks and houses, which are usually more competitively priced than those on the south side of the island. For a three-bedroom, low-rise apartment on a quiet street expect to pay HK$25,000 and up. Although Pok Fu Lam is of a considerable size and includes the original Chinese village of Pok Fu Lam, now almost wholly swallowed up by the high rises that surround it, it really doesn't have an independent town center and can feel quite isolated—for better or worse.

Farther west, Pok Fu Lam turns into Cyberport, a planned commercial development that was conceived as Hong Kong's miniature version of Silicon Valley. It's a cutting-edge hub for IT and digital technology companies that has had limited success. Home to a cinema, shopping mall, and much of the area's amenities, Cyberport also has some seriously luxurious high-rise apartment complexes, although considering the sterile surroundings and distance into downtown, rents could be considered stiff. The most famous and most palatial is the unfortunately named Belchers, where two-bedroom units start at around HK$30,000.

STANLEY AND ISLAND SOUTH

This is Hong Kong Island's rural retreat. What the south side of the island lacks in MTR access, transport, and amenities, it makes up for with golden beaches, silent nights, and the Hong Kong holy grail—houses. Because all the property out here is either low-rise townhouses or stand-alone houses, both prices and demand are very high and you're unlikely to find any leeway on rent. What you will find are properties that make the maximum out of their surroundings, with stunning sea views and jungle greenery on your doorstep. Most houses are built with families in mind, including three or four bedrooms, while apartment complexes are generally gated and feature parking, shared swimming pools, and other amenities. The area is popular with expats, so you should have little problem getting by in English.

The most luxurious villas are found in the neighboring enclaves of Deepwater Bay and Repulse Bay, which have long been exclusive residential communities. Palatial properties with equally royal prices can be found off Island Road/Repulse Bay Road, set a little way up the hill for expansive views of the sea. The communities here are small, private, and loaded and you can expect to be rubbing shoulders with CEOs, bankers, and other people who can handle a golf club. There are supermarkets and schools nearby, if little else. Repulse Bay, the slightly larger of the two, has The Repulse Bay, an upmarket shopping mall with a number of pricy restaurants. Both areas have beautiful beaches that are remarkably quiet during the week, although the sea itself is as dirty as week-old dishwater.

If you're looking for stand-alone houses, you'll find them tucked away behind Repulse Bay or sequestered behind long driveways near Stanley, the south side's main settlement. Set out on a peninsula, this seaside town is

© ROSS TALBOT

sunset over the beach on the south side of Hong Kong Island

popular with tourists and locals alike for its low-rise, laidback vacation appeal. Its small shopping mall, brand new arts center, and attractive promenade of restaurants and bars make it big enough and busy enough to justify its town tag, but it's lost little of its character and community appeal. Well, except on weekends. One of the major drawbacks of Stanley is the influx of tourists each Saturday and Sunday.

Prices and properties on the south side vary greatly, from a shared, three-bedroom low rise at HK$60,000 to small, three bedroom houses featuring gardens and sea views at HK$150,000. Because everything is aimed at the top end of the market most properties have been kept in good shape and boast a decent line of luxuries.

As ever, your major concern when considering an out of town location is the potential commute. For practical reasons-to get to school and the super-market—many people who live out here own a car. Unfortunately, Deepwater Bay, Repulse Bay, and Stanley, as well as everything in between, are effectively connected by a single winding road and by tunnel to Happy Valley; consequently, traffic can be horrendous. There are frequent bus services along the road between Central and Stanley, but this can be part of the problem, as you're often stuck behind slow double-deckers. Rush hours and weekends may leave you needing a massage, a whiskey, or both.

Much more affordable than the triumvirate of Deepwater Bay, Repulse Bay, and Stanley, secluded Shek O in the far southeastern side of the island is often overlooked by prospective tenants. This small seaside village remains largely

PRIME LIVING LOCATIONS

undeveloped, unpretentious, and engagingly ramshackle. The snaking lanes are home to both traditional village houses and more modern developments, while the green belt surrounding the village hides more ostentatious mansions and villas. Renting in Shek O is much in demand and, given its small size, very few houses actually make it on to the market. Instead, they are rented out by word of mouth in the village and if you want to rent here, the best plan is to arrive and ask around. The lack of available property also makes it hard to stick an average price tag on property in Shek O. Village houses with three or four bedrooms sometimes pop up for HK$60,000–100,000, depending on the view.

The village is about as isolated as you can get on Hong Kong Island and is only served by a 40-minute minibus service to Shau Kai Wan. In Shek O you'll find some basic grocery shops and a couple of restaurants and bars that cater to the tourists that invade on weekends.

Getting Around

Nowhere in Hong Kong enjoys better transportation links than Hong Kong Island, particularly the north shoreline. The south side is less well connected thanks to small, winding roads and although there is a constant parade of bus services, many people out here use a car. Mid-Levels' residents worried about sweaty climbs can utilize the Mid-Levels escalator, the longest system of outdoor escalators in the world.

MTR

The Island MTR line travels the whole length of the north shore, from Sheung Wan in the west to Chai Wan in the east and is scheduled to be extended to the south of the island and farther west to

© BARTOSZ KOŚCIELAK

Carting people down to work in the morning and back up the evening, the Mid-Levels escalator is part of the attraction of living in Mid-Levels.

Kennedy Town. It is both the most frequent and quickest way to get around. It also offers four underwater connections to Kowloon via Central, Admiralty, North Point, and Quarry Bay.

TRAMS AND BUSES

Above ground, Hong Kong's famous trams shadow the MTR from Kennedy Town in the west to Shau Kei Wan in the east, with a handy branch line running south to Happy Valley. The many bus services that crisscross the island can actually be a better way to get to and from places not directly on the MTR line and to get where you are going at night. Less useful is the Peak Tram, whose tourist prices mean the bus is a better way to climb the slopes.

FERRIES

The indomitable Star Ferry from Central, Wan Chai, and North Point continues to be a popular and cheap way to cross the harbor. Central is also Hong Kong's ferry hub and most of the outlying island ferries connect to it. From the Hong Kong–Macau ferry terminal ferries travel to Macau and the cities along the Pearl River Delta.

GREATER HONG KONG

Branching out into Greater Hong Kong may offer you the opportunity to find more budget-friendly housing, a less frenetic pace of life, and a chance to experience a bit of the rural countryside. Kowloon is favored for its proximity to Hong Kong Island by MTR, but the choice of accommodations and housing is slim, and leans towards the old and cramped side. Longer-term expat residents are drawn to the New Territories, sandwiched between Hong Kong and mainland China, where they can experience the isolation and traditions of tiny villages. The Outlying Islands, on the other hand, attract urban refugees fleeing the pollution and pace of Hong Kong Island and Kowloon. The pull is low-rise housing, friendly neighbors, and lazy days spent exploring the green hills and empty beaches.

© MARTYNA SZMYTKOWSKA

Kowloon

Separated from Hong Kong Island by Victoria Harbour and a mere three-minute MTR ride, some expats still call a trip to Kowloon a trip to the dark side; we even knew one girl who remained convinced Kowloon was in China, no matter how many maps we flung at her.

Kowloon is Hong Kong with some of the sheen stripped away: grittier, smellier, and louder than its cousin across the water and, in many people's opinion, a lot more authentic. The neighborhoods here are predominantly Chinese and the street markets, street food, and temples are more directly rooted in Chinese culture. Both the footprint of the British and the clamor of banks and business feel more distant, although it would be unfair to claim that Kowloon can't match Hong Kong in internationalism or commerce. The blue-collar neighborhoods have long been home to pockets of Thai, Vietnamese, and perhaps most famously Indian, Pakistani, and Bangladesh communities, some of whom can trace their roots back to families who splashed ashore with the British as police officers, sailors, and soldiers.

The main reservation for expats looking to make the move to Kowloon is the choice of accommodations, which tend to be old and extremely cramped. Mongkok is the most densely populated piece of real estate on the planet and the rows upon rows of decrepit apartment blocks that blot out the sun are few people's dream destination. Unfortunately, it sets the tone for much of Kowloon; but things are changing. The under-construction West Kowloon Cultural District now boasts a number of high-end luxury units, a major shopping mall, and what is soon to be Hong Kong's tallest skyscraper, while Kowloon Tong offers something most Hong Kongers believe is just a fairytale: a house.

LAY OF THE LAND

Officially Kowloon is a mere 47 square kilometers, which may account for why it feels so impossibly crowded. Historically, Kowloon was the area that ran from the Tsim Sha Tsui peninsula, which faces Hong Kong Island across Victoria Harbour, to Boundary Street in the north. Everything up to this point the British gained in perpetuity from the Chinese, while anything north of this line was the New Territories and only ceded for 99 years. Today, the built-up area north of Boundary Street is officially known as New Kowloon, but more normally just Kowloon.

At its northern end Kowloon is bounded by eight hills, known as the nine dragons, which are the source of the area's name. Legend has it that Kowloon

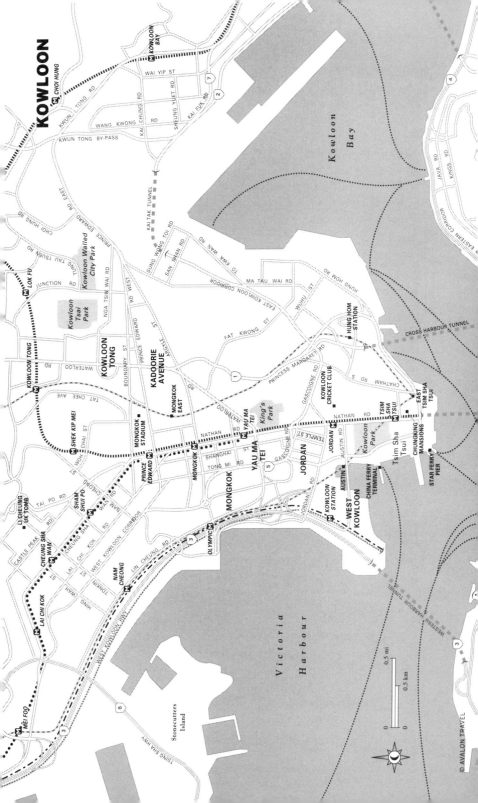

Nathan Road is the bustling commercial heart of Kowloon and the area's main thoroughfare.

© RORY BOLAND

was named when a Song-era Emperor spotted the eight hills and claimed they must be home to eight dragons, before one of his groveling groupies piped up that the Emperor was also a dragon so there were in fact nine dragons. It's a tear-jerking story.

In more recent times, thanks to being flat as a pancake, Kowloon was the site of Hong Kong's Kai Tak Airport prior to the opening of the new airport on Lantau. Strict height restrictions on the surrounding land kept Kowloon to medium-rise buildings in the shadow of the skyscrapers across the water. With the airport gone and the restrictions removed, Kowloon is quickly spreading skywards. Tying the whole area together is Nathan Road, a broad avenue that begins at the Star Ferry in the south and unfolds north through most of the area's key neighborhoods.

WHERE TO LIVE
West Kowloon

Hong Kong's fastest developing district, West Kowloon is supposed to be the face of new Kowloon, mirroring the high-end shopping and skyscrapers that have long taunted the peninsula from across the harbor. Free from the airport-building restrictions that once confined the area, West Kowloon is building big and building bold. At its heart is Union Square, a series of high-end residential complexes reaching 50 floors or more. These are some of the most luxurious apartment buildings in Hong Kong and the properties buck Hong Kong's taste for tiny, with extravagant floor spaces, as well as clubhouses and a leisure-center

The fast food spots in Chunking Mansions have the most authentic Indian food in Hong Kong.

list of extras, such as swimming pools and badminton courts. The Sorrento, Hong Kong's tallest residential building is here, and its ritzy apartments often fetch prices just as handsome as Mid-Levels across the water. The three- and four-bedroom apartments go for HK$30,000–60,000. Prices in nearby developments are similar, even for smaller living spaces.

The anchor piece of Union Square is Hong Kong's tallest skyscraper, the 118-floor International Commerce Centre which, at its base, rubs shoulders with the acclaimed Elements shopping center and Kowloon Station, where you catch the Airport Express. It's an undoubtedly impressive project that covers almost 12 million square feet. When they finally hammer in the last skyscraper it's likely to be one of Hong Kong's most important neighborhoods, although, given the constant wrangling, redesigns, and arguments, aliens may land first. West Kowloon is also penciled in as the site for the West Kowloon Cultural District, a development designed to be Hong Kong's prime arts and culture hub. It's certainly a good place for an investment. As of today, much of the primary residential and commercial building have been completed, although the area stills feels a little cutoff from the natural ebb and flow of Kowloon.

Mongkok, Yau Ma Tei, and Jordan

The guts of Kowloon are made up by the three adjoining neighborhoods of Mongkok, Yau Ma Tei, and Jordan, all of which can be summed up in one word: crowded. Mongkok is the most densely populated piece of real estate on the planet and the neighborhoods of Yau Ma Tei and Jordan, which it blends into, are not much roomier. At the best of times, it feels busy; at the worst of times, the constant noise and movement feels like being thrown around a Six Flags rollercoaster. Add in the humidity to all this humanity and after a few minutes you'll look like you were drenched on the log ride as well.

What these crowds do bring is an incredible energy and there is nowhere in Hong Kong where street life feels more vibrant. On its cramped streets everything spills onto the sidewalk and you'll find snake restaurants, the city's best dim sum joints, trendy teenage fashion stores, and mahjong halls all rubbing shoulders. It is without doubt one of Hong Kong's most atmospheric districts, but only the more adventurous expat or possibly the hard of hearing would want to live here. The markets and the shops go late, as do the noise and the crowds, up to midnight.

Most of the tenements here have been banged up and bandaged up and look like they've come out the wrong side of a tank siege. Conditions inside are usually no better, with up to three generations packing into single-bedroom flats. The only real attraction is the absolute bottom

Mongkok is the busiest place on the planet and Mongkok Station is usually jammed shoulder to shoulder.

of the barrel rents. While the grime and gloom is likely to outweigh the very bottom properties, there are more modest apartments on the market that offer bargain rates without the cockroaches. For the rooms that are little more than a wardrobe, you could conceivably pay less than HK$3,000—but then you could also sleep under a bridge for free. More acceptable apartments, with the wonders of plumbing and electricity, start around HK$5,000; a fully furnished, reasonably well-turned-out two-bedroom can cost as little as HK$10,000.

Kowloon Tong and Kadoorie Avenue

A massive neighborhood in northern Kowloon, Kowloon Tong may look a little rough around the edges, but at its heart are some of the plushest streets in the city. On the broad, leafy streets around Oxford Street is where the British government once housed its civil servants in considerable comfort and the low-rise luxury housing now attracts the city's middle and upper classes, including a couple of Cantopop warblers and kung fu stars.

There are some very grandiose mansions in the area as well as more pragmatic townhouses. Properties have usually been around the block a few times, but are well kept and can boast a lot more square feet for your dollar than on Hong Kong Island. When compared to houses in other locations, the HK$100,000–130,000

THE CANCER OF KOWLOON

Before the bulldozers brought it all crashing down in 1993, Kowloon Walled City Park was Hong Kong's very own slice of the Wild West: a lawless slum suburb that was home to illegal brothels, casinos, and drinking dens frequented by criminals. It also has quite a story.

The product of an international quirk of history, the city was first developed as a garrison town, set behind walls and watchtowers, from where the Chinese could keep an eye on the barbarian British who had been handed Hong Kong Island in 1841. By 1899 the British had added the New Territories to their big red colonial map, all be it on lease, but in their rush to get pens on paper the British allowed the Chinese to retain sovereignty over Kowloon Walled City, turning it into a virtual exclave within the colony. Predictably, less than a year later, the British tore up the treaty and marched the Qing officials and troops out of the city and back across the border. Inside, residents remained, but the walled city quickly disappeared down the diplomatic cracks, claimed by both parties but administered by neither.

During World War II, occupying Japanese forces did what the British had been threatening to do for a half a century, flattened the walls and the village, but as the war ended and the British sailed back into town to collect the keys to the colony, any hopes of the Kowloon City problem going away were dashed by a rush of squatters from the mainland who took up residence among the ruins. Knee-deep in five-year tractor plans and reading red books, communist China forgot about the exclave, except to periodically remind the British to keep their hands off whenever they threatened to clear the fast developing slum. Diplomatic niceties and the million-man army camped out across the border persuaded the British to stay out.

With no administration and no rules, the city descended into the depths of dystopia. Poorly-constructed high rises carpeted the city's 6.5 acres: standing only a few feet apart, they blotted out

asking price for a three-bedroom house here is very honest. Unfortunately, you aren't the only one who thinks so and relatively few houses actually make it onto the market. Over on Kadoorie Avenue, which is often included in Kowloon Tong, despite being closer to Mongkok East, are some of the most ostentatious houses, bold in both design and space. If the quiet neighborhood is the appeal, rather than the houses, spacious low-rise apartments also provide a good value, with two and three bedrooms costing as low as HK$15,000 and HK$35,000, respectively.

Unlike Mid-Levels, Kowloon Tong has a more enjoyable mix of locals and expats, with enough of the latter to find English is well spoken and supermarkets well stocked. The area is somewhat removed from the rest of Kowloon, an enjoyable oasis from the shop-clogged streets. Nevertheless, you'll find all the amenities you need nearby at the mammoth Kowloon Tong shopping mall, where you can also catch the MTR. Thanks to its former the sun and created a maze of dark, dank alleyways. To avoid the alleys and the constant climbing of stairs, residents erected makeshift walkways between buildings and rooftops, so flimsy they would have given Indiana Jones wobbly knees. With little municipal management, residents sank water wells, stole electricity from the Hong Kong power supply, and rubbish rotted in the streets or was dumped on the city outskirts. There was reportedly only a single postman assigned to the whole city.

Beyond the reach of the law, drug abuse, prostitution, and gambling flourished, although not without the help of the upstanding citizens of Hong Kong, who would often visit the "Cancer of Kowloon" to indulge in their particular vice. While there was no border, fence, or guards, most of the refugees and their families stayed in the city because they risked arrest if they tried to work in Hong Kong. Instead, sweatshops and workhouses provided employment, although the fact that you didn't need a license to operate here attracted failed doctors, dentists, and other tradespeople. Depending on who you listen to, local community groups kept the peace and attempted to bring some sort of order, pointing to the schools and clinics set up in later years; others claim that the only authority came from the Triad groups (criminal organizations) who thrived. By the 1980s it was estimated over 30,000 people lived in just over 6.5 acres of land, easily making the city the most densely populated place on the planet.

By 1987, Britain and China were friends again and as the handover of the whole of Hong Kong loomed, the Chinese finally gave the go ahead for residents to be re-housed and the city demolished. Today, the only remaining building is the Yamen, once the headquarters for the 19th century garrison, and now the centerpiece of Kowloon Walled City. Inside the Yamen, the City of Thousand Faces exhibition features photos and relics documenting the incredible life and times of Kowloon Walled City.

life as a civil servant retreat, there are also many international schools and clubhouses based here.

PUBLIC TRANSPORTATION

Best served by the MTR, Kowloon has five lines snaking through it, connecting the area both to Hong Kong Island and the New Territories. The East Rail even travels as far as Shenzhen. The most important are the red Tsuen Wan line, which connects Central with Tsim Sha Tsui, Jordan, Yau Ma Tei, and Mongkok, before swerving through the west of Kowloon towards the new town of Tsuen Wan, and the green Kwun Tong line, which starts at Yau Ma Tei and connects Kowloon Tong and many of the major neighborhoods in the east of Kowloon.

Kowloon is also a hub for transportation to China. The Hung Hom Train Station is the terminal for all intercity trains to Guangzhou, Shanghai, and

Beijing. From the Hong Kong China Ferry Terminal in Tsim Sha Tsui there are several scheduled ferry services to cities along the Pearl River Delta and regular ferries to Macau.

New Territories

Sandwiched between Kowloon and the Chinese border, the New Territories are Hong Kong's forgotten backyard. In stark contrast to the city's concrete-suit reputation, 85 percent of Hong Kong is actually rural and boasts a beautiful landscape of jungle greenery, mountains, and unspoiled beaches. But as pretty as all this is, the truth is, very few expats who move to Hong Kong are here to paint landscapes and play with plants and very few live in the New Territories. Those that do are often longer-term residents, drawn to the isolation and traditions of tiny villages. These provide an immersion into local Chinese culture and an unhurried, simple lifestyle, but feature few, if any, amenities. More recently, smaller towns on the south coast, with realistic quick city commutes have started attracting real estate–hungry but rent-shy city dwellers looking for their own slice of cheap peace and quiet.

Thanks to the lowest rents in Hong Kong, around half of the Hong Kong population has shifted to the New Territories in the past few decades, mostly wedged into New Town projects (the towns are actually known as the New Towns), such as Sha Tin and Tsuen Wan. Erected to house Hong Kong's swelling population, these bedroom communities provide high-rise housing at cheap rents, if little else. Lacking any real character, they are little more than domino rows of apartment buildings connected by the MTR to Kowloon.

© MARTYNA SZMYTKOWSKA

Much of the New Territories are covered by national parks and reserves, such as the Mai Po Marshes.

LAY OF THE LAND

Covering 747 kilometers from Kowloon in the south to the Chinese border in the north and banked in

© RORY BOLAND

Experience pure isolation in the New Territories.

the east and west by the South China Sea, the New Territories have traditionally been Hong Kong's great outdoors, home to mountains, valleys, and
wildlife-rich wetlands, as well as small fishing villages. Although it remains
a green getaway, half of Hong Kong now lives here and there are several New
Towns in various states of development. The biggest of these, Tsuen Wan, just
above Kowloon on the south west coast, is already racing towards a million
residents. Tuen Mun in the western New Territories and Sha Tin on the east
coast are the other major New Towns, boasting populations over 500,000 and
providing major hubs of transport and shopping for the surrounding villages.
In the southeast, Kowloon has nearly swallowed up Clearwater Bay into the
city, while the small but busy fishing town of Sai Kung remains protected by
its location, perched between sea and mountains. Thanks to the easy commute
times, the south coast, both east and west, has witnessed an increasing number of residential developments, such as Hong Kong Gold Coast. The further
north into the New Territories you go, the more isolated villages become and
villages near the border with China are off-limits to non-residents.

WHERE TO LIVE
Sai Kung
Those that fancy the laidback living and well-laundered lungs of the outlying
islands but are reluctant to become slaves to the ferry schedule are increasingly
considering Sai Kung as a place to live. Once a working-class fishing village, Sai
Kung is now more reliant on hooking tourists rather than fish and has essential
shops and services and a number of Western bars and restaurants. Despite this

development, it's lost little of its atmosphere or charm and remains enjoyably un-hurried, a place where you can walk down the street in sandals and shorts without getting knowing glances. Housing is all low rise, from village houses and three-floor apartment blocks in the town to more modern houses and more luxurious apartment complexes on its outskirts. Rents have, thus far, remained stubbornly low. In the town center you can pay as little as HK$12,000 for a two-bedroom basic apartment on one floor of a village house or HK$30,000 for a modern three-bedroom house next to the coastline with all the furnishings you want.

The catch? The commute. If you live in the town, buses can connect you to the MTRs in Hang Hau and Choi Hung in around 20 minutes and 30 minutes, respectively, although commutes into downtown Hong Kong Island are likely to top an hour, door-to-door. If you live outside of the actual town, realistically, you'll need your own set of wheels.

Clearwater Bay

Renting a house in Hong Kong usually means five-star mansions that come equipped with five bedrooms, white-gloved butlers, and sky-high rents. Un-fortunately, some people simply aren't built for apartment living, which is what makes Clearwater Bay and nearby Silverstrand such a fantastic find. Previously a rural peninsula in the far southeast of the New Territories, this area is increasingly resembling the middle-class suburb that Hong Kong has been missing. It combines low rise and medium density to come up with more modest and affordable houses, often complete with toy-sized gardens or roof

PRIME LIVING LOCATIONS

© RORY BOLAND

Grab yourself a live lunch from this Sai Kung seafood seller, before taking it across the road to be cooked at one of the seafood restaurants.

EXPAT PROFILE: MIRANDA LEE BREDING (WONG)

Hailing from a small town in Montana, Miranda Lee Breding (Wong) has always had an appetite to see more of the outside world, particularly China, and in 2002, fresh from high school, she landed in Hong Kong as a volunteer for YWAM (Youth with a Mission). She went on to see more of the Middle Kingdom before returning to Hong Kong in 2006, where she settled down with her husband and their son in a small village outside Yuen Long. Miranda is a journalist, an author, and a teacher.

Most people come to Hong Kong for the skyscrapers. How did you end up in a small village in the New Territories?

Well, when I first came to Hong Kong, I lived in the village we live in now simply because that was where the organization I was working with had their offices. But it became a sort of adopted hometown for me. When my husband and I returned later with our son, we chose it primarily because of my husband's daily commute to Shenzhen. He grew up on Hong Kong Island East and was nervous about moving so far out of the city, but it made more sense logistically.

But there were also less practical reasons. For me, as an American from the wide-open spaces of Montana, I never wanted to live in a shoebox apartment. For the same price or less as renting a 500-square-foot flat with no view in the city, we are able to rent two floors of a village house, which includes a covered roof area where we can have a BBQ and where we keep our washing machine and clothesline, as well as two balconies. In total, we have six bedrooms, two living rooms, two bathrooms, and two kitchens. We can look out our window and see trees and in Hong Kong that is quite the luxury.

What are some of the positives of village life?

I like the quality of life. Everything is small and recognizable. It's quiet – most of the time – the noise pollution is much less than in the city. We are near the wetlands park so we hear a lot of indigenous birds in the morning; there are even water buffalo who still roam through our village. People don't think of nature when they think of Hong Kong, but it surrounds us. There is a large, organic gardening co-op within walking distance from our house, we buy fresh produce including strawberries from the local gardeners, and we can even pick our own produce if we want to.

I also like that our village has a strong sense of history. Everywhere you walk there are ancestral homes, temples, and buildings that are literally hundreds of years old. In the city, these buildings often get demolished to make room for high-rise apartment complexes. For me, I enjoy the strong sense of place and history the old architecture exudes – it has a sense of permanence to it. The village is also proud of its heritage. For example, during Chinese New Year different family clans from this area hold lion dance competitions in our village and there are various other all-night festivals that the whole village attends. The community bonds are strong.

Speaking of community bonds, it's very unusual for expats to live in villages in Hong Kong, did the locals try and run you out of town?

We aren't the only expats: There are some Europeans and North Americans working for YWAM, African and Pakistani refugees attracted by the cheap rents, and a strong Nepalese community that dates back to a British army base that was once nearby.

Traditionally the villagers have been quite resistant to having people from outside the Tang clan live here – even Hong Kong locals from other parts of Hong Kong. But, over the past decade or so our village has increasingly opened up to "outsiders." At first, when we moved to the village, the local people somewhat ignored us. Our breakthrough came when my mother came to live with us for nine months. Age is respected in Hong Kong, particularly here, and they respected our "filial piety," which is incredibly important. After she left they were much friendlier towards us, although they have always liked my son.

Villages and villagers in the New Territories are often said to be more traditional than their city counterparts. To what extent have you found this is true?

Well, I think they may be more superstitious. At various cycles of the moon and surrounding holidays, you'll find the older people in the village lighting fire crackers and banging pots and pans at odd hours of the day – often in the very early morning hours, which can be startling. They are scaring away evil spirits. Our village house shares one wall with a small temple, so we often hear these types of noises.

They also tend to be a bit rougher around the edges, not as genteel as people in the city. They tend to speak more loudly and curse more; they're often pretty rude – even to one another. This has been observed not only by me but by quite a few of my Hong Kong Chinese friends. When you live in the village you're more likely to run into small-town activities, such as the many old women who occupy their time by trying to spy on you and then gossip about their findings. They're harmless, really, but it can be annoying – especially when they try and plug you with advice.

For many expats, career and cash are the main reasons to come to Hong Kong. Does the city have more to offer?

No doubt about it, Hong Kong is a great place to make money or start a business. But that's not the only reason to move here. It's also a wonderful place to meet people from all over the world; the population is constantly in flux. For people with families, HK offers you the chance to provide your children with a multilingual education and exposure to many different cultures. Hong Kong is also a very safe and well-run city with a low crime rate and excellent public transportation options. The public hospital system here is also a pretty great perk. If you are a Hong Kong Identity Card Holder (and you should be if you're employed here) then you have access to nearly free medical care. Most Americans can appreciate how cheap that is for quality medical care.

terraces. For HK$50,000 and up you should be able to secure a garden, car park, three bedrooms, and if you're lucky a sea view. Houses are modern and renovated and you'll find furnishings can be included in the deal for a small amount more. There are also a smattering of smaller hamlets in the area with older village houses and close traditional communities.

Beating at your back door are some fine beaches and jungle greenery, although that's about all you'll find. Like any suburb worth its salt, Clearwater Bay has poor transportation links, shockingly poor by Hong Kong standards. And, aside from the Park N Shop in Silverstrand, a lack of amenities means a car is pretty much essential. Once you hit the main roads, Hang Hau in Kowloon is only five minutes away and has a shopping mall and MTR station.

Sha Tin

There are more than 600,000 people in Sha Tin, although you'd never know it; most of them spend their time either working back in the city or tucked away in their bedrooms. Blocks and blocks of high-rise identical apartment blocks fill the skyline and, apart from New Town Plaza and City One Plaza malls, there is relatively little commerce on street level and few restaurants and bars. Still reading? In its defense, Sha Tin is clean and efficient: Streets are swept, garbage is picked up on time, and the traffic system actually works. There is also the Sha Tin racecourse and enjoyable Shing Mun River waterfront, but that's not really enough to sell what is essentially one massive housing estate. Instead, most people's motive for living here is the excellent rent to real estate ratios and apartment blocks that are modern and relatively spacious. A two-bedroom apartment in the newish City One block can cost as little as HK$7,000. Sha Tin is also one of the best connected towns in the New Territories, with a number of stations on both the Ma On Shan line and centrally-connected East rail line connecting to various estates in the conurbation. If you're considering a New Town for the low rent, you can expect pretty much the same picture as is painted above.

TAI PO

This market town of 250,000 may be no Cinderella to look at, but if it's personality that counts, Tai Po has it in spades. Shopping malls have yet to suck the life out of old Tai Po and the unassuming streets and rundown shop fronts in the center are enjoyably vibrant. While technically a New Town and with high rises to prove it, Tai Po still feels like a place where people live in, rather than just commute from.

Set around the main street of Kwong Fuk Road, the town center has a traditional feel with an excellent spread of shops, humble rice restaurants, and spit-

and-sawdust bars. For city comforts, there are fast-food joints, a supermarket, and the usual brand names at the Tai Po Mega Mall, as well as an MTR connection. Although Tai Po is a long way from the cosmopolitan streets of Central, physically and mentally, and you'll bump into few expats, it has enjoyed a modest boost in popularity among expats thanks to the luxury house and townhouse complexes built around its outskirts. These houses and townhouses deliver a lot of floor space for not a lot of money with a four-bedroom townhouse at the luxury, gated—if somewhat ambitiously named—Beverly Hills complex renting for around HK$35,000 with sea view. Away from the developments, prices drop steeply and you can easily find a three-bedroom renovated village house apartment in one of the hundreds of villages in the area for around HK$8,000 or less.

Gold Coast

Pack your *Grease* album and relive your summer vacations at the Hong Kong Gold Coast, a luxury residential resort set in relative seclusion on the built-up south coast, between Tsuen Wan and Tuen Mun. Similar to a package vacation resort you'd find in Cancún, this private development features tennis courts, swimming pools, and access to a private beach. Hard day at work? Unwind in the tropical garden. The Gold Coast is an interesting idea, and one that doesn't appeal to everyone as it can feel a little like living at Disneyland. The Gold Coast Piazza, for example, is the development's compact mall, but the faux-Mediterranean design and inflated prices feel contrived and no one needs a Lady Gaga impersonator crooning at them when all they came down for was a pack of toilet paper.

Home to around 5,000 residents, including many expats, the luxury apartments here are some of the best priced in Hong Kong considering their long line of amenities. Two-bedroom apartments start at HK$14,000, inclusive of management fee, with a fixed two-year term, while the much sought-after beach houses are a hefty HK$45,000 for a two bedroom and HK$125,000 for four bedrooms and a garden. The major drawback of living on the Gold Coast is that transportation is largely limited to the hourly shuttle bus, which connects to Tsuen Wan MTR in around 15 minutes and to Central in around 35 minutes, although there are private minibuses on the roads outside the complex.

GETTING AROUND

Thanks to the rapid development of the New Territories' New Towns, the region is now well plugged into the MTR. Four MTR lines pass through the New Territories, linking it to Kowloon and Hong Kong Island, although there is little inter-region connection. The East Rail line is perhaps the most useful of the four, running from Hung Hom through Sha Tin, Fo Tan, and Tai Po, all the way across the Chinese border at Lo Wu and into Shenzhen. An addition to this line is the Ma On Shan line that runs from Tai Wai in Sha Tin along the northeast coast, through several Sha Tin estates. In the west, the Tsuen Wan line connects Tsuen Wan directly to stops in Kowloon and Hong Kong Island, including Central. This line has an interchange at Mei Foo with the West Rail, which connects Tuen Mun with TST. Tuen Mun acts as a hub for the comprehensive Light Rail service that covers more than 60 stops across 38 kilometers of track.

Of course, the MTR isn't much help, if you're living in a smaller town or village. Minibuses do reach all but the tiniest hamlets, but service can be infrequent. In reality, if you want to be able to get around freely or get into town when you want, you'll need a car. The New Territories does have an excellent road network.

Outlying Islands

Relatively untouched by the city sprawl that affects the New Territories, the Outlying Islands are a wholesale change from the cosmopolitan Hong Kong advertised in guidebooks, and the opportunity to explore a more traditional Cantonese lifestyle is often part of the attraction. If you want to eat Cantonese food, speak Cantonese, and live in Chinese Hong Kong, the villages on the Outlying Islands are ideal. Of course, low rents for big spaces are also a convincing attraction. This has usually meant affordable houses outside small villages, but today people are braving the boat journey for an increasing number of fair-priced luxury apartments and dedicated low-rise developments, such as the one in Discovery Bay.

Despite their far-flung reputation, moving to the islands doesn't require tears and white handkerchiefs waved at the port, although the commute to the city is likely to be a major factor in deciding where to live. The two main inhabited islands of Lantau and Lamma are only 30 minutes away from Hong Kong Island by ferry and Lantau has both an MTR and road connection to Kowloon. Nevertheless, island living isn't ideal for those who need to commute daily to the city. You'll constantly have one eye fixed on your watch and one hand on your briefcase, ready to dash to your next ferry departure. On the islands, access to facilities, public services, and shops varies from village to village and island to island. Lantau already has international schools, supermarkets, and, penciled into its future, a hospital, while Lamma residents need to use the ferry for all three. However, despite the belief of some expats that living on the Outlying Islands is similar to bedding down inside a crater on the moon, services such as cell phone coverage and broadband are widely available in all but the smallest villages. Prices for goods, including food, are generally a little lower, but then so is the selection.

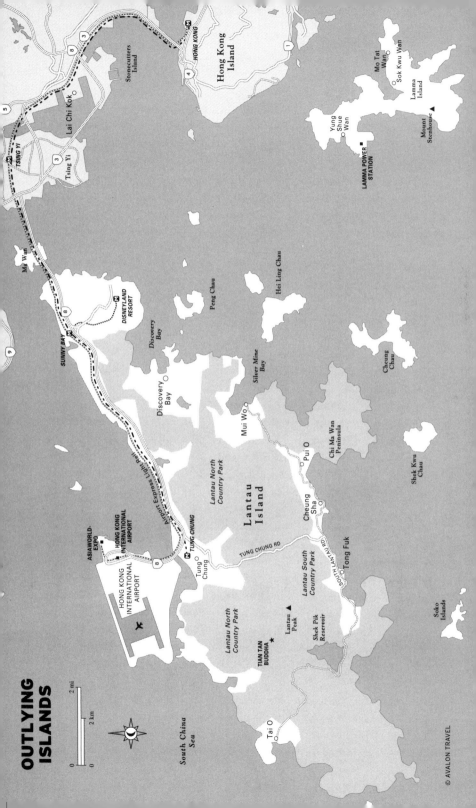

OUTLYING ISLANDS

South China Sea

Tai O

TIAN TAN BUDDHA ★

Lantau Peak ▲

Shek Pik Reservoir

Lantau North Country Park

Lantau South Country Park

SOUTH LANTAU RD

TUNG CHUNG RD

Tung Chung

TUNG CHUNG

Lantau Island

Lantau North Country Park

Cheung Sha

Tong Fuk

Pui O

Chi Ma Wan Peninsula

Mui Wo

Silver Mine Bay

Discovery Bay

Discovery Bay

DISNEYLAND RESORT

SUNNY BAY

Airport Express Light Rail

HONG KONG INTERNATIONAL AIRPORT

ASIAWORLD-EXPO

HONG KONG INTERNATIONAL AIRPORT

Feng Chau

Hei Ling Chau

Cheung Chau

Shek Kwu Chau

Soko Islands

Lamma Island

Yung Shue Wan

Mo Tat Wan

Sok Kwu Wan

Mount Stenhouse ▲

LAMMA POWER STATION

HONG KONG

HONG KONG Island

Stonecutters Island

Lai Chi Kok

Tsing Yi

Ma Wan

5

8

3

8

9

8

1

4

3

2 mi

2 km

© AVALON TRAVEL

LAY OF THE LAND

On paper there are over 235 islands to choose from, although in practical terms only a handful of these will be on your real estate radar. The majority are little more than a collection of rocky outcrops or desert island strips home only to sunbathing seagulls. Around a dozen or so of the larger islands once housed lively fishing villages, but as the fishing industry has died so have the villages and all that is left is a skeleton crew of inhabitants largely cutoff from the rest of Hong Kong. Substantial population centers and civilization are only found on Lantau, Lamma, and Cheung Chau, which, along with Peng Chau, are the only islands with regular ferry schedules.

WHERE TO LIVE
Lantau

Bigger than Hong Kong Island but home to less than 100,000 people, Lantau's mountainous interior, half of which is a national park, is carpeted by a thick rug of greenery that hides peaceful monasteries and wandering water buffalo. Famed for its jungle-like hiking trails and powder puff beaches, the island's traditional fishing villages are some of the most enjoyable and isolated in Hong Kong. Unfortunately, it was only a matter of time before some suit discovered all this empty real estate lying around and Hong Kong's land-starved developers well and truly stuck their bulldozers into the island. Alongside Hong Kong Airport and Disneyland, the island has seen the rise of the new town of Tung Chung and the trimmed-lawn, white-picket-fence development of Discovery Bay. There are roads across much of the island, including a bridge to Kowloon, and a selection of schools and supermarkets.

It's certainly not the life and times of Robinson Crusoe, but Lantau can be a good place to balance a rural retreat lifestyle with the comforts of the big city. Where you choose to live on Lantau very much depends on the lifestyle you're seeking. The north end and middle of the Island are the focus for much of the development, including Disneyland, Hong Kong Airport, and Tung Chung. The south side remains relatively untouched—for now.

With a sub-30-minute MTR connection to Central, the Citygate shopping mall and cinema, and various supermarkets, Tung Chung has very much become the focal point for Lantau life. In a little over 20 years it's gained a population of 70,000, a number expected to swell three fold. In truth, unless you like the sound of the Airbus A380 and can appreciate the vicinity of Hong Kong Airport, there is little to recommend about living in this dull new town. It offers none of the advantages of living on the islands—you'll still be surrounded by high-rise concrete clutter—along with all the disadvantages, namely the commute into the city. What it does offer is luxury developments such as the Caribbean Coast, Tung Chug Crescent, and Seaview Crescent, which have clubhouses, pools, and prices that are cheap compared to the city. Apartment buildings are usually priced by phase, which indicates their age, and by distance to the MTR. For a new but unfurnished two-bedroom apartment in Seaview Crescent expect to pay HK$9,000, doubling to HK$18,000 for four bedrooms. Snag the sea-view penthouse for HK$40,000.

Nearby Discovery Bay, or DB as it's also known, is Hong Kong's stab at an American suburb. It's a pretty convincing imitation and has proved a resulting success with expats eager to recreate suburban living. Completely at odds with the excitement and chaos that characterizes Hong Kong, DB is owned by a single developer and everything is micromanaged to perfection: The grass is given a weekly buzz cut, the streets scrubbed daily, and there's even a well-groomed, artificially-made beach for residents. Some people love it, especially families, who fall for the low-rise living, green spaces, and safety. But the toy-town appeal isn't for everyone and it can feel a little like living on the set of the Stepford Wives. Distinctly humdrum when compared to the city and with just under 20,000 residents, the community can be a little claustrophobic, although it is hugely international.

© MARTYNA SZMYTKOWSKA

Lantau Peak dominates Lantau Island.

Housing in Discovery Bay is new, luxurious, and low rise. While you can't completely escape the apartment towers, much of the real estate consists of mid-sized townhouses, duplexes, and stand-alone houses with gardens. These are mostly large properties aimed at families, often with three or more bedrooms, and there is usually more options to rent them out fully furnished. Rent-wise you will get more for your money in Discovery Bay than similar properties on Hong Kong Island, but there are few bargains and real estate is pitched at the top end of the market. Four- and five-bedroom houses with gardens cost upwards of HK$130,000, while a luxury apartment in the new Chianti Towers with three bedrooms comes in around HK$25,000. The occasional studio also pops up with prices around HK$6,000. Price tends to be dictated by the distance to the ferry pier and central plaza and the phase of the building.

DB is mostly self-sufficient and there is an onsite Fusion supermarket, squarely aimed at expats, and a Wellcome, as well as essential shops and services clustered around the plaza, clubhouses, and restaurants. Be warned: Shops and restaurants seem to consider it their sworn duty to relieve the weighty wallets of residents, and locals are held hostage to inflated prices, especially for food.

For an island community, DB enjoys enviable transport links to the city, with a fleet of super speed, Wi-Fi-enabled catamarans making the journey to Central in less than 30 minutes. These run 24 hours a day, so living in DB needn't curtail your 4 A.M. cocktail habit. There are also buses to Tung Chung, Hong Kong Airport, and the MTR stop at nearby Sunny Bay. No private cars are allowed into Discovery Bay, including public taxis, although shuttle buses can shuffle you around the complex. If you want to get around in motorized transport, you'll need to sell your dignity and buy or rent one of the ridiculous and ridiculously-overpriced golf buggies.

South of Discovery Bay, the busy streets of Mui Wo, also known as Silvermine Bay in English, have all the atmosphere of a traditional Cantonese town. Considered the de facto capital of the island, before the government conjured Tung Chung out of the ground, Mui Wo and its 5,000 residents remain an important center for villages in the surrounding area and South Lantau. Spread around several roads, it's packed with markets, shops, and restaurants, including a couple of Western spots, has a ferry connection to Central, and feels substantial enough to justify its town label. It also has the beautiful Silvermine Beach and access to many of Lantau's best hiking trails. While Mui Wo has been given a shampoo and a shave in recent years, its buildings do show their age and it looks shabby. Housing can be similarly unappealing and is generally in older, low-rise apartment blocks and although rents are very low, it's hardly anyone's ideal rural retreat.

Instead, the town's small but noticeable number of expats find peace and quiet in the surrounding countryside or nearby villages, where you can find roomy and often renovated village houses, shared duplexes, and three-story villas, all at bargain prices. More established villages in South Lantau where you'll have more than water buffaloes as neighbors include Poi O, Tong Fuk, and Cheung Sha. Rents for a village house are wide open, from HK$8,000 for the village shed to HK$30,000 and up for fully renovated, fitted, and furnished places. Rates drop the farther away from Mui Wo you move. At the very bottom of the island is Tai O, a picturesque fishing village where Tanka boat people live in houses that stand on bamboo stilts. Popular with tourists for its tumbledown charm, the village is unfortunately in decline. But, with more than 1,000 residents, it still has a useful selection of shops, amenities, and seafood restaurants.

There are no bona fide ESF schools on Lantau and the English-language schools that do exist are seriously oversubscribed. Discovery College in Discovery Bay, which offers primary and secondary education, is affiliated with ESF but doesn't operate a dedicated catchment area for Lantau. Instead, Lantau children are included in the Bradbury School primary and West Island School secondary catchment area. Also in Discovery Bay, Discovery Bay International School is a private school that operates from kindergarten to the secondary level. It does offer preferential enrollment for Discovery Bay residents. Lantau International School in Pui O and Tong Fok has kindergarten and primary classes. There are both public healthcare outpatient clinics and private healthcare centers in Tung Chung, Mui Wo, and Discovery Bay. There are no public or private hospitals, although one is scheduled to be built.

Lamma

Just over 14 kilometers in size, smothered in botanical greenery, and ringed by golden beaches, Lamma has—aside from a Soviet Union–styled powerplant—dodged the development that many people feel has blighted Lantau. And, with no cars and no high rises, it feels more ruggedly rural. Alongside the roughly 6,000 resident fisherfolk and farmers, the island has attracted a substantial expat community who are often characterized by jealous office rats in Central as hippy dropouts who drink fair trade coffee, recycle their trash, and plot the downfall of capitalism. The splendid isolation and lungs full of fresh air certainly do attract those looking for a healthy alternative lifestyle, but contrary to popular belief, you don't need to wear tie-dye T-shirts and know the words to the Bob Dylan back catalog to live on Lamma. Many freelance professionals and families have also relocated here simply because it's more relaxing than the city and property is considerably cheaper. During the week the island is quiet, peaceful, and can feel remarkably remote, but on weekends, you may find your bonding with Buddha interrupted by hordes of day-trippers traipsing across hiking trails to the seafood restaurants.

The island's main settlement is Yung Shue Wan, an atmospheric one-street village whose family-run shops spill out over the sidewalk. Grocery shops, although no supermarkets, a bank, and most other essentials are available in the village, as well as many relaxed restaurants and bars, including some expat-owned businesses. Thanks to Yung Shue Wan's ferry connection to Central, which alternates between fast (30 minutes) and slow ferries (45 minutes), most people live in and around the village. On the far side of Lamma

© RORY BOLAND

Perhaps the greatest plus of living on Lamma Island is access to some of Hong Kong's best beaches.

is the island's second village, Sok Kwu Wan, which is famed for its hook 'em and cook 'em seafood restaurants and also has a ferry connection. Aside from that, there are a handful of hamlets, with little more than a village shop, scattered around the coastline.

Housing on Lamma is all low rise, restricted to three stories or less and a mix of triplex and duplex apartment buildings and stand-alone houses. Buildings in Yung Shue Wan tend to be shabbier and given that you've come this far, it would be a shame not to spring for an actual house in the surrounding hillside. In the past, these houses often looked like they had survived a direct nuclear strike and needed more than a screwdriver to fix them up. Today, an increasingly large pool of professional residents means many places are renovated and modernized. Rental rates are some of the most affordable in Hong Kong and embarrassingly cheaper than the city. With a little persistence, you can grab a modest, two-bedroom village house that's in reasonable shape for HK$15,000, while a first-class house with garden, sea views, and your own swimming pool can be found for HK$50,000. Lamma can also be a good place to find shared rooms for as little as HK$2,000.

Generally the farther you move away from the ferry ports, the more prices will drop, although it's worth remembering all transport on Lamma is on two legs or with two peddles, so distance can be important. Hills or not, Lamma is a location very much in demand and there is not a huge amount of rental real estate available; you may need to be patient in any Lamma house hunt.

There are no ESF or International Schools on Lamma Island, although there is a bilingual kindergarten. The island falls into the catchment area for the ESF's Bradbury School primary and West Island School primary and many expats send their children by ferry to these schools. The Lamma Clinic offers outpatient services and limited emergency care, including care for bites and stings, but for anything more exciting you'll be helicoptered to the city.

GETTING AROUND

Unlike the other islands, Lantau has both a bridge connection to Kowloon and an MTR line that connects it with the city, alongside the traditional ferry routes. Tung Chung is Lantau's transport hub, with its MTR line connecting to Central in less than 30 minutes and public buses from here serving south Lantau, the Airport, and Kowloon. There are also a handful of infrequent ferry services. Mui Wo has the most useful ferry route on the island with alternate fast and slow ferries connecting to Central in 40 minutes and 55 minutes, respectively. It's also a bus hub for transport to south Lantau. The island's road network continues to improve, for better or worse, and residents can either obtain a special permit to drive cars on the island or use the 50 or so Lantau taxis.

By contrast, Lamma has no motorized transportation, bar your own legs, and bicycles are a popular way to commute to the ferry pier. Regular fast and slow ferries connect Yung Shue Wan with Central as often as every 20 minutes during peak periods, with less frequent services also servicing Sok Kwu Wan. Both Cheung Chau and Peng Chau also enjoy regular ferry services.

With cars banned on Lamma Island, the only way to get around is on two wheels.

RESOURCES

Embassies and Consulates

IN THE UNITED STATES

As part of China, Hong Kong is represented overseas by Chinese embassies and consulates. The addresses listed here are for the main embassy or consulate, but keep in mind that at some locations the visa and passport service may be at a different address. Phone ahead before you jump in the car.

CONSULATE-GENERAL OF THE PRC IN CHICAGO

100 West Erie St.
Chicago, IL 60654
tel. 312/803-0095
www.chinaconsulatechicago.org

CONSULATE-GENERAL OF THE PRC IN HOUSTON

3417 Montrose Blvd.
Houston, TX 77006
tel. 713/520-1462
www.chinahouston.org

CONSULATE-GENERAL OF THE PRC IN LOS ANGELES

443 Shatto Pl.
Los Angeles, CA 90020
tel. 213/807-8088
http://losangeles.china-consulate.org

CONSULATE-GENERAL OF THE PRC IN NEW YORK

520 12th Ave.
New York, NY 10036
tel. 212/244-9456
www.nyconsulate.prchina.org

CONSULATE-GENERAL OF THE PRC IN SAN FRANCISCO

1450 Laguna St.
San Francisco, CA 94115
tel. 415/674-2940
www.chinaconsulatesf.org

THE EMBASSY OF THE PEOPLE'S REPUBLIC OF CHINA IN THE UNITED STATES

2201 Wisconsin Ave., N.W. Suite 110
Washington, D.C. 20007
tel. 202/337-1956
www.china-embassy.org

OUTSIDE THE UNITED STATES

THE EMBASSY OF THE PEOPLE'S REPUBLIC OF CHINA IN AUSTRALIA

15 Coronation Dr.
Yarralumla, ACT 2600
tel. 02/627-34780
http://au.china-embassy.org

THE EMBASSY OF THE PEOPLE'S REPUBLIC OF CHINA IN CANADA

515 St. Patrick St.
Ottawa, Ont. K1N 5H3
tel. 613/789-3434
http://ca.china-embassy.org

THE EMBASSY OF THE PEOPLE'S REPUBLIC OF CHINA IN IRELAND

40 Ailesbury Rd.
Ballsbridge, Dublin 4
tel. 01/269-1707
http://ie.china-embassy.org

THE EMBASSY OF THE PEOPLE'S REPUBLIC OF CHINA IN NEW ZEALAND

2-6 Glenmore St.
Kelburn, Wellington
tel. 04/472-1382
www.chinaembassy.org.nz

THE EMBASSY OF THE PEOPLE'S REPUBLIC OF CHINA IN THE UNITED KINGDOM

49/51 Portland Pl.
London W1B 1JL
tel. 020/72994049
www.chinese-embassy.org.uk

IN HONG KONG
AUSTRALIAN CONSULATE GENERAL HONG KONG
23/F Harbour Centre, 25 Harbour Rd.
Wanchai, Hong Kong
tel. 852/2827-8881
www.hongkong.china.embassy.gov.au

BRITISH CONSULATE GENERAL HONG KONG
1 Supreme Court Rd.
Admiralty, Hong Kong
tel. 852/2901-3000
http://ukinhongkong.fco.gov.uk

CONSULATE GENERAL OF CANADA IN HONG KONG
12/14F, One Exchange Sq.
Central, Hong Kong
tel. 852/3719-4700
www.canadainternational.gc.ca

CONSULATE GENERAL OF THE UNITED STATES IN HONG KONG AND MACAU
26 Garden Rd.
Central, Hong Kong
tel. 852/2523-9011
http://hongkong.usconsulate.gov

IRISH CONSULATE HONG KONG (HONORARY)
Suite 1408, Two Pacific Place, 88 Queensway
Admiralty, Hong Kong
tel. 852/2527-4897
www.consulateofireland.hk

NEW ZEALAND CONSULATE GENERAL HONG KONG
6501 Central Plaza, 18 Harbour Rd.
Wanchai, Hong Kong
tel. 852/2525-5044
www.nzembassy.com/hong-kong

Planning Your Fact-Finding Trip

HONG KONG TOURISM BOARD
www.discoverhongkong.com
This government-run website boasts encyclopedic coverage of the city's sights, attractions, and events, if you can ignore the relentlessly upbeat propaganda urging you to shop till you drop.

ZUJI
www.zuji.com.hk
This is a travel-booking search engine with the most competitive prices and steal deals on Hong Kong hotels and package stays in the city.

Making the Move

LIVING IN HONG KONG
ASIAXPAT
http://hongkong.asiaxpat.com
Not quite as user-friendly or useful as geoexpat, the forums over at asiaxpat are still worth a poke around.

GEOEXPAT
www.geoexpat.com
From debates on the deteriorating air pollution to where to buy Monterey Jack Cheese, there isn't a question about Hong Kong that

hasn't been answered on geoexpat. Its forums are a wealth of information and regularly used by even the most seasoned expats.

HONG KONG BLOGS REVIEW
www.hong-kong-blogs-review.com
From criticism and commentary on Hong Kong's politics and culture to blow by blow accounts of expat life in the city, Hong Kong has some outstanding English-language bloggers; find most of the best sites aggregated here.

RESOURCES

MOVING COMPANIES AND SHIPPING

ALLIED PICKFORDS
www.alliedpickfords.com
One of the world's biggest and best removal and relocation firms, although their services don't come cheap.

CROWN RELOCATION
www.crownrelo.com
International removal and relocation services.

FTC LOGISTICS
www.ftc.hk
Local firm with specialized experience of moves in and out of Hong Kong.

SEVEN SEAS WORLDWIDE
www.sevenseasworldwide.com
Useful for shipping the odd crate or three.

VISAS AND IMMIGRATION

You can find out everything you need to know about visas on the exhaustive Hong Kong Immigration Department website (www.immd.gov.hk). For most people, contracting a specialized firm to do your application is completely unnecessary (and expensive), but if you're expecting or experiencing difficulties, try one of the specialists listed here who have been known to massage miracles. Be warned: There are also some cowboys on the market.

EMIGRA
www.emigra.com.hk
International immigration consultancy that can assist in cases involving all visa types, but specializes in business and investment visas. They can be particularly useful in complex cases involving setting up a business in Hong Kong.

VISAPRO
www.visapro.com.hk
Local firm that offers no visa, no fee, and reasonable rates.

Language and Education

LANGUAGE SCHOOLS

CHINESE LANGUAGE CENTRE (THE CHINESE UNIVERSITY OF HONG KONG)
www.cuhk.edu.hk/clc

HONG KONG LANGUAGE LEARNING CENTRE
www.hkllc.com

YMCA
www.ymcahk.org.hk

ONLINE LANGUAGE TOOLS

CANTONESE SHEIK
www.cantonese.sheik.co.uk
Well-explained introduction to Chinese and Cantonese, vocabulary lists, tests, and an excellent and active forum.

LEARN CHINESE ONLINE
www.learnchineseez.com
Listen to key words and phrases in both Cantonese and Mandarin.

SCHOOLS

AMERICAN INTERNATIONAL SCHOOL
www.ais.edu.hk

AUSTRALIAN INTERNATIONAL SCHOOL
www.aishk.edu.hk

CANADIAN INTERNATIONAL SCHOOL
www.cdnis.edu.hk

EDUCATION BUREAU
www.edb.gov.hk
Information and resources on Hong Kong's public education system, including school listings, both public and private, by district.

ESF (ENGLISH SCHOOLS FOUNDATION)
www.esf.edu.hk
Website for the English Schools Foundation with general admission information and links to all of their kindergartens, primary schools, and high schools.

HONG KONG INTERNATIONAL SCHOOL
www.hkis.edu.hk

PRIVATE TUITION AND GENERAL EDUCATION RESOURCES
ALPHA ACADEMY
www.alphaacademy.com.hk
Well-respected private tuition school that offers one to one tutoring across all academic subjects and preparation for both local and international examinations.

ITS
www.tuition.com.hk
ITS is a private tuition school that offers group and private tutoring on all subjects and preparation for specific examinations, such as IELTS or SATs. Their information-packed website is also an essential first stop for anyone about to dive into the complexities of Hong Kong's education system. If you have a couple of kids to enroll at different levels, you might even consider buying their book, *The Unique Hong Kong Schools Guide.* Their website also features a map that shows all of Hong Kong's international schools.

UNIVERSITIES
THE CHINESE UNIVERSITY OF HONG KONG
www.cuhk.edu.hk

THE HONG KONG POLYTECHNIC UNIVERSITY
www.polyu.edu.hk

STUDY HK
http://studyinhongkong.edu.hk
Government-funded website with information and resources specifically geared towards international students considering enrolling at a Hong Kong university.

THE UNIVERSITY OF HONG KONG
www.hku.hk

RESOURCES

Health

DOCTORS, DENTISTS, AND HOSPITALS

CHINESE MEDICINE COUNCIL OF HONG KONG
www.cmchk.org.hk
List of registered Chinese medicine practitioners.

HONG KONG DENTAL ASSOCIATION
www.hkda.org
Offers a list of all registered practitioners and a database of dentists searchable by location, consultation hours, public/private, and specialty.

HONG KONG DOCTORS HOMEPAGE
www.hkdoctors.org
This useful page is maintained by the Hong Kong Medical Association and features a database of registered doctors in Hong Kong that is searchable by location, consultation hours, public/private, and specialty.

THE HONG KONG PRIVATE HOSPITALS ASSOCIATION
www.privatehospitals.org.hk
Links to all of Hong Kong's private hospitals.

THE HOSPITAL AUTHORITY
www.ha.org.hk
The official website of Hong Kong's central hospital authority, with information on hospital districts, healthcare eligibility, and fees.

HEALTH INSURANCE

AIA
www.aia.com.hk

BUPA
www.bupa.com.hk

PACIFIC PRIME
www.pacificprime.com
Based in Hong Kong, Pacific Prime is an international insurance broker that is able to aggregate offers from many of the biggest firms to find suitable coverage at the best price.

WILLIAM RUSSELL
www.william-russell.com
This U.K.-based firm specializes in expat healthcare coverage for all nationalities and is popular with expats in Hong Kong.

AIR POLLUTION

CLEAR THE AIR
www.cleartheair.org.hk
Local charity Clear the Air pulls no punches in their lobbying for the Hong Kong government to clean up its act on the city's chronic air pollution problems. Some of their statements can be alarmist, but the statistics featured on their webpage reveal the ugly truth about the problem.

GREENPEACE
www.greenpeace.org/eastasia
Keep an eye on the city's air quality with live reports from the good folks at Greenpeace and their monitoring stations around the city.

OTHER RESOURCES

ACCESS GUIDE
www.accessguide.hk
Aimed at tourists visiting the city, this website has information and guides on the accessibility of public transport, sights, and detailed listings on facilities at hotels for the disabled.

HONG KONG OBSERVATORY
www.hko.gov.hk
It's important to know what the weather is doing in Hong Kong and the source of all weather warnings and typhoon alerts is the Hong Kong Observatory.

Employment

JOB SEARCH

JOBSDB
www.jobsdb.com.hk
Free to join, JobsDB is a job-hunters playground, with a massive database of Hong Kong jobs advertised in English and aimed at professionals.

MONSTER
www.monster.com.hk
The local arm of this international job recruitment website has a broad selection of jobs across all professional sectors.

RECUIT.NET
www.recruit.net
Search engine for Hong Kong job listings.

SCMP CLASSIFIED POST
www.classifiedpost.com
The online and more extensive version of the *SCMP*'s weekly Classified Post section; most of the jobs here are aimed specifically at expats.

TEACHING

DAVE'S ESL CAFÉ
www.eslcafe.com
Occasional job postings for TEFL teachers in Hong Kong and forums discussing Hong Kong schools and common issues, problems, and grumbles with teaching in the city.

EDUCATION BUREAU
www.edb.gov.hk
Information and forms for enrolling in the Native English Teacher recruitment process.

SETTING UP A BUSINESS

INVEST HK
www.investhk.gov.hk
Government-funded agency that advises and assists those looking to invest or set up a business in Hong Kong.

Finance

BANKS AND BROKERS

BOOM
http://baby.boom.com.hk
Local, online stock brokerage that generally charges less than the banks and includes picks, FAQs and guides.

CITIBANK
www.citibank.com.hk

HSBC
www.hsbc.com.hk

TAX RESOURCES

HONG KONG INLAND REVENUE
www.ird.gov.hk
Information on tax liability and tax brackets in Hong Kong as well as e-filing.

U.S EMBASSY LIST OF TAX CONSULTANTS
http://hongkong.usconsulate.gov/acs_ustax-consultants.html
List of tax consultants based in Hong Kong who are experienced in doing battle with the IRS and filing U.S. tax returns.

SHOPPING

PARK N SHOP
www1.parknshop.com
Major Hong Kong supermarket chain with products, prices, and locations online.

WELLCOME
www.wellcome.com.hk
There is slightly less selection for expats at Hong Kong's second supermarket chain.

Communications

NEWSPAPERS
SCMP
www.scmp.com
The *South China Morning Post* is Hong Kong's biggest-selling English-language daily and possibly the best informed English-language paper in the region (online subscription only).

THE STANDARD
www.thestandard.com.hk
Hong Kong's second local paper runs a free website with stories on most major happenings in the city.

CHINA DAILY (HONG KONG EDITION)
www.chinadaily.com.cn/en/hk
The official English-language mouthpiece for Beijing has toned down its propaganda in recent years and is worth a browse for its free online news and a few laughs.

BOOK AND MAGAZINE SELLERS
BOOKSTORE AT FENWICK PIER
The Fleet Arcade at Fenwick Pier
Lung King St.
Wan Chai
tel. 852/2511-3611
www.fenwickpier.com
Specialist in American books and magazines with fair prices.

DYMOCKS
Shops 201-203
1-3 Pedder St., Central
tel. 852/2826-9248
www.dymocks.com.hk
Australian bookstore chain with several outlets in Hong Kong.

FLOW
1/F
40 Lyndhurst Ter., Central
tel. 852/2964-9483
www.facebook.com/flowbookshop
Hong Kong's best and beloved English-language secondhand bookstore.

PAGE ONE
Shop 922, 9/F
Times Square
1 Matheson St.
Causeway Bay
tel. 852/2506-0381
www.pageonegroup.com
Bookstore chain that stocks solely English-language books.

TELEPHONE, INTERNET, AND MULTIMEDIA
HGC
www.hgc.com.hk
Internet and phone provider.

I-CABLE
www.i-cable.com
Alternate cable TV, Internet, and phone line provider.

PCCW
www.pccw.com
Hong Kong's dominant telecommunications provider has Hong Kong's widest coverage and offers cable TV, Internet, and phone services.

CELLPHONE NETWORKS
CHINA MOBILE
www.hk.chinamobile.com
Also offers IDD.

ONE2FREE
www.one2free.com
Services also include broadband and IDD.

SMARTONE VODAPHONE
www.smartone-vodafone.com
Also offers broadband.

3
www.three.com.hk
Hong Kong's leading cell phone provider also offers fixed phone line services, IDD, and the city's quickest broadband connections.

Travel and Transportation

AIR

CATHAY PACIFIC
www.cathaypacific.com
Hong Kong's flagship carrier.

DRAGON AIR
www.dragonair.com
Cathay Pacific's little brother has the most connections between Hong Kong and China and many budget regional routes.

HONG KONG AIRPORT
www.hongkongairport.com
Check out which airlines fly to the city.

TRAIN

MTR
www.mtr.com.hk
Fares and schedules for Hong Kong's metro.

MTR INTERCITY
www.it3.mtr.com.hk
Fares, timetables, and online purchasing for intercity trains to China.

FERRY

CHU KONG PASSENGER TRANSPORT
www.cksp.com.hk
Ferries between Hong Kong and mainland China.

DISCOVERY BAY TIMETABLE
http://db.tdw.hk/
Ferries to Discovery Bay.

HONG KONG AND KOWLOON FERRY
www.hkkf.com.hk
Ferries to the Outlying Islands.

NEW WORLD FIRST FERRY
www.nwff.com.hk
Ferries to the Outlying Islands and Macau.

STAR FERRY
www.starferry.com.hk
Hong Kong's venerable cross-harbor ferry.

TURBO JET
www.turbojetseaexpress.com.hk
Hong Kong to Macau and Shenzhen ferries.

GENERAL TRANSPORTATION

GOVERNMENT TRANSPORT INFORMATION
www.gov.hk/en/residents/transport/public-transport/
Information on driving licenses, vehicle registration, and all the other bureaucratic form-filling required to drive a car. There is also general information on public transport in the city.

TRANSPORT DEPARTMENT MAP
http://ptes.td.gov.hk
Plug in your point of origin and destination to this interactive map to be shown the quickest route via public transport.

TRAVEL AGENCIES

CHINA TRAVEL SERVICE
www.ctshk.com
Quasi Beijing-owned operation that always seems to know all the right names and numbers when it comes to getting hold of complex China mainland visas in a hurry. They also offer tours and packages.

TRAVEL EXPERT
www.travelexpert.com.hk
One of Hong Kong's biggest travel agency chains with branches throughout the city, Travel Expert has fantastic deals on weekend getaways to regional destinations.

ZUJI
www.zuji.com.hk
Travel-booking portal with some of the best prices available on long-haul flights and excellent packages to short-haul destinations, including China.

RESOURCES

Housing Considerations

CENTURY 21
www.century21-hk.com
With dedicated branches in most of Hong Kong's districts, Century 21 has a huge selection of listings.

GOHOME.COM.HK
www.gohome.com.hk
Many of the city's rentals, particularly at the mid-range of the market, end up on this comprehensive property listing website. They also have sales listings.

MIDLAND REALTY
www.midland.com.hk
One of Hong Kong's biggest realtors, Midland has branches throughout the city.

RATING AND VALUATION DEPARTMENT
www.rvd.gov.hk
Head to the Property Market Statistics section on the Rating and Valuation Department's website to find up-to-date, if broad, statistics on average rentals by area and class and a list of recently completed sales transactions.

SQUAREFOOT.COM.HK
www.squarefoot.com.hk
A property listings website featuring properties to rent and buy as well as some insightful articles into the Hong Kong real estate scene.

Prime Living Locations

GENERAL
ANGLOINFO
www.hongkong.angloinfo.com
Expat-orientated guide to the city with well-informed guides to common issues and problems expats encounter.

ASIAXPAT
www.asiaxpat.com
The forums provide good expat information and they have a useful classified section.

CAB (COMMUNITY ADVICE BUREAU)
www.cab.org.hk
Tailored towards English-speaking expats, this superb local charity is based on the Community Advice Bureaus in the United Kingdom and offers free legal, financial, and welfare advice.

GEOEXPAT
www.geoexpat.com
There are few questions about Hong Kong that the legion of seasoned expats over at geoexpat haven't been asked; just search

their forums. It's a great palace to share fears and frustrations about expat life and get advice on how to make things easier.

HONG KONG GOVERNMENT
www.gov.hk
Recently revamped, the Hong Kong government portal contains a tome of information on everything from taxes and immigration to swimming pools and shark nets. Well presented and well written, with a refreshing lack of bureaucratic babble, it can answer a lot of your questions.

OUTLYING ISLANDS
DISCOVERY BAY FORUMS
www.discoverybayforum.com
Heated discussions on ferry timetables, Park N Shop prices, and everything DB over at the Discovery Bay forums.

LAMMA-ZINE
www.lamma.com.hk
The closest thing Lamma's residents have to a newspaper, Lamma-zine features news, information on the island, and listings, as well an active forum and classified section.

Community

ORGANIZATIONS
AMERICAN CHAMBER OF COMMERCE
www.amcham.org.hk

AMERICAN WOMEN'S ASSOCIATION
www.awa.org.hk

AUSTRALIAN ASSOCIATION
www.ozhongkong.com

AUSTRALIAN CHAMBER OF COMMERCE
www.austcham.com.hk

BRITISH CHAMBER OF COMMERCE
www.britcham.com

CANADIAN CHAMBER OF COMMERCE
www.cancham.org

NEW ZEALAND SOCIETY OF HONG KONG
www.nzshk.org

THE ROYAL SOCIETY OF ST. GEORGE
www.royalsocietyofstgeorgehk.com

ST. ANDREW'S SOCIETY
www.standrewshk.org

ST. DAVID'S SOCIETY
www.saintdavids.hk

ST. PATRICK'S SOCIETY
www.stpatrickshk.com

EXPAT PUBLICATIONS
BC MAGAZINE
www.bcmagazine.net
Bi-weekly pop and culture listings focused on happenings in Wan Chai (website is not updated).

CITYLIFE
www.citylifehk.com
Primarily aimed at tourists, the monthly *CityLife* magazine has some useful listings on dining and shopping in Hong Kong.

HONG KONG MAGAZINE
http://hk.asia-city.com
An expat institution, *Hong Kong Magazine* has long been highlighting the best of the city's restaurants, nightlife, and culture and chronicling both expat life and hot-button social issues.

TIME OUT
www.timeout.com.hk
Same name, new city; *Time Out* includes listings and features on events, nightlife, and restaurants.

SPORTS CLUBS
HONG KONG FOOTBALL CLUB
www.hkfc.com.hk

KOWLOON CRICKET CLUB
www.kcc.org.hk

VALLEY RFC
www.valleyrfc.com

PRIVATE CLUBS
THE AMERICAN CLUB
www.americanclubhk.com

FOREIGN CORRESPONDENTS CLUB
www.fcchk.org

M FOR MEMBERSHIP
www.mformembership.com
Information on the entry requirements and fees for enrollment into approximately half of Hong Kong's private clubs.

VOLUNTEERING
HANDS ON HONG KONG
www. handsonhongkong.org
Project database putting charities in touch with volunteers.

HO SUM
www.ho-sum.org
Another searchable project database

with a wide selection of volunteering opportunities.

VOLUNTEER MOVEMENT
www.volunteering-hk.org
Less comprehensive government website with volunteering openings.

PARENTS' GROUPS
ABERDEEN MARINA CLUB
www.aberdeenmarinaclub.com

AMERICAN WOMEN'S ASSOCIATION
www.awa.org.hk
Voluntary organization and club that runs a number of social activities for members, including a moms and tots group.

LADIES RECREATIONAL CLUB
www.lrc.com.hk

YMCA
www.ymcahk.org.hk

YWCA
www.esmdywca.org.hk

Other Kids Resources
BOY SCOUTS OF AMERICA HONG KONG
http://dragonnet.hkis.edu.hk/community/scouts/
Official troop of the Boy Scouts of America in Hong Kong.

GEOBABY
www.geobaby.com
Active and helpful forum of expat and English-speaking parents based in Hong Kong.

HONG KONG GIRL GUIDES ASSOCIATION
www.hkgga.org.hk

HONG KONG LITTLE LEAGUE
tel. 852/2504-4007
www.hkll.org

LEISURE AND CULTURAL SERVICES DEPARTMENT
www.lcsd.gov.hk
Information, opening hours, and rates on swimming pools, sports grounds, and community clubs, as well as theaters, libraries, and other performance venues.

GAY AND LESBIAN GROUPS
FRUITS IN SUITS
www.fruitsinsuits.com.hk
Very active group of gay professionals who host regular mixers and social events. Their website has some useful background information and articles on gay life in Hong Kong.

GAY AND LESBIAN HONG KONG
http://sqzm14.ust.hk/hkgay
This local site has useful and regularly updated information on Hong Kong's gay and lesbian scene, including tips on gay-friendly establishments, counseling helplines, and general discussion and news.

OTHER COMMUNITY CONTACTS
AMERICAN COMMUNITY THEATER
www.acthongkong.com
American-orientated community theater group.

COFFEE MATCHING
www.coffeematching.com
Speed-dating club aimed at single professionals.

HASH HOUSE HARRIERS
http://www.wanchaih3.com/otherhashes.htm
Hong Kong is home to several Hash House Harrier Groups, or kennels as they are also known. They host regular cross-country runs, washed down with large quantities of beer, which are popular with expats. The full list of kennels can be found through the link above.

HONG KONG PLAYERS
www.hongkongplayers.com
English-speaking community theater group.

Phrasebook

PRONUNCATION

Cantonese is a tonal language. This means that an individual word may have several meanings based on the pitch used on certain syllables. For example the word fan below has six different meanings, depending on the pitch used to pronounce the word. The pitch is indicated by diacritics or accents, and in the case of the Yale system used in this guide, by the placement of the letter h. The pronunciation guide below indicates what pitch to use with each accent or diacritic mark. It can be very difficult to get the pitch correct but from the context of the situation Cantonese speakers can often guess what a foreigner is trying to say—no matter how strange it sounds.

Unlike Mandarin which has an official and widely used system for romanizing words, Cantonese has several rival systems. In this guide we have used the simplified Yale system simply because it is one of the best known and generally acknowledged to be the easiest system for English speakers to follow and pronounce. Pinyin is primarily a communication tool, trying to allow people to speak and be understood, but the muddle of systems used for Cantonese can make it seem confusing. Different systems use different combinations of letters and syllables to recreate the right sounds, so the transliterations you see in Hong Kong will not always match the ones in the phrasebook, although they are usually similar.

PRONUNCIATION GUIDE

TONE	DESCRIPTION	EXAMPLE	CHINESE	TRANSLATION
1	accent above the letter a indicates a high-flat tone	fān	分	divide
2	accent above the a indicates a mid-rising tone	fán	粉	powder
3	no accent, indicates a mid-flat tone	fan	糞	manure
4	accent above the a, followed by letter h indicates a low falling tone	fàhn	焚	burn
5	accent above the a, followed by letter h indicates a low-rising tone	fáhn	憤	resent
6	letter h indicates a low-flat tone	fahn	忿	fury

The three flat tones have only a slight inflection up or down, whereas the falling or rising tones represent a rise or fall in pitch on the syllable. The letter h is not pronounced and is used to indicate tone.

NUMBERS

ENGLISH	CHINESE	PINYIN
1	一	yāt
2	二	yih
3	三	sāam
4	四	sei
5	五	ńgh
6	六	luhk
7	七	chāt
8	八	baat
9	九	gáu
10	十	sahp
20	二十	yih sahp
50	五十	ńgh sahp
100	一百	yāt baak
500	五百	ńgh baak
1000	一千	yāt chīn
10,000	一萬	yāt maahn
100,000	十萬	sahp maahn
500,000	五十萬	ńgh sahp maahn
1 million	一百萬	yāt baak maahn

DAYS OF THE WEEK AND MONTHS OF THE YEAR

ENGLISH	CHINESE	PINYIN
Monday	星期一	sīng kèih yāt
Tuesday	星期二	sīng kèih yih
Wednesday	星期三	sīng kèih sāam
Thursday	星期四	sīng kèih sei
Friday	星期五	sīng kèih ńgh
Saturday	星期六	sīng kèih luhk
Sunday	星期日	sīng kèih yaht
January	一月	yāt yuht
February	二月	yih yuht
March	三月	sāam yuht
April	四月	sei yuht
May	五月	ńgh yuht
June	六月	uhk yuht
July	七	chāt yuht
August	八月	baat yuht
September	九月	gáu yuht
October	十月	sahp yuht
November	十一月	sahp yāt yuht
December	十二月	sahp yih yuht

TIME

ENGLISH	CHINESE	PINYIN
today	今日	gām yaht
yesterday	尋日	chàhm yaht
tomorrow	聽日	tīng yaht
morning	上晝	seungh jau
afternoon	下晝	hah jau
evening	夜晚	yeh máahn
overnight	通宵	tūng siū
this week	呢個星期	nī go sīng kèih
next week	下個星期	hah go sīng kèih
this month	呢個月	nī go yuht
next month	下個月	hah go yuht
now	依家	yi gā
later	遲啲	chìh dī
earlier	早啲	jóu dī
twenty four hours	廿四個鐘	yah sei go jūng
fifteen minutes	十五分鐘	sahp ńgh fān jūng
half an hour	半個鐘	bun go jūng
an hour	一個鐘	yāt go jūng
What time is it?	幾點?	géi dím?
eleven o'clock	十一點	sahp yāt dím
quarter past	十五分	sahp ńgh fān
half past	三十分	sāam sahp fān
quarter to	四十五分	sei sahp ńgh fān
weekdays	平日	pìngh yaht
weekends	週末	jāu muht

GREETINGS AND USEFUL PHRASES

ENGLISH	CHINESE	PINYIN
Hello.	你好	Néih hóu.
Good morning.	早晨	Jóu sàhn.
Good afternoon.	下晝好	Hah jau hóu.
Good evening.	晚上好	Máahn seuhng hóu.
Nice to meet you.	好高興認識你	Hóu gōu hing yihng sīk néih.
Fine.	唔錯	M`h cho.
Ok.	仲可以	Juhng hó yíh.
My name is____.	我叫____	Ngóh giu____.
Goodbye.	拜拜	Bāai baai.
yes	係	haih
no	唔係	m`h haih
Thank you.	多謝	Dō jeh. (for a gift)
Thank you.	唔该	M`h gōi. (for a service)
Please.	请	Chíng.

Excuse me.	唔好意思	M`h hóu yi sī.
Do you speak English?	你識唔識講英文?	Néih sīk n`gh sīk góng yīng mán?
I don't speak Cantonese.	我唔識講廣東	Ngóh m`h sīk góng gwóng dūng wá.
I don't understand.	我唔明	Ngóh m`h mìhng.
Could you please repeat slowly?	你可以慢慢重覆嗎?	Néih hó yíh maahn máan chùhng fūk ma?
I am American.	我係美國人	Ngóh haih méih gwok yàhn.
British	英國人	yīng gwok yàhn
Australian	澳洲人	ou jāu yàhn
Canadian	加拿大人	gā nàh daaih yàhn
a New Zealander	紐西蘭人	náu sāi làahn yàhn
Irish	愛爾蘭人	oi yíh làahn yàhn

SHOPPING

ENGLISH	CHINESE	PINYIN
How much is this?	呢個幾多錢?	Nī go géi dō chín?
Where can I find?	可以係邊度搵到?	Hó yíh hái bīn douh wán dóu?
that one	果個	gwó go
cheap	平	pèhng
expensive	貴	gwai
too expensive	太貴	taai gwai
more	多啲	dō dī
less	少啲	síu dī
Can you lower the price?	平啲得唔得?	Pèhng dī dāk m`h dāk?
convenience store	便利店	bihn leih dim
supermarket	超市	chīu síh
shopping mall	商場	sēung chèuhng
market	市場	síh chèuhng
wet market	街市	gāai síh
opening (time)	營業	yìhng yihp
closing (time)	落班	lohk bāan

FOOD

ENGLISH	CHINESE	PINYIN
beef	牛肉	ngàuh yuhk
beer	啤酒	bē jáu
bottled water	樽裝水	jēun jōng séui
chicken	雞肉	gāi yuhk

fish	魚	yùh
fruit	生果	sāang gwó
meat	肉類	yuhk leuih
noodles	麵	mihn
pork	豬肉	jyū yuhk
rice	飯	faahn
seafood	海鮮	hói sīn
soft drinks	汽水	hei séui
soup	湯	tōng
vegetables	蔬菜	sō choi
wine	紅酒	hùhng jáu
No ice.	唔要冰	M`h yiu bīng
We have a reservation.	我地訂咗檯	Ngóh deih dehng jó tòih.
Do you have an English menu?	有冇英文餐牌?	Yáuh móuh yīng mán chāan pàaih?
I would like this.	我想要呢個	Ngóh séung yiu nī go.
Can I have the bill please?	埋單吖, 唔該	Màaih dāan ā, m`h gōi?
cash	現金	yihn gām
credit card	信用卡	seun yuhng kā
I'm a vegetarian.	我食齋	Ngóh sihk jāai.
gluten free	唔含穀膠	m`h hàhm gūk gāau
Does it have MSG?	有冇味精?	Yáuh móuh meih jīng?
Do you have cutlery/ and fork?	有冇餐具/ 刀叉?	Yáuh móuh knife chāan geuih / dōu chā?
to takeaway	拎走	v. līng jáu

GETTING AROUND

ENGLISH	**CHINESE**	**PINYIN**
bus	巴士	bā sih
train	火車	fó chē
subway	地鐵	deih tit
ferry	渡輪	douh lèuhn
car	私家車	sī gā chē
taxi	的士	dīk sí
plane	飛機	fēi gēi
station	車站	chē jaahm
bus/tram stop	巴士站/電車站	bā sí jaahm / dihn chē jaahm
Stop please.	唔該有落	M`h gōi yáuh lohk.
ticket	車票	chē piu
How much is the fare?	車費幾多钱?	Chē fai géi dō chín?

English	Chinese	Pinyin
Where is?	係邊度?	Haih bīn douh?
Which direction?	邊個方向?	Bīn go fōng heung?
left	左	jó
right	右	yauh
north	北	bāk
south	南	nàahm
east	東	dūng
west	西	sāi
straight on	直行	jihk hàahng
far	遠	yúhn
near	近	káhn
near to___	響___附近	héung___fuh gahn
opposite	對面	deui mihn
I'm lost.	我蕩失咗路	Ngóh dohng sāt jó louh .

HEALTH AND EMERGENCIES

ENGLISH	CHINESE	PINYIN
help	救命	gau mehng
police	警察	gíng chaat
ambulance	救護車	gau wuh chē
fire brigade	消防隊	sīu fòhng deuih
I need___.	我要___	Ngóh yiu___.
My___hurts.	我嗰___好痛	Ngóh go___hóu tung.
It hurts here.	呢度好痛	Nī douh hóu tung.
I'm allergic to___.	我對___敏感	Ngóh deui___ máhn gám.
I'm ill.	我病咗	Ngóh behng jó .
allergy	敏感	máhn gám
antacid	抗酸劑	kong syūn jāi
antibiotics	抗生素	kong sāng sou
antihistamine	腎上腺皮膚素	sahn seuhng sin pèih fū sou
arm	手臂	sáu bei
asprin	阿士匹靈	a sih pāt lìhng
back	背	bui
bandage	敷膏藥	fū gōu yeuhk
birth control pills	避孕藥	beih yahn yeuhk
chest	胸口	hūng háu
cold	感冒	gám mouh
cold medicine	感冒藥	gám mouh yeuhk
condoms	避孕套	beih yahn tou
cough	咳	kāt
dentist	牙醫	ngàh yī
diarrhea	肚屙	tóuh ō
doctor	醫生	yī sāang
fever	發燒	faat sīu

head	頭	tàuh
headache	頭痛	tàuh tung
hospital	醫院	yī yún
itch	癢	yéuhng
leg	腳	geuk
lump	腫塊	júng faai
neck	頸	géng
pain	痛	tung
painkillers	止痛藥	jí tung yeuhk
pharmacy	藥房	yeuhk fòhng
pill/tablet	藥丸/藥片	yeuhk yún / yeuhk pín
sleeping pills	安眠藥	ōn mìhn yeuhk
stomach	胃	waih
swelling	腫	júng
tampons	衛生棉條	waih sāng mìhn tíu
temperature	溫度	wān douh
tooth	牙	ngàh
vomiting	嘔吐	áu tou

Glossary

amah domestic helper or nanny

aiyah expression of surprise, exasperation or disappointment. 'Aiyah, you've left the toilet seat up again.'

ah term of endearment used before a name. "ah-Michael." Dangerously easy to mix up with aiyah

Cantopop Cantonese pop music; the soundtrack to your stay in Hong Kong

Canton capital of Guangdong province and known today as Guangzhou

catty Chinese unit of weight that is still used in wet markets. One catty is equivalent to 1.33 pounds

choy sum popular Chinese vegetable

accident and emergency hospital emergency room. Also known as A&E or Casualty.

congee rice porridge often eaten at breakfast

coolie manual laborer. Sometimes used as an ethnic slur.

chop stamp or seal of a person, company or organization; often required on official documents

cha chan teng cheap, neighborhood diners famed for their own unique take on western dishes. Hong Kong comfort food.

Ding Ding colloquial name for the tram

dai pai dong open air street stalls serving bargain priced noodle and rice dishes and other snacks; Hong Kong fast food

face the complicated concept of respect and status that governs relationships between individuals

feng shui Chinese concept of geomancy that believes the placement and orientation of objects and buildings can positively or negatively affect energy flows, Influential in Hong Kong architecture.

FILTH derogatory acronym meaning 'Failed in London Try Hong Kong' that was once popular during colonial days but has understandably lost its currency

godown warehouse

gweilo meaning ghost man or white devil, gweilo refers to a foreigner in Hong Kong. Originally derogatory, these days it's lost much of its bite.

gwaipo Gweilo is used for both genders but gwaipo is specifically for women.

hong refers to Hong Kong's most influential companies, particularly those with long established roots in the city, such as Jardine Matheson.

hostess bar occasionally a strip club, more usually fronts for brothels. Also known as girlie bars.

junk once ubiquitous, junks are flat bottomed boats with bat winged sails that were a Hong Kong icon but that have long since disappeared from Hong Kong harbor. More commonly heard today as a junk trip, meaning the pleasure cruises locals take on motor yachts and boats around the South China Sea.

kaido small motorized ferry or boat

kowtow bowing to show respect or subservience. Traditionally associated with the Emperor and Imperial China, in recent years it has taken on a broader meaning to mean subservience. 'She has to kowtow to her boss first.'

Lai See red envelopes containing money given at Chinese New Year

LegCo Legislative Council

love hotel hotels that rent beds by the hour for 'romantic' liaisons

Mainland used in Hong Kong and Macau to refer to China proper.

Mainlanders refers to people from mainland China

mamasan manager of a hostess bar or brothel, usually found trying to man-handle drunk sailors inside clubs on the streets of Wan Chai.

mah jong popular Chinese game played with domino sized tiles that involves skill, chance and usually gambling

MPF Mandatory Provident Fund. Compulsory pension fund

Mark Six Hong Kong's lottery

pinyin Romanization system used to transcribe Chinese characters into the Roman alphabet

praya waterfront promenade

putonghua official spoken language of China and the preferred name for the language as opposed to Mandarin

sampan Small boats often used as private water taxis

SAR Special Administrative Region (Hong Kong and Macau)

SCMP South China Morning Post

SEZ Special Economic Zone (Shenzhen)

shroff payment kiosk often used at government institutions such as hospitals

PRC People's Republic of China

tai chi martial-arts based exercise popular with Hong Kong's older population

taipan once used to describe western bosses at large companies; now used more broadly to refer to any powerful businessman

tai tai ladies of leisure whose schedules revolve around lunches, galas and handbag shopping. Far fewer in number than in their heyday, *tai tai* culture still survives.

tiffin less common since the Union Flag was hauled down, *tiffin* is afternoon tea

triad Hong Kong's very own breed of mobsters, as exported to just about every city in the United States. Handy with cleavers.

uncle/auntie term of respect and or endearment when talking about older people.

VCD Video Compact Disc; less expensive and of poorer quality than DVDs, the majority of the city's ubiquitous video shops stock VCDs. They play on most Asia region DVD players

Suggested Reading

GENERAL

Booth, Martin. *Gweilo*, Bantam, 2005. Wonderfully evocative and colorfully detailed memoir of a young child's experiences growing up in colonial Hong Kong.

Chamberlain, Jonathan. *King Hui*, Blacksmith Books, 2007. Based on interview transcripts with the man himself, few people have lived as many lives as King Hui. This very personal journey of Hong Kong from pre-war to the handover follows the exploits, triumphs and disasters of one of Hong Kong's greatest operators; a hustler and playboy who knew everyone and was willing to do anything to make a buck.

Coates, Austin. *Myself a Mandarin. London: Frederick Muller*, 1966. Tasked with administering British jurisdiction to the then very far flung New Territories in post war Hong Kong, Myself a Mandarin deals with Coates earnest attempts to get to grips with the nuances of local culture and politics to comic effect.

Dragon Syndicates: The Global Phenomenon of the Triads, Basic Books, 2001. This excellent history of the triads pulls back the curtains on one of the world's most secretive society, from their origins as a revolutionary brotherhood to their violent success as one of the world's biggest criminal enterprises with much of the backdrop being Hong Kong.

Feng, Chi-shun. *Diamond Hill*, Blacksmith Books, 2009. An unabashedly candid and warm account of the author's humble childhood in the slums of Diamond Hill, where he documents the poverty, crime and corruption that stalked 1950's Hong Kong but also the sense of community, belonging and spirit of hard work that helped carve out the city's success.

Lambot, Ian. *City of Darkness: Life in Kowloon Walled City*, Watermark Publications, 1993. An incredible photo documentary of life inside Hong Kong's infamous Kowloon Walled City.

Morris, Jan. *Hong Kong*, Vintage, 1997. With less emphasis on the facts and figures seen in a traditional history book and more on the stories and anecdotes, this book by veteran journalist and HongKongophile Jan Morris is a thoroughly engaging and entertaining introduction to the city.

HISTORY AND POLITICS

Contemporary Hong Kong Politics: Governance in the Post 1997 Era, HKU Press, 2007. There are very few English books for the casual reader covering post 1997 Hong Kong politics and the intricacies of the political system here and while Contemporary Hong Kong Politics remains instructional it is still probably the most accessible.

Dimbleby, Jonathan. *The Last Governor*. Little Brown and Co, 1998. Granted unprecedented access to Chris Patten himself, Dimbleby traces the governor's last minute drive for democracy in the lead up the Hong Kong handover. His opinionated and engrossing narrative reveals the backstabbing, mudslinging and brawling that went on as the two sides bitterly wrangled over the city's future.

Loh, Christine. *Underground Front: The Chinese Communist Party in Hong Kong*, University of Washington Press, 2010. Academically written but readable examination of the Chinese Communist Party's role in Hong Kong, both officially and unofficially.

Patten, Christopher. East and West, Random House, Pan Books, 1999. Hong Kong's last and famously outspoken governor sounds a slightly more conciliatory tone as he ties up his experiences as governor with his thoughts on democracy, the free market and how Hong Kong works best.

Tsang, Steve. *A Modern History of Hong Kong 1841-1997*, I.B. Tauris, 2004. In depth but readable history of Hong Kong spanning the whole period of British rule.

Welsh, Frank. *A History of Hong Kong*, HarperCollins Publishers Ltd, 1997. Considered history of Hong Kong with an emphasis on colonial affairs.

FICTION

Clavell, James. *Tai-Pan*, Hodder Paperbacks, 1966. Based on the historical events surrounding Britain's seizure of Hong Kong, this epic saga is a swashbuckling, tabloid turner of rivalries, ambition, passion and war.

Milnes, David. *The Ghost of Neil Diamond*, whattraditionbooks, 2008. Long term expats will recognize many of the entertaining characters in Milne's bitingly funny and touchingly honest tale of one man's attempt turn around his fortunes as a Neil Diamond impersonator in Hong Kong.

Mason, Richard. *The World of Suzie Wong*, Amereon Ltd 1957. Whether you read the book or watch the movie, this tale of a good girl prostitute and a British painter falling in love in a small town called 1950's Hong Kong can't fail to pull at the heartstrings.

Mo, Timothy. *The Monkey King*, Paddleless Press, 1978. Set in post war Hong Kong, Monkey King is the heartfelt and hilarious misunderstandings and misadventure of Wallace Nolasco as he tries to come to terms with his eccentrically dysfunctional new in-laws, the Poons.

Pierce, Alan B. *Cheung Chau Dog Fanciers Society, Asia 2000, 1996*. Despite the triads, drug dealers and corrupt cops, this crime thriller about an expats accidental involvement in a money laundering operation really shines for its uncanny and funny portrayal of the characters and community on Hong Kong's outlying islands.

Theroux, Paul. *Kowloon Tong*, Penguin Books, 1997. Wonderfully divisive book that it's best not bring to dinner parties. Painting a picture of local expats as arrogant and inept and the Chinese as vulgar and greedy, Theroux managed to offend just about everyone in Kowloon Tong but his tale of a British Hong Konger factory owner bullied into selling his business by a mainlander during the run up to the Hong Kong handover captures the atmosphere of unease and anxiety that stalked the city.

Xi, Xu. *Unwalled City*, Chameleon Press, 2001. Exploring the lives of a young, local, wannabe canto-pop star, a high flying Eurasian executive and single mother, the wife of a loaded businessman stuck in a string of infidelities and a stuck in a rut photographer, Xu Xi's quiet and unimposing portraits are the story of Hong Kong's many lives and many identities.

Xi, Xu and Ingham, Mike. *City Voices*, HKUPress, 2003. Trying to find English language fiction about Hong Kong that doesn't involve either the blood and bluster of the colonial heyday or fairytales of tea ceremonies and cheongsams can be difficult. For something a little less sensational and a little more local, don't miss City Voices, a seminal anthology of post war to present, English language fiction, poetry and essays. Joint editor Xu Xi is one of Hong Kong's most exciting and accomplished English language writers and her fifty-fifty anthology where forty local writers consider the question 'What are Hong Kong's odds as it counts down 50 years of the S.A.R. is equally unmissable.

RESOURCES

FILMS

Chan, Fruit. *Made in Hong Kong,* 1997. Fruit Chan's tale of an alienated teenager forced into a spiral of Triad violence to pay for his girlfriend's operation is an atmospheric and reflective exploration of identity and alienation in the run up to the Hong Kong handover.

Chow, Stephen. Shaolin Soccer. 2001. An infectiously funny slapstick comedy that follows a group of former Shaolin Monks who form a soccer team and use their superhero martial art skills to defeat Team Evil

Clouse, Robert. *Enter the Dragon,* 1973. Debate over Bruce lee's best film continues to be the topic of late night shouting matches, but with many of his most accomplished and celebrated martial art fights Enter the Dragon is certainly a contender.

King, Henry. *Love is A Many Splendored Thing,* 1955. Set in 1949, this melodramatic love story between a Eurasian doctor and American correspondent played out to the backdrop of the Chinese communist revolution is worth a watch for an all too rare screen portrayal of colonial Hong Kong and the racial predjuces it was riddled with.

Kar Wai, Wong. *Days of Being Wild,* 1990. One of Hong Kong's most accomplished Directors, Cannes winner Wong-kar

wai's breakthrough film is a steamy tale of raw emotions and desire set in a stylishy sultry 1960;s Hong Kong.

To, Johnnie. *Election,* 2005. Follow the deception, dishonesty and double dealing in this suspense filled drama that snakes through the twists and turns of a Triad power struggle.

Tsui, Hark. *Once Upon a Time in China,* 1991. Jet Li fights the dastardly forces of colonialism in 19th century Canton in a sweeping epic that proves that martial arts films are allowed to have explosive fight sequences and an actual plot.

Yuen, Woo-ping, *Drunken Master,* 1978. A fresh faced Jackie Chan delivers one of his best and most understated comedy performances as a young man sent to learn the way of the Drunken Master martial art from his ruthless uncle.

Wai-keung, Lau. *Infernal Affairs,* 2002. An absolute barnstorming, blockbuster of a film that pitches the triads against the police force in a gripping plot of backstabbing and betrayal.

Woo, John. *A Better Tomorrow,* 1986. Guns, Guns and a little gore made this bad guys, good guys shoot em up a box office record breaker in Hong Kong and launched the action wizard John Woo's leap into Hollywood and the film career of heartthrob Chow Yun-fat.

Index

Acknowledgments

This book is dedicated with all my love to my sister, Gemma, and to my parents, who brought us up to believe that we could go anywhere and achieve everything. Gemma, your courage will always be an inspiration. I miss you every minute.

Thank you to the many people who have shared their stories, experiences and tips about living in Hong Kong. The book is broader and better for them. In particular, I'd like to thank Alison Collingridge and Lawrence Tang at InvestHK, Eliza Cheng at the HKTB, the helpful staff at the Hong Kong Immigration Department, Sue Smith for letting me grill her on the world of Hong Kong education, Danny Harrington, Ellen Mak, Brendan Kinne, Iris Pak and Jane Chan as well as the wise old heads over at geoexpat.com for their advice and insights. Special mention goes to my translator, Minran Pu for her dedication in getting me to grasp the intricacies of Cantonese. I'm also grateful to my interviewees Mike Rowse, Angie Wong, JC Cortez and Miranda Lee Breding (Wong) who gave their time so generously. Several people were kind enough to offer up their superb photographs, including Martyna Szmytkowska, Agnieszka Szmytkowska, Ross Talbot, Bartosz Kościelak and the incredibly talented duo of Magda Hueckel and Tomasz Śliwiński at Muzungu-art.

I also owe a debt of gratitude to everybody at Avalon who worked on the project but particularly to my commissioning editor Grace Fujimoto for the opportunity, and my editor Shari Husain for her enduring patience, understanding, and hard work. There aren't enough flowers in the world to thank my partner, Martyna; not only for her help in organizing large parts of the book and her impeccable eye for detail, but for her endless encouragement and infectious enthusiasm. I couldn't have done it without you.

www.moon.com

DESTINATIONS | ACTIVITIES | BLOGS | MAPS | BOOKS

MOON.COM is ready to help plan your next trip! Filled with fresh trip ideas and strategies, author interviews, informative travel blogs, a detailed map library, and descriptions of all the Moon guidebooks, Moon.com is all you need to get out and explore the world—or even places in your own backyard. While at Moon.com, sign up for our monthly e-newsletter for updates on new releases, travel tips, and expert advice from our on-the-go Moon authors. As always, when you travel with Moon, expect an experience that is uncommon and truly unique.

f ✈ KEEP UP WITH MOON ON FACEBOOK AND TWITTER

JOIN THE MOON PHOTO GROUP ON FLICKR